FROM CRITICAL THEORY OF SOCIETY TO THEOLOGY OF COMMUNICATIVE PRAXIS

Rudolf J. Siebert

199375

University Press of America™

DEDICATION

In remembrance of my wife, Margie, for whom theology was
the consciousness that the world is appearance and not
the absolute and ultimate truth and the longing that the
injustice which characterizes the world will not be the
last word and the hope that the murderer will not triumph
over the innocent victim. And who lived, loved, acted,
suffered and died in this consciousness and with this
longing and in this hope.

ACKNOWLEDGEMENT

This book developed out of papers which I read and
discussed with many scholars in the *Philosophy of
Religion and Theology Section* of the American Academy
of Religion Meeting in San Francisco in 1977 and in the
international course on *The Future of Religion*, which I
have initiated in the Inter-University Centre for Post
Graduate Studies in Dubrovnik, Jugoslavia. I thank
particularly Professor Dr. Jürgen Habermas for participating
in the second course on *The Future of Religion* in the IUC
in April 1978 and for affirming that the part of this book
concerned with his critical theory of religion, particularly
the chapters VI-VIII, does him justice. My thanks go to
Vice President Cornelius Loew at Western Michigan University
who in his previous function as Dean of the College of Arts
and Sciences gave me a leave of absence and financial
support, so that I was able to direct the course on *The
Future of Religion* and develop further in discourse with
colleagues from the Americas and Eastern and Western
Europe the fundamental issues of this book. I am grateful
to Dr. Samuel Clark, Director of the Honors College of
WMU, for providing me with a research assistant on the
basis of the Russel Seibert Fund. My thanks go to the
Research Committees of WMU and of King's College,
University of Western Ontario, London, Ontario, Canada
who gave me a substantial grant, without which this book
would not have been possible. I am grateful to Mrs.
Dolores Condic, secretary of the Religion Department of
WMU, for typing the first drafts of this book and to
Mrs. Jean Murphy, secretary of the Social Sciences
Department of King's College, University of Western Ontario,
for typing the final draft. I am grateful to the board
of the University Press of America for its courage, tolerance
and great help in relation to this holistic-humanistic
work. Another publisher found me difficult to publish
since I want "to say everything about the given topic",
while the market in a postivistically oriented society
is more inclined to fragmented knowledge.

I am infinitely grateful to my late wife Margaret, who
dying from cancer herself nevertheless helped to edit
the final draft of this book. She is particularly
responsible for the ideas expressed on negative theology,
Chapter XIII and on communication theology, Chapter XIV.

On her very deathbed Margaret applauded and affirmed once more the statements contained in Chapter XIII on the present epidemic of cancer and the pain and suffering it produces for the victims. Particularly Chapter XIV on the "innocent other" who has been destroyed, but is hopefully rescued from total destruction and on the "practical, paradoxical, anemnetic solidarity" with the "innocent other", Margaret and I intended to be our spiritual testament. The book would never have been written without the impulses my late wife gave to it through her life, love, thoughts, actions, suffering and death. Margaret's fate stands concretely behind the theodicy question, which constitutes, so to speak, the very *entelechia* of this book. Contrary to the positivistic tradition, in this book we are emphatically committed to the differentiated unity of the theory and the praxis of life and death in the immediate life world.

INTRODUCTION

It is the purpose of this book to develop Jürgen
Habermas's critical theory of religion out of its origin
in Georg W.F. Hegel's philosophy of religion, Karl Marx's
critical theory of religion and Max Horkheimer's and
Walter Benjamin's dialectical theory of religion.1
Furthermore, it is the intent of this study to confront
Habermas's dialectical sociology of religion with Talcott
Parsons' and Niklas Luhmann's functional theory of religion.
To the historical materialism on the Left and the social
evolutionism on the Right we oppose Hans Küng's negative
theology, Helmut Peukert's theology of communicative
praxis, and Theodor Haecker's and Georg W. Rudolphi's
theology of history with practical intent.2 The theodicy
concern moves like a red thread through all chapters of
this book. We conclude this book with Hegel's answer to
the theodicy problem and with a critical renewal of his
attempt to unite an idealistic with a materialistic
interpretation of religion in general and of Christianity
in particular.3

The scientific-theoretical discussion of the 20th century
and the interdisciplinary discourse about a normative
theory of communicative action in recent decades have led
to boundary problems, which raise the question concerning
the very foundation of the science of religion as well as
of the theology of religions and the theology of Christianity.4
The main question of this book is: How can such a foundation
and out of it a theology of the subject, society and history
be developed, which is accountable in an interdisciplinary
way.

Wolfhart Pannenberg, Küng, Johannes B. Metz and Peukert
make the attempt to develop in continual contact with
the science-theoretical discussion, a proposal for a
fundamental theology, i.e., a basis theory of theology.5
Peukert starts from the assumption that between the
present considerations of the foundation of theology
on one hand, and the results of the science-theoretical
research of recent decades, a certain convergence can
be observed. The point of convergence lies in a theory
of communicative practice. In our study we will
concentrate on this point of convergence in the form of
Habermas's critical theory of society and religion.

The central idea of Peukert's work consists in the attempt to develop the proposal for a fundamental theology as theological basis theory for a political theology out of a theory of communicative action. We will follow Peukert as he develops his basis theology of subject, society and history out of Habermas's theory of communicative praxis, more specifically, his critical theory of religion which is an integral part of the former, and in opposition to Parsons' and Luhmann's functional sociology of religion.

Peukert, as well as Küng, proceed methodologically in such a way that they push forward the fundamental problems of the philosophy of science and of the theory of action to such an extreme, that the theological dimensions of communicative action as well as the possibilities of their theoretical comprehension become visible in dialectical boundary reflection. We follow Peukert's dialectical method as we trace Habermas's critical theory of communicative practice and Parsons' and Luhmann's structural-functional sociology to the point where they become theories of religion, and reveal as such the theological dimensions. In these dimensions are situated Hegel's attempt at the resolution of the theodicy problem as well as his attempt at a reunion of the idealistic and materialistic aspects of religion, especially Christianity, Haecker's and Rudolphi's practical theology of history, Küng's functional theology and Metz's and Peukert's fundamental theology as foundation of a political theology of the subject.6

TABLE OF CONTENTS

FROM CRITICAL THEORY OF SOCIETY TO
THEOLOGY OF COMMUNICATIVE PRAXIS

Rudolf J. Siebert

CHAPTER I

CLAIMS OF A CRITICAL THEORY

According to Peukert, the claims of a critical theory of
society after Hegel, August Comté, Marx, Charles Darwin,
Benjamin, Horkheimer, Habermas, Parsons and Luhmann, which
reaches beyond partial spheres of social life and turns toward
such a phenomenon as the total human action system, are
threefold.1 First, such a theory must try to comprehend
the object of the theory in its constitution. Secondly,
such a theory must make evident the interdependence
between the mode of the constitution of the object and
the constitution of the subject, including his or her
ability to theorize. Thirdly, such a theory must make
understandable these objective and subjective processes
of constitution out of the over-reaching process of
natural and social evolution. Since Hegel, the
fundamental problems of such a global type of theory,
including a theory of religion, are under debate. Since
Hegel also, the science of religion and the theology of
religions and the theology of Christianity must seriously
take into consideration theories of this type.

According to all the recent research of Peukert, Küng and Metz
as well as of Pannenberg and Trutz von Rentorff in the
field of the philosophy of science, the science-theoretical
discussion seems to have the result that the construction
of an over-reaching process, into which reflection could
supercede itself in an identifying manner, leads to inner
contradictions and absurdities. In this, their aporia,
the science theoretical constructions are again and again
directed back toward the factual existence of men and
women and their communicative actions searching for mutual
understanding. According to Peukert in this aporetic
situation of all forms of positivism -- the historical
positivism of Comté, the neo-positivism of the Vienna
School, and Popper's reform positivism or critical
rationalism -- Habermas and his collaborators in the
Frankfurt School have undertaken the attempt to develop
a theory of communicative action, which avoids the
positivists' hypostatizations as well as their aporias,
but does nevertheless justice to the claims of a critical
theory of the interdependence of the constitution of the
object and the constitution of the subject and their
genesis.2

1

On the basis of Habermas's critical theory of society and particularly of his theory of religion, his collaborator R. Döbert was able to make plausible the thesis that the religious development of mankind can be comprehended as manifestation of man's communicative competence.3 In the perspective of Döbert in the total course of the development of the religious consciousness a process of reflection manifests itself. In this process of reflection humankind is able to produce for itself an increasing measure of clarity concerning its own essence. Mankind acquires in the sequence of positive religions -- Taoism, Hinduism, Buddhism, etc.- -- as so many systems of interpretation and orientation, the theoretical and practical means to shape its life autonomously. Like Hegel and Habermas before, Döbert asserts in his fundamental thesis, that the religious systems of interpretation follow in their development an inner logic, which makes it possible to reconstruct certain sequences of positive religions judiciously and sensibly: e.g., the expansion of the profane sphere in relation to the sacred dimension; the tendency from far-reaching heteronomy to increasing autonomy; the emptying out of religious world views concerning all cognitive contents; the trend from cosmology to purely moral systems; the tendency from tribal particularism to universalistic and at the same time individualistic orientation; the increasing reflexivity of the mode of faith.4 At the end point of this development of the history of religion appears the competence of the subjects to test in linguistically mediated inter-subjective action, finally a discourse, assertions and behavioural expectations by a procedure of reciprocal reflexivity and make them so evident for each other, that ultimately this understanding and insight implies also the transparency and perspecuity of the communicating partners for themselves and for each other.

Peukert and Küng are mainly interested in the claim of Habermas's theory of religion, that in the present stage of social evolution the previous religious systems of interpretation and orientation, including the implicit theologies, have become hopelessly obsolete.5 Habermas ascribes to each positive religion and its theology a specific limited location in the process of human evolution. Peukert explains and illustrates this claim of Habermas by showing how he characterizes the development of the critique of religion since Hegel's death in 1831, particularly on the Hegelian Left.6 According to Habermas's characterization, the metaphysics of Modern Time up to and including Hegel, was still very much in the position to sublate by interpretation to the

2

level of the notion -- as the differentiated identity
of universality, particularity and singularity -- the
idea of the one God, as it had been developed in the
high religions, through the idea of the One or the
Absolute.7 Thereby metaphysics could take the place of
religion. So at least Habermas thinks, not Hegel.8

According to Habermas, as Peukert understands him, the
manifestation of religious revelation could be thought
of by the metaphysicians as process of reflection and
that way could become transparent and perspicuous for
their thought.9 In Habermas's view, the post-metaphysical
thinking of the later 19th and 20th centuries does not
contest or dispute any determinate theological assertion.
The positivists on the Right and the dialecticians on
the Left rather state categorically the meaninglessness
of all metaphysical and theological propositions. They
intend to prove that in the fundamental conceptual system
in which the Judeo-Christian tradition has been dogmatized
and thereby rationalized, theologically meaningful
assertions can in no way be posited. Furthermore, at
least since Marx, a self-reflection, limited to the sphere
of the human species-history, has taken the place of the
ultimate proof of metaphysics. At the same time modern
philosophy -- particularly the critical theory of religion
of Horkheimer, Theodor W. Adorno, Herbert Marcuse, Erich
Fromm, Benjamin, Ernst Bloch, Roger Garaudy, Milan
Machovec, Vitezslav Gardavsky, etc. -- has integrated
into itself the utopian contents of the religious traditions
as well as an interest in liberation and reconciliation,
which so far in man's evolution had been interpreted in
religious terms. With Bloch we can speak of such
philosophy of religion as meta-religion or religion in
heritage.10

According to Habermas the rising primacy of the practical
philosophy allows the philosopher of religion to detach
the rational core of the utopian contents from their
irrational clothing and to take it over.11 Religious
utopia is separated sharply from religious ideology, i.e.,
false consciousness, rationalization of irrational content,
necessary appearance.12 In Habermas's perspective the
connection between the practical philosophy and the
empirically secured theories of action delivers to the
philosopher the means of interpretation by which what so
far had been interpreted in religious terms can now be
understood in its real meaning and can, as such, be
appropriated. Thereby Habermas's theory of religion
claims meta-theoretical status in relationship to the
history of religion and theology. Habermas's own
practical philosophy of communicative praxis, particularly

his critical theory of religion, has integrated into itself the originally religious utopia of a communicative community, characterized by communication without domination, by liberation and reconciliation, by the absence of ideological distortion.*13* It is itself meta-religion or religion in heritage.

For Peukert, as for Metz and Küng, Habermas's theory of religion poses the following fundamental problem: Does a theo of action of this type reach a position from which the history of mankind as history of religion can be unkeyed, and from which human history, after being newly interpreted, can be reconstructed, so that any earlier religious interpretation of this history is out of date and falls into sheer obsolescence and also every theology has become an anachronism?*14* Since according to Peukert's analysis, the problem positions of theological, as well as science-theoretical discussions in a certain sense converge, particularly in the Anglo-Saxon development, in a theory of communicative action, he can ask the question: Is it possible to show, in the framework of a theory of communicative practice, dimensions in the constitutive structure of communicative action, which by themselves elicit in a new way the further inquiry into the Judeo-Christian tradition, possibly also into other religious traditions?

Peukert's, Metz's and Küng's affirmative answer to this quest can fully be understood only after Habermas's critical theory of religion has been explored further. Since Habermas derives his critical theory of religion mainly from Hegel, Marx, the early Horkheimer and Benjamin it can be comprehended only against the background of their dialectical theories of religion. In this book we will trace the development of the critical theory of religion from Hegel over Marx, Horkheimer and Benjamin to Habermas, Parsons and Luhmann, in order then to describe Peukert's resp to the challenge of Habermas's dialectical theory of religion in the form of his fundamental or basis theology of communicative praxis, prepared by statements on Küng's negative theology.

CHAPTER II

RELIGION AND STATE

Hegel defines the notion of religion in his *Phenomenology of Spirit* as the consciousness of Absolute Being.[1] According to Hegel's *Philosophy of Religion* the notion of religion consists of three fundamental moments: (a) God as the absolute truth; the universality which is in and for itself; the all-determining, all-comprehending and all-supporting essential reality, from whom everything comes and to whom everything returns, on whom everything depends and outside of whom no other being has absolute, true independence; the absolute spirit; the absolute love; the absolute freedom. (b) The religious relationship as God's relationship toward nature and history, man and society. (c) The cult as man's concrete and practical reunion with God.[2] It includes man's socio-ethical transition from the dimension of religion to communicative practice in the spheres of family, society, state and history. Hegel's philosophy of religion is dialectically connected with his philosophy of right and history.[3] They are different from each other, but also identical. They reproduce each other.

According to Hegel, the state as the synthesis of family and society is the true mode of the reality of communicative action.[4] In the state, the true, socio-ethical will of man comes into the reality of communicative action. Here the spirit of man lives in its veracity. For Hegel, religion is God's theology, his knowledge of himself, as well as man's knowledge of God and man's anthropology, his knowledge of himself in God. This is the divine wisdom and the dimension of absolute truth. But there is for Hegel a second wisdom, the wisdom of the world, of secular communicative practice in family, society, state and history. Hegel is throughout his life, from his early theological writings through his Jena system fragments, his phenomenology and his logic to his philosophy of right, history and religion concerned with the relationship of the wisdom of the world to the divine wisdom, of non-positivistic natural and social science to theology.

In Hegel's view, the religion and the foundation of the communicative action in the state are one and the same.[5] They are in and for themselves identical. Religion is

5

the foundation of the communicative practice taking
place in the state. In the patriarchal relationship of
the Jewish theocracy, religion and the foundation of the
state are not yet differentiated and are still externally
identical. But religion and the foundation of the state
are also different. So they are *de facto* strictly
separated from each other in the further course of world
history. At a later stage of history religion and the
foundation of the state will again be posited as truly
identical.

In Hegel's perspective, religion is the knowledge of the
highest truth, and this truth, more concretely determined,
is the free spirit.6 In religion man is free before God.
While man makes his particular will pursuant to God's
universal will, he stands not in opposition to the divine
will, but he finds himself in God's will. Man is free
when he has achieved in the cult to overcome the disunion
between his own particular and God's universal will.

In Hegel's view, the state is only the freedom in the
world, in the reality of man's communicative praxis.
Here everything depends on the notion of freedom, which
a nation carries in its self-consciousness. This is so,
since the notion of freedom is realized in the communicative
practice of the state. To this realization in communicative
action belongs essentially the consciousness of freedom.
Nations who do not know that man is free in and for himself
-- old African and Asian nations, the old Greeks and
Romans -- live in a more or less intense dullness in
relation to their political constitution as well as to
their religion.7

For Hegel there exists *one* notion of freedom in religion
and in the political interaction of the state. This one
notion of freedom is the highest which man has. Man
realizes this notion of freedom in his communicative
praxis in state, society, marriage and family. The
nation which has a poor concept of God has also a bad
state, a corrupt government, bad laws, systematically
distorted communication everywhere.

According to Hegel, the common people do have some
consciousness about the relationship between religion
and the state, including family and society.8 But they
do not comprehend the absolute connection between religion
and the foundation of the state. In Hegel's view this
is known only in philosophy on the phenomenological
level of the notion as the differentiated unity of
universality, particularity and singularity, the peak of
his logic.9 People merely know this relationship

between religion and state in general on the notionless phenomenological level of representation or imagination.[10] They represent this relationship to themselves in pictorial thinking. This mythical representation of the relationship between religion and the communicative practice of the state expresses itself in the way that the laws, the authorities, the political constitution are considered to be originating from God. They are thereby authorized or legitimated by the highest authority, which is given to peoples' representation. The laws are the development of the notion of freedom. This political notion of freedom, as it reflects itself through the laws upon existence, i.e., peoples' communicative action, has for its foundation and truth the notion of freedom as it is conceived, grasped, held and contained in religion. Thereby is expressed and conveyed the fact that these laws of social morality, of right, are eternal and unchangeable rules for communicative action of men and women; that they are not arbitrary, but will exist and be valid as long as the particular positive religion exists which legitimates them. Hegel finds the representation of this connection between religion and the foundation of the state in all nations. It is sociologically universal.

In Hegel's view, the relationship between religion and state can be expressed on the level of representation also in that form, that one says people obey God when they follow the laws and the authorities, the powers, which hold the state together.[11] In Hegel's view this sentence is partially correct. But this sentence is also exposed to the danger that it can be taken in an entirely abstract form. In this case it is not determined how the laws are explicated, and which laws are suitable for the fundamental constitution. That sentence expressed formally says: One ought to obey authorities and laws, they may be how they want to be. In this case the governing and the legislation is left entirely to the arbitrariness of the government. Religious formalism leads to political ideology. Long before Hegel, Marx engaged in differentiated ideology critique, i.e., critique of necessary appearance, false consciousness, the rationalization of irrational conditions.

In the view of the Lutheran Hegel, this authoritarian relationship has taken place in the Protestant states.[12] It can only take place in Protestant states, since only here the unity of religion and state is present. Here the laws of the state are valid as rational and as divine, because of this presupposed original harmony between religion and state. Unlike in Catholic states, in

7

Protestant states religion does not have its own principles which contradict those which are valid in religion. So in Catholic states, the religious vows of chastity, poverty and obedience contradict the principles, rules, norms and laws which govern the communicative action of people in the modern family, society and state.13

But Hegel sees very clearly that Protestant states, since they stop with that formal sentence - one ought to obey authorities and laws no matter how irrational they may be - give thereby free play to arbitrariness, despotism, and oppression.14 Hegel observes that this has particularly come forth in Protestant England under the last kings of the House of Stuart. Here a passive obedience was demanded. The Sentence was valid that the regent was accountable only to God concerning his actions. Thereby the pre-supposition is made that only the regent knows exactly what is essential and necessary for the state. This is so since in the will of the regent lies the more concrete determination that he is an immediate revelation of God. According to Hegel, through further consequence this principle is developed in that direction, that it turns over dialectically into its very opposite. This happens, since the difference between priests and lay people is not present in Protestantism. The priests are not privileged to possess the divine revelation. There exists still less in Protestantism a privilege which would belong exclusively to a layman. Therefore, against the principle of the divine authorization of the regent, is posited the principle of the same legitimation which belongs also to the layman in general. So in England a Protestant sect arose -- the Puritans -- which asserted that it had been informed by divine revelation how the people are to be governed. After such inspiration of the Lord the Puritans instigated an insurrection and beheaded their king. From all this, Hegel concludes that even if it is certain in general that the laws are constituted through the divine will, it is nevertheless an as important aspect to recognize and discern concretely this divine will. This knowledge is nothing particular. It belongs to all people. Hegel is indeed a champion not of formal, but of substantial democracy.

In Hegel's view, to recognize what is rational in communicative action in state, society and family is a matter of the education of thought and particularly a matter of practical philosophical discourse.15 In this sense philosophy can very well be called world wisdom. It does not matter for Hegel in which external appearance the true laws have made themselves valid, if they have been pertained from the regent by persistence or not.

8

The further development of the notion of freedom, right, humanity among men in the form of philosophical discourse is necessary in itself. In Hegel's view, concerning that truth, that the laws are the divine will, all depends on the determination which precisely these laws are. In Hegel's perspective, principles as such are merely abstract thoughts. They have their truth only in their development in philosophical discourse. These principles held on to in their abstraction are the complete untruth i.e., ideology in the critical sense. Hegel himself is engaged precisely in such practical philosophical discourse.16 At present the Hegelian Habermas pushes forward this very same philosophical discourse, standing on the shoulders of Hegel, Marx and Horkheimer.17

Hegel criticizes the subjective idealists from Kant over Kichte to Schleiermacher and his followers, because they do not posit the knowledge of God, which is the very essence of religion into the comprehending dialectical reason of man.18 For them the consciousness of God rather originates exclusively in the sphere of man's feeling. The relationship of man to God lies merely in the sphere of feeling. It must not be drawn over into the dimension of dialectical thought. According to Hegel, if God is excluded from the area of rational insight, the necessary substantial subjectivity of man, then there remains nothing else to be done, than to assign to him the area of the contingent subjectivity, i.e., feeling. Schleiermacher, Hegel's opponent, does indeed define religion as *feeling* of dependence.

Hegel is surprised to see that theologians like Schleiermacher and his followers attribute to God any objectivity at all any longer.19 In Hegel's view the bourgeois materialists -- empiricists, historicists, naturalists or whatever else they may be called -- are at least much more consistent than Schleiermacher and other subjective idealists. While the bourgeois materialists are taking the spirit and thinking for something material and are of the opinion to have reduced them to mere sensations, they identify also God as a product of feeling and deny him objectivity. The result of bourgeois materialism is atheism. So for the bourgeois atheistic materialist God is nothing else than a historical product of man's weaknesses, fear, joy or selfish hope or avarice or thirst for power, as they arise from his adaptive behaviour or communicative action in family, society, state and history and motivate it at the same time. In Hegel's view, what is merely rooted in an individual's feeling is only for him or for her, his or her possession, but not its own property. It is

9

not independent in and for itself. Therefore Hegel finds
it necessary in his philosophy of religion first of all
to show that God has not only the feeling of the individual
for his root. God is not merely the God of this singular
individual. Therefore the pre-Kantian metaphysicians
have always first of all proven that *a God is* and not
merely a *feeling of God*. In Hegel's view, his philosophy
of religion has to respond to the demand to prove God
as a reality in and for itself and independent from
human subjectivity and inter-subjectivity and communicative
action in state, society and family. Hegel anticipates
the attempt of present day critical political theologians
to deprivatize Christianity and to motivate a political
proof of God.

According to Hegel, in theology we have God simply for
himself before us.20 Of course, then also God's
relationship toward men is of importance. While this
relationship in earlier pre-Kantian usual representation
did not seem to belong essentially to theology as the
teaching of God, the modern theology in contrast is more
concerned with religion than with God. Modern theology
merely demands that man ought to have religion. This is
the main concern! Modern theologians posit it even as
entirely indifferent, if people know something of God
or not. Modern theologians consider the knowledge of
God to be something entirely subjective. In reality one
cannot know what God is. This is bourgeois agnosticism.21
Contrary to this, the medieval theologians considered
and determined more the being or the essence of God.
Hegel recognizes nevertheless the truth in the modern
position, which lies in the fact that modern theologians
do not consider God separately from man's subjective
spirit. But the modern position is not true because God
is the *theos agnotos*, but because God is essentially
spirit, i.e., knowing, loving, free subject. Therefore
there is a relationship between God's absolute Spirit
and man's finite spirit. This relationship from Spirit
to spirit is the foundation of religion.

In Hegel's perspective, the older theologians have
comprehended the innermost depth of the divine essence.22
The modern theologians cannot fathom this divine depth
through the notion. They should therefore leave it
alone. For Hegel, theology is the comprehension of the
absolute religious content. The modern theologians
should admit that they are not able to comprehend the
religious content. But they should not want to judge
the act of comprehending, the least so with such
expressions as "pantheism". For Hegel the contemporary
Protestant theologians, "who have merely critique and

and history", have put aside entirely philosophy and dialectical science. In Hegel's view Master Eckhart, the late medieval Dominican monk and mystic, defines most adequately the very essence and foundation of religion when he says in one of his sermons about this innermost depth of the divine essence:

"... the eye, with which God sees me, is the eye with which I see God, my eye and his eye is one. In justice I am weighed in God and He in me. If God was not, I would not be. If I was not, God would not be."[23]

Master Eckhart does not forget to point out that it is not necessary for the common people to know about the religious relationship between God's infinite and man's finite spirit, since these are things which are easily minunderstood and which can only be comprehended in the notion.[24]

Hegel traces in the power of the dialectical notion as the differentiated identity of universality, particularity and singularity, the history of religion through three stages: (1) The stage of nature religion -- direct and indirect magic, Taoism as religion of measure, Hinduism as religion of fantasy, Buddhism as religion of inwardness. (2) The stage or religion of spiritual individuality or subjectivity -- Persian Religion as religion of light and darkness or good and evil, Syrian religion as religion of pain, Egyptian religion as religion of riddle, Jewish religion as religion of sublinity, Greek religion as religion of fate or beauty, and Roman religion as religion of purposiveness and utility. (3) The stage of the religion of truth and freedom -- primitive Christianity, Catholicism and Protestantism.[25]

Hegel compares the stages of the history of religion with the developmental stages of the individual human being.[26] The first stage of man, the child, is still in the immediate unity of will and nature, his own inner nature as well as the nature surrounding him. The second stage, adolescence, the individuality becoming for itself, is the living spirituality. The boy does not yet posit a particular purpose for himself. He urges toward, aspires after, and takes interest in everything. The third stage, manhood, is the age of work for a particular purpose. The adult subordinates himself to this particular purpose. The mature man devotes his energies to this purpose. Finally, the last stage in a man's development is old age. The old man has the universal before himself as purpose. He recognizes this universal purpose. He has returned from particular vivacity and work to the universal, absolute, ultimate purpose. The old man collects himself out of the broad multiplicity of existence into the infinite depth of the being-in-one self. These determinations are those which are logically determined through the nature of the dialectical notion. At the end stands the insight, that the first immediacy is not as mere immediacy, but is also mediated. The child himself is begotten. For Hegel everything between heaven and earth is mediated.

According to Hegel's science of religion, the religion of freedom which emerges from the religion of nature and the religion of spiritual individuality, at the same time gives itself the meaning in terms of the dialectical logic, that what is first posited as that what follows is rather the absolute prius of that through which it appears as mediated and as the truth of which it is known.27 The *a posteriori* is the *a priori*. In Hegel's dialectical perspective the religion of freedom, Christianity, is the absolute prius of the religion of nature and the religion of subjectivity through which it appears to be mediated and as the truth of which it is known in the dialectical philosophy of religion.

In Hegel's view it is the way and the goal of the history of religion that the spirit achieves its own notion, that what it is in itself.28 Spirit reaches what it is, only in this mode which is indicated in the abstract moments of the history of religion, its different stages, the different positive religions. The revealed religion, Christianity, is the manifest religion, since in it God as the Absolute Reality has become completely open. Here God empties himself. In Christianity everything is adequate to the notion of religion. There is nothing secret any longer as far as God's relationship to man is concerned. Here in Christianity Hegel finds the consciousness of the developed notion of the spirit, of God and man being reconciled not only in beauty, in serenity, as it happens in the Greek religion, but in the spirit. The manifest religion, while it was on all pre-Christian stages of the history of religion, always concealed, i.e., not in the truth, has arisen in the fullness of time. For Hegel this time of the arrival of Christianity is not merely contingent time, an arbitrariness, a brainwave. But it is rather time determined in the essential, eternal decision, i.e., in the eternal reason, wisdom of God. It is the notion of the thing itself, i.e., religion, the divine notion, the notion of God itself, which has determined itself to this development, the history of religion, and has posited its goal -- the appearance of religion. Christianity is the absolute religion.²⁹ Contrary to the present day evolutionists Hegel knows of no homogeneous and empty time. For him the flow of time is broken by the messianic fulness of time again and again. For him time is filled and fulfilled per se.

According to Hegel, Christianity is the end of the history of religion. No really new religion is to be expected any longer after Christianity, since in it all essential moments of the notion of religion have been or are still being actualized. Marx agrees with this conclusion of Hegel's philosophy of religion. But while Hegel's philosophy of religion was one mainly from above, an elaboration of the Anselm of Canterbury's proof of God, Marx lays the foundations for a theory of religion from below, from man and society.³⁰

CHAPTER III

BASIS AND SUPERSTRUCTURE

A generation after Hegel, the young Marx develops his own critical theory of religion out of, as well as against, the subjective-idealistic philosophies of religion of Kant and Fichte, the objective-idealistic theory of religion of Schelling and particularly the objective and absolute idealistic philosophy of religion of Hegel.[1] He does this mainly by dialectically-materialistically reinterpreting Hegel's theory of religion.

Already in his early writings Marx argues against Hegel's philosophy of right, that the profane existence of error, the verbal, instrumental and communicative practice of civil society, is discredited after its heavenly *oratio pro aris et focis* has been rejected.[2] Man, who looked for a superman in the fantastic reality of heaven and found nothing there but the reflection of himself, will no longer be disposed to find but the semblance of himself, the non-human (*Unmensch*) where he seeks and must seek his true reality. In any case, the sacred is a mere reflection of the profane and the former has to be taken back into the latter.

For Marx the fundamental sentence of irreligious criticism is: Man makes religion, religion does not make man.[3] In other words, religion is the self-consciousness and self-feeling of man who has either not yet found himself or has already lost himself again. But man is no abstract being squatting outside the world. Man is the world of man, the state, society and family. Man's verbal, instrumental and communicative practice in state, society and family produces religion, a reversed world-consciousness, because the social world is a reversed world. Religion is the general theory of the verbal, instrumental and communicative action in that world, its encyclopaedic compendium, its logic in a popular form, its spiritualistic *point d'honneur*, its enthusiasm, its moral sanction, its solemn completion, its universal ground for consolation and justification. It is the fantastic realization of the human essence, because the human essence has no true reality in the interaction of bourgeois family, society and state. For Marx the struggle against religion is

therefore mediately the fight against the systematically
distorted, verbal, instrumental and communicative
practice of the bourgeois world, of which religion is
the spiritual aroma.

Religious distress, so Marx argues against Hegel's theory
of bourgeois family, society and state, is at the same
time the expression of real distress and the protest
against real distress.4 Religion is the sigh of the
oppressed creature, the heart of a heartless world, just
as it is the spirit of a spiritless situation. It is
the opium of the people involved in systematically
distorted and as such, crippling verbal, instrumental
and communicative action in family, society, state and
history.

According to Marx, the abolition of religion as the
illusory happiness of the people is required for their
real happiness.5 The demand to give up the illusions
about its condition is the demand to give up a condition
which needs illusions. For Marx the criticism of religion
is therefore in embryo the criticism of the vale of woe,
the instrumental and communicative practice systematically
distorted by oppression and domination in bourgeois family,
society and state, the halo of which is religion.

In the view of Marx, bourgeois and socialistic materialistic
and atheistic criticism has plucked the imaginary flowers
from the chain not so that man will wear the chain without
any fantasy or consolation, but so that he will shake off
the chain and cull the living flower. The criticism of
religion disillusions man to make him think and act and
shape his reality like a man who has been disillusioned
and has come to reason, so that he will revolve round
himself and therefore round his true sun. Religion is
only the illusory sun which revolves round man as long
as he does not revolve round himself. Religious cult is
to be replaced by undistorted verbal, instrumental and
communicative action, by communication without domination.

The task of history, as Marx sees it, once the world beyond
the truth has disappeared, is to establish the truth of
the world.6 The immediate task of philosophy, which for
Marx is at the service of history, once the saintly form
of human self-alienation has been unmasked, is to unmask
self-alienation in its unholy forms as it occurs in the
distorted communication of bourgeois family, society,
state and history. Thus the criticism of heaven turns
into the criticism of right and the criticism of theology
into the criticism of politics, of distorted communicative
practice in family, society, state and history. In

opposition to Hegel, Marx reduces divine wisdom to secular wisdom, theology to philosophy, history and science.

Marx's critical theory of religion reaches its full maturity in the first volume of the *Capital*.7 Here Marx lays out the fundamental methodological structure of a future dialectical materialistic theory of religion, fully to be developed only in the 20th century by neo-Marxists like Bloch, Horkheimer, Adorno, Erich Fromm, Herbert Marcuse and Habermas.8

In the *Capital* Marx states that the technology reveals the active behaviour of man toward nature, the immediate process of production of his life, instrumental action, and thereby also his social life relations, his communicative practice, as well as the spiritual, particularly religious ideas rising from them. In Marx's view, all history of religion which abstracts from this material basis, is uncritical. In Marx's estimate it is indeed much easier to find through analysis the earthy core of the religious fog formations than vice versa, to develop out of each real life condition, its instrumental and communicative practice, its deified form. The former is the bourgeois materialistic method, which reduces religious phenomena to psychic phenomena like fear, pleasure, will to power, search for meaning, etc.9 According to Marx, the latter is the only real, i.e., dialectical materialistic and therefore truly scientific method in the history of religion. Marx combines the bourgeois materialistic critique of religion with Hegel's dialectical logic, and thereby transcends the former and demystifies, so at least he thinks, the latter. Against Hegel, Marx recommends a philosophy of religion from below. The pattern of the ontological proof of God is broken in the philosophy as well as in the art and the religion of the 19th and 20th centuries.

Marx restates in the *Capital*, what he had already argued against Hegel's philosophy of right, namely that the religious world is but the reflex of the real world.10 But then he describes civil society much more concretely than before as a society based upon the production and exchange of commodities. In such a bourgeois society the producers in general enter into social relations with one another by treating their products as commodities and values. Thereby they reduce their individual private labor to the standard of homogenous human labor. According to Marx, for such a liberal capitalistic society, Christianity with its cult of abstract man, more specifically its bourgeois developments, i.e., unitarian, Protestantism, Deism, etc., is the most fitting form of

religion. For Marx as for Hegel before, Christianity is
the end stage of the history of religion. But while for
Hegel, Christianity is to be sublated in his philosophy,
and thereby not only to be negated in its mythical form
but also to be rescued and elevated in its truth core, for
Marx it is to be transformed into pure humanism.

Marx finds in the old Asiatic and other ancient modes
of production, that the conversion of the products into
commodities, and therefore the conversion of men into
producers of commodities, holds a subordinate place.11
But the conversion of products into commodities increases
in importance as the primitive communities approach nearer
and nearer to their dissolution. Trading nations properly
so called, exist in the ancient world only in its
interstices, like the "gods of Epicurus in the inter-mundia",
or like the "Jews in the pores of Polish society". Those
ancient social organisms of production are, as compared
with modern bourgeois society, extremely simple and
transparent. But they are founded either on the immature
development of man individually, who has not yet severed
the umbilical cord that unites him with his fellow men
in a primitive tribal community, or upon direct relations
of subjection. They can arise and exist only when the
development of the productive power of labor has not yet
evolved beyond a low level, and when, therefore, the social
relations within the sphere of material life, between
man and man, and between man and nature, are correspondingly
immediate and close.

According to Marx, this closeness is reflected in the
ancient worship of nature and in the other elements of
the popular religions. For Marx, as for Hegel before,
the first stage in the history of religions is the
religion of nature. According to Marx, the religious
reflex of the real world can, in any case, only then
finally vanish when the practical relations of everyday
life offer to man none but perfectly intelligible and
reasonable relations with regard to his fellow man and
to nature. That could not happen in primitive, archaic,
intermediate-historical or even modern society. It has
to await the arrival of a post-modern socialistic and
communistic society.

In Marx's view, the life-process of society, which is
based on the process of material production, does not
strip off its mystical veil until it is treated as
production by freely associated men, and is consciously
regulated by them in accordance with a settled plan.12
This, however, demands for society a certain material
groundwork or set of conditions of existence, which

in their turn are the spontaneous product of a long and painful process of development. Its result is the realm of freedom beyond the realm of necessity, i.e., nature and material production or instrumental practice.13 The free realm of communicative praxis lies beyond the realm of nature, adaptive behaviour, material production. Communism is the technical name for the realm of freedom as balance between the universal and the particular, the collective and the person. Today communism exists nowhere.

Marx admits that bourgeois political economy has indeed analyzed, however incompletely, value and its magnitude, and has discovered what lies beneath these forms.14 But bourgeois political economists, like Adam Smith, Says or Ricardo, never once asked the question why labor is presented by the value of its product, and labor time by the magnitude of that value. These formulae bear stamped upon them in unmistakable letters, that they belong to a state of society in which the process of production has the mastery over man instead of being controlled by him. Such formulae appear to the bourgeois intellect to be as much a self-evident necessity imposed by nature as productive labor itself. Hence forms of social production that preceded the bourgeois form, e.g., slavery or serfdom, are treated by the bourgeois political economists in much the same way as the "fathers of the church treated pre-Christian religions". These economists have a unique manner of proceeding. They differentiate only two kinds of institutions, those of art and those of nature. Feudal institutions are artificial institutions, those of the bourgeoisie are natural institutions. In this the bourgeois economists resemble the bourgeois enlightenment theologians, who also establish two kinds of religion. Every religion but their own is an invention of men, while their own religion is an emanation from God. Thus, so Marx concludes, there has been history, but there is none any longer. In the 20th century the great protestant theologian Karl Barth continues this line of religious thought.

In Marx's view, truly comical is the bourgeois economist M. Bastiat.15 He imagines that the ancient Greeks and Romans lived by plunder alone. But when people plunder for centuries, so Marx argues, there must always be something at hand for them to seize. The objects of plunder must be continually reproduced. It would thus appear that even Greeks and Romans had some process of production, consequently an economy. This economy just as much constituted the material basis of the Roman world, as capitalistic economy constitutes that of our Modern World. Marx speculates that perhaps Bastiat means that a mode of production based on slavery, is based on a system of plunder. In that case he treads on dangerous ground. If a giant thinker like Aristotle, so Marx argues, erred in his appreciation of slave labor, why should a bourgeois dwarf-economist like Bastiat be right in his appreciation of wage labor?

At this point Marx seizes the opportunity of shortly answering an objection made by a German newspaper in America against his work, *Critique of Political Economy* of 1859. In the estimation of that paper, Marx's view that each special mode of production and the social relations corresponding to it, in short, that the economic structure of society, is the real basis on which the juridical and political superstructure is built, and to which definite social forms of thought correspond, that the mode of production determines the character of the social, political and intellectual life generally -- all this is very true for our own times, for civil society in America and Europe, in which material interests preponderate, but not for the Middle Ages, in which Catholicism, nor for Athens and Rome, where politics reigned supreme. In the first place, it strikes Marx as an odd thing for anyone in America or Europe to suppose that these well-worn phrases about the Middle Ages and the Ancient World are unknown to anyone else. According to Marx, this much, however, is clear: That the Middle Ages could not live on Catholicism, nor the Ancient World on politics. On the contrary, it is the mode in which they gained a livelihood that explains why here politics and there religion, i.e., Catholicism, played the chief part. For the rest, so Marx states against the American paper, it requires but a slight acquaintance with the history of the Roman Republic, in order to be aware that its secret history is the history of its landed property. On the other hand, Don Quixote long ago paid the penalty for wrongly imagining that knight errantry was compatible with all economical forms of society. For Marx the dialectics of economic basis and cultural superstructure is the very essence of his critical theory of religion. Max Horkheimer, Walter Benjamin and Jürgen Habermas have further developed and thereby differentiated and refined Marx's dialectical basis -- superstructure theory. This has influenced greatly their critical theories of religion.[16]

CHAPTER IV

INFINITY AND FINALITY

In the 20th century, Horkheimer, the founder of the
critical theory of society of the *Frankfurt School*,
reinterprets Marx's theory of religion which has been
developed in liberal capitalistic society under the
new circumstances of advanced capitalistic society.[1]
Horkheimer emphasizes more than Marx the protest character
of religion versus its opium character. Unlike for Marx,
for Horkheimer the religious ideas are more than mere
fog formations. This is particularly true for the
central religious idea -- the God concept. Horkheimer
wrote in 1935, during the second year of his exile from
Nazi Germany, in New York a very short essay, "On
Religion", which remained nevertheless the very foundation
for his whole critical theory of religion as it was to be
developed during the next 40 years in the U.S.A. and,
particularly after World War II, in Germany.[2] Here
Horkheimer states that the concept of God was for a long
time the place where the idea was kept alive that there
are other norms besides those to which nature and society
give expression in their operation. For Horkheimer, as
for Marx before him, dissatisfaction with earthly destiny
is the strongest motive for the acceptance of a transcendental
being. If justice resides with God, then it is not to be
found in the same measure in the world, in the verbal,
instrumental and communicative practice of family, society,
state and history. For Horkheimer, religion is the record
of the wishes, desires and accusations of countless
generations.

Horkheimer is as certain as Marx that mankind loses
religion as it moves through history.[3] As for Hegel and
Marx, so is also for Horkheimer, Christianity the end
stage of the history of religion. But like Hegel, and
unlike Marx, Horkheimer stresses that this loss of
religion leaves its mark behind. According to Horkheimer,
part of the drives and desires which religious belief
preserved and kept alive through the centuries are
detached from the inhibiting religious form and become
productive forces in the communicative praxis of family,
society, state and history. In Horkheimer's view, in
this process even the immoderation characteristic of
shattered religious illusions, which already Marx observes,

acquires a positive form and is truly transformed.
Horkheimer understands his own critical theory of society
and religion as the positive form and transformation
which the immoderation, characteristic of shattered
religious illusions, acquires at the end of the history
of religion, if not total nihilism should be the last
word.

According to Horkheimer, in a really free mind the concept
of Infinity is preserved in an awareness of the finality
of human life and of the inalterable aloneness of man.4
It keeps society from indulging in an idiotic optimism,
an inflation of its own scientific and technological
knowledge into a new religion. This happens *de facto*
in historical positivism, the neo-positivism of the
Vienna School and in the reform positivism of Karl Popper,
his critical rationalism.5 From its very beginning
Horkheimer's theory of religion is characterized by a
deep pessimism.6 This he derives not from Marx, whose
theory of religion is rather optimistic in a humanistic
sense. The pessimism in Horkheimer's theory of religion
comes partially from Hegel, whose philosophy is less
optimistic than his archenemy Arthur Schopenhauer
thought.7 But ultimately the pessimism in Horkheimer's
theory of religion derives from Schopenhauer's philosophy
of the world as will and representation.8 Horkheimer was a
Schopenhauer follower, long before he began to study Hegel
and Marx. But unlike the pessimism of Schopenhauer, that of
Horkheimer refers merely to nature society and history, not
to the theological dimension. Horkheimer is not like
Schopenhauer a theological, but merely a sociological pessim.

In the year 1936, during the third year of his exile in
America, Horkheimer developed his theory of religion
further in a brilliant critique of Theodor Haecker's
new book, *The Christian and History.*9 Haecker who came
from Kierkegaard, had converted to Catholicism under the
influence of the writings of Cardinal Newman.10 He
became an outstanding philosopher of history, essayist
and culture critic in the Germany of the early 1930s.
He reinterpreted the traditional Catholic theology of
history existentially in the spirit of Kierkegaard and
Newman. Horkheimer has deep respect for the truly
religious faith of Haecker, but without being able to
share it. Horkheimer admires Haecker's Christian
humanism: the announcement of the infinite value of the
person, the faithfulness to the inborn right of the
individual, the struggle against the ideologies of race,
nation and leadership in the midst of the barbarism of
Nazi Germany. Horkheimer values greatly Haecker's and
his friends' courageous resistance against totalitarianism

in Nazi Germany on the basis of their Christian faith. But for Horkheimer, Haecker's theology of history is nevertheless still fundamentally ideology, i.e., false consciousness, necessary appearance, rationalization of the irrational conditions of society, state and history. Horkheimer's theory of religion is like that of Hegel and Marx ideology critique. Horkheimer's theory of religion is, as ideology critique, more radical than that of Hegel and as radical as that of Marx.

Horkheimer's critique of Haecker's theology of history shows that his attitude toward Catholicism and toward religion in general is not only negative, but rather materialistically dialectical.11 So Horkheimer admires the greatness and wisdom of Catholicism, not to dilute completely the thought of eternity and to separate it altogether from material wishes, as it is the rule in the Protestant form of Christianity. According to Horkheimer, while the materialistic bourgeois verbal, instrumental and communicative praxis in liberal and organized capitalistic society represents in a certain sense the truth of Catholic theology, the critical theory which holds up the mirror to that practice, does not simply reject the theological motifs, as they can be found, e.g., in Haecker's work, but supercedes, i.e., negates, preserves and elevates them. Horkheimer takes back, of course, in his critical theory of religion, the theological hypostatization of the abstract human being of civil society, by developing the concept of God from determinate historical conditions. Horkheimer's assumption that modern Christian theology is nothing else than the hypostatization of the abstract man of bourgeois society follows, of course, directly Marx's critical materialistic theory of religion.

Horkheimer like Marx before, takes the abstraction of man animated and sanctified by faith as the result of the social dynamic of liberal and organized capitalistic society. According to Horkheimer, the critical theory of religion teaches that men - as they do no longer encounter each other mainly as masters and slaves in civil society, but as free workers, and as the social whole reproduces itself through exchange -- posit their activities, the products of their work as being equal to each other and thereby come to the representation of man as such, i.e., man without time and place and without a definite fate. In Horkheimer's, as in Marx's view this popular idea of the abstract man is completed in the God concept of modern time, particularly in unitarian Protestantism and Deism. For Horkheimer really real are the historically determined factual men and women who are connected with

each other in the form of the social life, the verbal,
instrumental and communicative interaction of civil society,
its need-production and exchange system. These men and
women are the real subjects of that abstraction of man
which is the content of the bourgeois God-concept -- the
supreme being. To be sure, this abstraction reflects the
social being of liberal and advanced capitalistic society
only inaccurately, that is, abstractly. For Horkheimer the
hypostatized, eternalized concept of this abstraction, is,
at this stage of his intellectual development, entirely unrea

Horkheimer, like Bloch, has a critical attitude toward
the Marxian basis-superstructure theory.*12* For Horkheimer
not every structure of thought, every connection of
knowledge is a socially conditioned and necessary
appearance, i.e., ideology. But, according to Horkheimer,
as to Marx before, the notion of God of the last three
or four centuries proves itself nevertheless to be bound
to a transient form of social being, i.e., to the social
formation of civil society as a specific mode of
production and exchange. Horkheimer has no doubt that
modern Christians, like the Catholic Haecker, Romano
Guardini, Jacques Maritain or Reinhold Schneider, share
in this God concept of modern time. They are
fundamentally bourgeois ideologists. But the critical
theory of religion, including all its psychoanalytical
and sociological hypotheses -- mainly its Freudian and
Marxian elements -- does not hinder Horkheimer in the
least from considering the Christian religion as a
decisive cultural progress beyond the pagan forms of
religion -- magic, Taoism, Buddhism, Zoroastrianism,
Babylonian religion, etc. As for Hegel, so also for
Horkheimer, Christianity is not only the end of the
whole history of religion, but also its fulfillment
and completion.

In Horkheimer's perspective the critical theory does in
no way minimize or cover up the truth, the importance
and the implications of the thoughts, which have
connected themselves with Christianity throughout the
centuries.*13* Quite to the contrary! As the critical
theory negates the theological ideas of the resurection
of the dead, the last judgement, the eternal life as so
many dogmatic positions, the need of men and women for
infinite happiness becomes completely manifest and comes
into opposition to the evil earthly conditions, the
systematic distortion of communicative practice in
civil society. Horkheimer's critical theory of religion
liberates, so to speak, Christianity to itself, to the
truth and freedom promised by it, by letting its
fundamental theological concepts emmigrate into the

profane realm. Horkheimer's critical theory of religion
is to a large extent Christian meta-religion, which of
course is as little any longer genuine positive Christian
religion as meta-science is still positive science.
Horkheimer's theory of religion aims at total emancipation.

In Horkheimer's view, it is not true that the theoretical
materialist or critical theorist, similar to the
bourgeois materialist, must posit transitory goods --
pleasure, power, wealth as absolutes in order, as
atheists to be able to endure finitude as Christian
apologists like Haecker have asserted again and again
with great intellectual effort.14 The critical theorist
merely knows that the wish for the eternity of happiness,
this religious dream of humanity, cannot be fulfilled.
Horkheimer is fully aware of the fact that the thought
is really monstrous that the prayers of the persecuted,
the sick, the dying in their greatest need, the prayers
of the innocent victims who must die without clearing
up and explanation of their case, that the last hopes
for a superhuman instance reaches no goal; and that the
night, which no human light illuminates, is also not
penetrated by any divine light. Horkheimer makes these
statements in his Haecker-critique in New York, when in
Germany the concentration camps begin to operate, in
which in the next 9 years, thousands of Jews and
Christians would pray to the Lord for help, without
receiving any answer except the death commands of petite
bourgeois SS men, and in which thousands of socialists
and communists would be tortured and massacred without
even trying any longer to pray. Here Horkheimer asserts
absolute finitude.

Horkheimer knows only too well that the eternal truth
has without God as little a foundation and a hold as the
infinite love or freedom. Eternal truth and love become
without God unthinkable notions. But, so the critical
theorist asks, has monstrosity ever been a valid and
sound argument against the assertion or the denial of the
facts of the case. Does logic, postivistic or dialectical
contain the law, that a judgement is false if its
consequence would be desperation? According to Horkheimer,
the error that this small earth is a predestined space
and in the immense number of stars a selected and
priviledged star, this pious faith, which Haecker sees
once more verified by statements from modern astronomers
and on the basis of experiences, corresponds to a longing,
which also bourgeois materialistic atheists have
understood in the past, and which also critical theorists
comprehend very well today, the longing for perfect
justice and infinite happiness.

Clearly Horkheimer states about the relationship between religion and materialism in his critique of Haecker:

"All these wishes for eternity and particularly for the entrance of the universal justice and goodness the materialistic thinkers have in common with the religious ones, in opposition to the dullness of the positivistic attitude."15

Concerning the longing for eternal truth and love and universal justice and kindness, Horkheimer -- the materialistic thinker -- agrees fully with religious thinkers from Hegel to Haecker.16 But according to Horkheimer, while the religious thinker acquiesces in the thought, that the Christian revolution has already happened in the Christ event and that the wish for justice and love is thereby fulfilled anyhow, the materialistic thinker is embued with the feeling of the limitless abandonment of man. Up to his death in 1973, for Horkhewmer this feeling of the limitless loneliness of man is the only true answer to the impossible hope of Christianity and any other positive religion.

In Horkheimer's view, contrary to Haecker's opinion, the materialistic critical theorist must not necessarily fall into insanity in the face of man's abandonment, loneliness and finitude.17 Horkheimer admits that a metaphysical sorrow can very well be felt in the writings of the great materialists, in the tradition of whom he himself stands. This melancholia can also be perceived in Horkheimer's critical theory as well as in that of his close friend Adorno, and it is also not completely lacking in Habermas's theory of religion.18 Such sorrow is the price the critical theorist has to pay for his longing for the truth. Positivists or vulgar Marxists who criticize the pessimism of the critical theory, could overcome it effectively only by disproving its assertion of man's finitude, abandonment, suffering, and death. Of course this metaphysical sadness may not at all be limited to great materialist thinkers only. It can certainly be found in Hegel's philosophy as well who is the greatest of the modern idealists, and as such is in principle committed to a theological optimism.

Horkheimer knows very well that materialistic thought is essentially concerned with pleasure, delight and desire.19 But the materialist Horkheimer is too truthful and honest to deny the fact that pleasure carries in itself already as phenomenon the consciousness of transitoriness and of the bitterness of the end. This knowledge belongs to the essence of pleasure. The critical theory integrates into itself not only the heritage of Feuerback and Marx, but also that of Schopenhauer and Freud. The latter heritage balances out the former in the critical theory of the Frankfurt School.

But for Horkheimer, as for Marcuse and other critical theorists, the revolt against the senselessly curtailed and impaired life of the majority of all men and women, the affinity to hedonism and the historical partiality for the opressed, which constitute the critical sociology of religion, has its origin in the experience of the irretrievability of human happiness. The remembrance of the sufferings of the dead is at the heart of the critical theory.

In Horkheimer's perspective, the question why a behaviour and conduct toward the world, for which also the good seems -- according to its very essence -- to be connected with a negative, does not turn over into desperation, this psychological problem which the Christian Haecker disposes of and dismisses *a priori*, can be solved less through the analysis of atheism than through the proof that the ability for pleasure is not bound to the egotistic personality structure of most religious people.[20] The psychological structure, on the basis of which Haecker, in contradiction to certain aspects of his work, considers the perseverance in the materialistic theory to be impossible, constitutes, of course, a widespread special case, which -- so Horkheimer believes -- will cease to be natural and normal someday in the future -- i.e., the bourgeois personality structure. In Horkheimer's very realistic historical perspective, when not only the mass delusion and insanity by which, according to Haecker's true word, the experience of the irreparable transitoriness of man is drowned and sealed off in the 1930's in the nations, but also the consolation of religion loses its power, i.e., with the entrance of conditions, which can exist without myth or legends, then certainly only the social, not also the natural ground of the melancholy in man would fall away. But in Horkheimer's view, not only would this natural ground, i.e., death, change its appearance under conditions in which the particular purpose of the individuals would be superceded in the social whole. In the reconciled society this would happen very differently from the way that is the case in competitive bourgeois society. The individual would devote himself or herself lovingly and creatively to the reconciled society and it would enhance the realization of the persons' productive forces. Beyond that, so Horkheimer states finally in his critique of Haecker, death can escalate limitlessly the solidarity of all living beings, after once under the condition of

a post-modern, post-capitalistic, reconciled society it
will be stripped of the religious and non-religious
ideologies. Throughout his life Horkheimer resisted
alternative Future I - the totally administered society
and alternative Future II - world wars, and fought for
alternative Future III - the reconciled society.[21]

According to the materialist Horkheimer, the religious
faith in the new creation of the world, the new heaven
and the new earth, which the Christian Haecker professes,
goes a short space too far in the fight against
melancholy.[22] Therefore Horkheimer must reject it.
There is no doubt that the early Horkheimer's critical
theory of religion is and will remain for some time to
come as serious, respectable and viable an opponent and
competitor and a challenge to Christianity, as presented
by Haecker in late civil society, as stoicism once was
in the late Roman empire.[23] That Horkheimer's critical
theory of religion is by far superior to all in advanced
capitalistic society extant forms of positivism as well
as the positive religions, which share in it and its
dullness, must not even be mentioned. Horkheimer's
realistic humanism is reinforced by that of Walter
Benjamin and Jürgen Habermas.

CHAPTER V

In the year 1932, four years before Horkheimer the
critical theorist of religion Benjamin had written an
excellent critique of the theologian Haecker's new book
*Virgil, Father of the Occident.*1 At this time - a year
before Hitler came into power in Germany - Benjamin was
extremely upset and alarmed concerning the political
events in Germany.2 Without wanting to be a prophet,
Benjamin knew that the threatening victory of German
fascism signified a second world war with immense
consequences.

According to Benjamin, Haecker in spite of the fact that
he is a Catholic, is also a disciple of Sören Kierkegaard
and this not only as a theologian, but also as a
polemicist.3 The philologist Benjamin understands
Haecker's more theological than philological work in
terms of its polemical intent. In his book Haecker is
concerned with two subject matters: the dissolution of
the traditional negative valuation, which puts the late
Roman poet Virgil into the shadow of the early Greek
poet Homer, and the annulment of any non-theological,
more precisely non-Catholic interpretation of Virgil.

In Benjamin's view, Haecker transforms the Virgilian
presentation of the wanderings and war troubles of
"*pater Aeneas*" from an old heroic legend, which intends
the mythological establishment of the corresponding hero
cult, into a kind of life of a saint similar to the
biblical stories. This saint story introduces a not-
to-be foreseen sequence of deeds, which have not really
been accomplished by Aeneas himself but rather by the
heirs of his mission. It merely serves as a prelude to
an immense enfolding of fate, in the face of which
Aeneas feels himself to be not so much the originator as
the forerunner of the promised salvation and as the
instrument of God. In short, Haecker posits Virgil's
conception of history between the bible and St.
Augustine's masterpiece *De Civitate Dei.*

According to Benjamin, the mystical-interpretative
procedure gives Haecker's work the character of a
theological *tractatus*. To this fits likewise Haecker's

elevated language, his linguistic mysticism as well as
the authoritarian determination through which he connects
Christian dogmas or *dicta* with each verse of Virgil.
Sometimes Haecker gives the last line of a verse a
Pascalian turn. Concerning the famous expression of
Virgil "*lacrima rerum*", Haecker conjures the idea of
religious justification. Then Haecker interprets the
fullness of Virgilian humanity as the readiness to honor
the *mysterium*, i.e., to believe in a divine *fatum* without
injury of the free will and the responsibility of man.
Haecker then determines more precisely this *mysterium*
as a double *mysterium*, which is supposed to be fulfilled
through Christianity in the *beneplacitum* of the
trinitarian God, who is spirit, life; a *beneplacitum*
Dei which is inscrutable, inaccessible as the old Greek
Fate. But it is not dark through night, but dark
through light. It does not bring suffering out of
arbitrariness, but out of wisdom. It does not only give
perfect justice, but also ardour and flame of love.

In Haecker's theological reflections, God is true and
good and beautiful. As soon as a poet like Virgil
touches only the seam of the beauty of God - whereby he
touches also at the same time the hem of the true and
the good - there is in his work necessarily an absolute
and an imperishable element.

Certainly Benjamin can find in Haecker's book deeper and
more fundamental statements about Virgil. But for
Benjamin, that does not change the fact that Haecker's
resolute neglect of a profane, i.e., proper, really true
Virgilian philology makes him completely unable to
recognize the *theologumena* in Virgil's Aeneas as what
they actually are: models and patterns out of the
cultural heritage of the belletristic late romanticism
of the declining Roman slave-owner society.

According to Benjamin, Haecker is very significantly
and very offensively and shockingly unable to go beyond
the individual psychic space of Virgil, the *anima*
naturaliter Christiana. Haecker never gains the vista
into the Roman religion - the religion of political
utility according to Hegel - and its specific piety,
which is so important for Virgil.4 Haecker is no longer
vividly interested in the practices of the Roman state
religion, nor generally in the whole heaven of Roman
gods. According to Haecker, this heaven was mainly -
except for the farmer gods - already for Virgil merely
beautiful poetry. It is only of external symbolicial
significance. All these Roman religious practices and
gods are of interest merely to science, particularly

religiology. Haecker is a theologian, not a religiologist.

Characterizing in the context of the Roman religion the
opposition between state religion and piety, Haecker states,
according to Benjamin, that in the "pure spirit" there is
no longer the possible opposition between external piety,
which is none, and an internal piety, which holds in contempt
the external one or calumniates it. This is so for Haecker,
since in the pure spirit everything is interior: form as
well as content. But in man, as he is historically, there
is nevertheless this opposition between external and internal
piety.

For Benjamin the inconspicuous, auxilliary concept of the
"pure spirit", which appears here in Haecker's work, deserves
greatest attention. This is so, since nobody else except
this pure spirit is the owner of the peculiar privileges,
which signify a thinking as Haecker practices it. According
to Benjamin, this privileged thinking is authoritarian.
But there is something peculiar about authority. Certainly
it must be strong and unshakable. But it must also be
inviting and engaging. It must be visible far away. It must
be a fortress, but with a thousand doors. Knowing better,
is also a firm castle, except that one has the privilege to
live alone in it. Benjamin's attack aims at Haecker's
spiritualism and idealism. He opposes a false spiritualism
which gilds the unjust world rather than to change it.
Benjamin puts his own materialistic, realistic humanism
from below, inherited from Marx - against the Christian
Haecker's idealistic and spiritualistic theology and humanism
from above. He does this in complete agreement with the
dialectical historical materialism later expressed in
Horkheimer's Haecker critique.5

In Benjamin's view, there have always been many intellectuals
in Germany and there are particularly many there in the
early 1930's, who are of the opinion that what they know and
the fact that they know it, constitutes now the lever of all
social relations and from there on things must become different.
But these people have only the most shadowy ideas, in *which
mode* this knowledge is to be communicated to the masses.
One must simply communicate and stress the communique!
From these intellectuals the thought is very distant, that
a knowledge which contains no instruction concerning its
possibility of dissemination does not help much. It is in
reality no knowledge at all. If Benjamin tells these
intellectuals in Germany, that every true knowledge proves
its truth only in such a way that it makes itself on the
way to new ignorance, he makes them shy and diffident.
Nothing characterizes the helplessness, the lack of a sense
of reality of German Christian intellectuals like Haecker

so crassly as the lamentable immediacy, with which the pure spirit in them turns to "the man" without making any bones about it. The man and the spirit have, in the heads of people like Haecker, concluded a ghostly friendship. So united, man and spirit can also be encountered in Haecker's book on Virgil.

According to Benjamin, Haecker declares already in the introduction to his book on Virgil - in a, maybe, superfluous apology of "the man" and "the human" - which enjoy anyway all the honors of fashionable words - that there is almost nobody who considering the countlessly different species of plants and animals and directing his main attention particularly to the differentiation of these species, can in view of this forget or deny that there is *the* plant and *the* animal with eternally unchangeable characteristics. But there are indeed such people today, who seem to believe in a radical change of the nature of man in the course of the times.

In Benjamin's perspective, in case of a scholastically trained scholar like Haecker, such a statement needs an unusual freedom from intellectual scruples. This is so, since nowhere the question of whether there are such genus-substantialities (formae substantiales), if they are *ante rem*, in re or postrem, has been fought through with similar exasperation as in the universalia-struggle, which nominalists fought against the realists, throughout the late Middle Ages.6 But Benjamin does not find Haecker's urgent partisanship *post festum* for medieval realism so curious as it may look. One will find Haecker's defense curious only so long as one has not yet grasped what it does achieve for the mentioned privileges of the pure spirit.

Here Benjamin returns once more to the "man" as the "spirit" sees him.7 Haecker says in a later connection in his book on Virgil, that the occidental man has had the dominion over all other nations and races for over 2,000 years. This, brought into the ultimate formula, means for Haecker that the occidental man has had in principle the possibility - which in a tactical sense he often did not realize - to understand all other men. In this is included Western man's factual and potential political domination. According to Haecker, this possibility occidental man has had through his faith. The Catholic poet Reinhold Schneider had similar thoughts and allied himself with fascists like Salazar in Portugal.8

It is, in any case, certainly not Benjamin's fault, when Haecker moves the real-political equivalent of his idea of man so painfully close to fascist ideology becoming daily stronger at this time and so becomes somewhat similar to Carl Schmidt, the most intelligent pioneer of national socialism, also a Catholic theologian. 9 According to Benjamin, this in a drastic sense privileged understanding of the non-western world is characterized through the working in each other of capitalistic exploitation and Christian mission. That way, as a matter of fact, the contraband usually looks, which, wrapped up in the muslin of the pure spirit, the travellers bring along to cloud-cuckoo town.

According to Benjamin, theology least of all should be such a cloud cuckoo town. There were indeed theological thinkers, who appeared, particularly in his generation, in order to take up the struggle against the idolatry of the spirit. One was the Jewish theologian Franz Rosenzweig, who came from philology like Benjamin himself. The other was the Protestant theologian Florens Christian Rang, who came from political science.

Benjamin knows, of course, that also Haecker considers himself to be a language-thinker. Benjamin knows that Haecker is also a politician, in spite of the fact that he may have preferred not to count as such. In Benjamin's judgement, this precisely excludes Haecker from the rank of the genuine theological thinkers, that he is of the opinion that he could handle the philosophy of language as well as of politics from the position of pure spirit, without being willing to engage himself either in philology or in economics.

Certainly – and only this way the whole matter moves into the right light for Benjamin – Rosenzweig and particularly Rang are heretically oriented men, for whom it is not impossible to carry the tradition on their own back, instead of administering it in a settled and established way. In Benjamin's view, it is his Lutheran moderatism which deprives Haecker of the fruits of his efforts. What does even a most radical return to the sources help, the even greatest art of interpretation, if the consciousness itself clings to convention. The traitorous distinguishing mark of this conventionalism is, in Haecker's case, the dilettantish question, what Virgil means to us today? Certainly this question corresponds precisely to the false immediacy with which the spirit turns to the men. According to Benjamin as to Hegel, Schopenhauer, Horkheimer and Adorno, it is the greatest political significance of the Jewish and Christian doctrine of the fall to have finished once and for all this type of immediacy and interiority.10

In Benjamin's perspective, Haecker should have penetrated to
the genuine mediate question: What does the history of
the Virgilian poetry and of its exploration teach us at
this point in time, when both are menaced by their
involuntary closing?[11] In case Haecker would have asked
this question, he would have proven his brilliant
literary talents without directing attention to his very
modest intellectual gifts. On this way, there is no
lack of models. Benjamin thinks of the scientific
modesty with which the historian and religiologist
Betzold explored the continuation of the gods of
Antiquity in medieval humanism. Whoever takes this
model into consideration, will understand how much more
significantly the presentation of the embeding of Virgil
in the medieval literature would have done justice not
only to the poet, but also to scholasticism. But
Haecker's formulas repeat fundamentally once more only
those with which once the "magician Virgilius" was
conjured.

Benjamin is not entirely disinclined to agree with
Haecker, when he states that a humanism which is
completely emptied from theology cannot resist the
present flood of barbarism. But for Benjamin, the joke
simply goes too far, when Haecker recommends Thomism as
a remedy for an age, in which this humanism is compromised
in theory and practice alike. Haecker lives in an ivory
tower, out of the highest window of which he looks,
abusing the world around him. The worst is that the
ground, on which this tower has been built, is in the
process of caving in. How else is it possible that a
man like Haecker can handle the notion of the adventistic
paganism as a customary expression and, in spite of that,
does not feel or perceive that which is coming toward our ow
days, which is indeed something adventistic, even if it
marches, e.g., the SA battalions in their brown shirts.

It is utterly amazing for Benjamin, that a man like
Haecker identifies a mere philological-aesthetical
explanation of Virgil's work as a falsum, a decomposition
of the whole, executed by disintegrated spirits, and
nevertheless, nowhere finds words for the barbarous
conditions to which every present-day humanism is
necessarily bound in late capitalistic society. In
Benjamin's view, the insincerity and the haughtiness of
the spiritual is responsible for this inconsistency.
These same traits allow men like Haecker to accept the
designation "spiritual persons" without blush, since
they are not able to render an account of their position
in the capitalistic process of production and exchange.
In case Haecker had taken into account his position in

the production process of German bourgeois society, an essayist of his rank could not possibly have avoided taking into consideration the problem of any interpretation of Virgil, Marxist, Christian or positivist: the very *possibility* of the humanist in our time. The reflection upon the privileges in the power of which one can still be a humanist today would have liberated Haecker from their hardest deposition: that privileged knowledge of the right way, which constitutes the most fateful and disastrous metamorphosis of the educational privilege in general.

Benjamin was not surprised by Hitler's victory, when it occurred a year after he had written his critique against Haecker.*12* As Jew and undesirable author, exposed to boycott, Benjamin is able for some time to publish under pseudonyms in Frankfurt and elsewhere in Germany. Finally, also Benjamin must decide for emmigration. He moves to Paris, where he had always felt at home and safe. At the beginning of the war, Benjamin is interned for three months in Paris.

In 1940, Horkheimer, who had emigrated with his Frankfurt Institute for Social Research to Columbia University, New York, in 1933, was able to procure for Benjamin an affidavit and a visa for the U.S.A. Since after the defeat of France only the way over Spain remained open, Benjamin joined a group of emigrants, who attempted to cross the Pryennes mountains. In the Spanish border town of Port Bou, the Alcalde made an extortion attempt against a small group of refugees. Benjamin took seriously the threat of the Alcalde to deliver the refugees back to France and into the hands of the Gestapo, if they would not yeild to this extortion attempt. In the night of September 26, 1940, Benjamin poisoned himself. He was still alive the next morning. But with his last energy, he hindered any attempt to pump his stomach out. His death had the effect, that the officials let the refugees pass. Benjamin rescued the refugees through his sacrificial death.

The last written reflection Benjamin produced he called "Theological-Political Fragment."*13* Of all the critical theorists, Benjamin would have been most able, had he survived, to discover the theological glowing fire in the depth dimension of historical materialism.*14* Brecht could have rescued his friend's, the marxist playwrite Bertholt Brecht's materialistic atheism as inversed theology, in the form of a negative theology.*15* Because of Benjamin's early death this task to go beyond mere ideology critique of Haecker, Jacques Maritain, Romano Guardini, Reinhold Schneider and other Christian theologians and to discover

the theological core of dialectical materialism fell to
Horkheimer, Adorno, Marcuse, Fromm and Habermas. They
at least moved, in Benjamin's spirit, this task closer to
its possible realization, as can very well be seen from
Kung's functional theology and Metz's and Peukert's
critical political theology of the subject.16

CHAPTER VI

BEYOND IDEOLOGY CRITIQUE

Habermas - like Marx, Horkheimer, Adorno and Benjamin before him - starts his theory of religion out of and against Hegel's philosophy of religion.1 According to Habermas, at the end of his course on the philosophy of religion at the University of Berlin, Hegel undertook to define his views with respect to the delicate question of the sublation of religion into philosophy. It gained momentous significance after Hegel's death, through the controversies among his pupils on the Hegelian Right and the Hegelian Left. In Habermas's view, here Hegel sets the task for philosophy of justifying the contents of religion, especially of Christianity as the absolute religion or religion of truth and freedom, before the higher authority of reason by divesting these contents of the form of faith. To be sure, Habermas's interpretation of Hegel's intent at the transfer of the contents of Christianity from the form of representation or imagination to the form of dialectical reason belongs itself to the tradition of the Hegelian Left.2

In any case, Habermas is correct when he states that, according to Hegel, reflection had broken in upon religion during the course of bourgeois enlightenment.3 It had split the Christian community into three antagonistic groups -- naive believers, educated believers and dialectical believers. This inner antagonism threatens Christianity with destruction. According to Hegel, critical thinking, which has begun this way through the bourgeois enlightenment, has no place to rest any more. It pushes on to its conclusion. It empties the psyche, the heaven and the knowing spirit. The religious content then takes refuge in the dialectical notion. Here it must receive its justification. According to Habermas, now, because of its philosophical nature, this critical knowledge which replaces faith cannot be universally disseminated. Habermas criticizes Hegel that he regresses in this behind the intentions of the bourgeois enlightenment. He thereby withdraws himself -- to speak with Paul Tillich -- from the bourgeois principle and subordinates himself to the feudal principle or the romantic principle of the myth of origin.4 This charge was made by the liberals against Hegel's social

philosophy already before the Hegelian Left came into
existence.5

Habermas is critical of Hegel because he has never
departed from the soil of the basic Parmenidean prejudice,
which has lived on in Western Philosophy: That the Many
are excluded from participation in Being.6 For Habermas
this is the reason why the truth of religion, as soon as
it takes refuge in the dialectical notion, must emigrate
from the community of the faithful to make its abode with
the philosophers, and thus lose its universal recognition.7
The public atheism of so-called cultivated people will
also seize hold of the poor, who until that time have
lived in a state of ingenious religiosity. Even the
power of the state can do nothing against this decline
of faith. The consequences of demythologization cannot
be arrested. The fulfillment of the epoch, whose sign
is the need for justification by means of the dialectical
notion, is accompanied precisely by a demoralization of
the people. Habermas quotes from the end of Hegel's
philosophy of religion:

> "When the gospel is no longer preached to the poor,
> when the salt has become dumb, and all the
> foundations have been quietly removed, then the
> people for whose permanently limited reason truth
> can only exist in the representational image, no
> longer know how to find aid for their inner
> religious urge."8

It appears from Habermas's interpretation, as if the
atheism of the masses was a result of the truth of
religion taking refuge in the notion and emigrating
from the community of the faithful to make its abode
with the philosophers.9 According to Hegel, the
destruction of the Christian community because of its
inner division in naive and enlightened believers in the
context of the general decline of the Western Civilization
in the present world-historical transition period, makes
the rescue of the Christian truth -- the trinity, the
incarnation, the unity of divine and human nature, the
absolute reconciliation -- by a philosophical theology
or theological philosophy necessary once more at the
end of the European world as before, during the fall of
the Roman world.10 In Hegel's view, the philosophy is
in this relationship a separate sanctuary, and its
servants form an isolated priesthood which must not go
together with the late bourgeois world, and which must
guard the possession of the absolute truth of Christianity.

Habermas finds remarkable the stoical placidity and

composure with which Hegel anticipates the ruin of Christianity.11 According to Habermas, Hegel speaks cooly of a "false note" that is present in reality.12 This disharmony is resolved for and by philosophy, for it recongizes that the idea is inherent in the Christian Revelation. But this reconciliation is only a partial one. It has validity only for the isolated priesthood of the philosophers. The reaction which the transition from one stage of absolute spirit -- religion -- to the next -- philosophy -- effects in the world of objective spirit -- bourgeois family, society, state and history -- this tremor which shakes the moral totality of Western Civilization cannot be alleviated by philosophy. Habermas quotes the last sentence of Hegel's philosophy of religion:

> "How the temporal, empirical present can find a way out of this dilemma, how it is to form itself, that must be left to this world and is not the immediate practical task, is not the business of philosophy."13

According to Habermas, this continence of the Hegelian theory, which mirrors its superiority, and at the same time its impotence in the face of a danger so full of practical consequences -- demythologization of the masses in civil society followed by their demoralization - is consistent with the meaning of the Hegelian system's compelling logical presupposition.

Habermas misunderstands as stoical placidity and composure what in reality is Hegel's Christian faith in the face of the disaster of Christendom and Western Civilization, the symptoms of which he discovered long before Marx, Friedrich Nietzche, Sigmund Freud and Horkheimer and his Frankfurt School, at latest in his phenomenology.14 Hegel can look the negativity of the transition period, in which he lives and Marx, Nietzsche, Freud and Horkheimer will live, in the eye without illusion and ideological distortion because he has, at the end of his philosophy of religion, the fundamental faith, which they can no longer share, that:

> "... the kingdom of God has been founded for eternity, the Holy Spirit as such lives eternally in his community and the gates of hell will not overcome the church."15

In Hegel's view, this faith has survived the ruin of the Roman Empire.16 In Hegel's perspective, the truth content of this faith -- the absolute reconciliation -- philosopher -theologians like himself are to carry through the dark age of the present transition period into the more

rational post-European, post-modern, post-bourgeois
American or Slavic world of a very distant future, as
once the Benedictan monks, who fled the declining Roman
civilization, preserved the Christian truth and thereby
laid the foundations for a new, the medieval culture.[17]

According to Habermas -- using the words of Friedrich
Schelling, the early friend and later opponent of Hegel,
reaching back into Western mysticism -- the distorted
world and a humanity that is concealed from itself
manifest their curse in the domination of the external
over the internal, of the lower over the higher, of
anger over love, of the force of the dark sentiments over
purity and clarity.[18] Habermas argues that on this same
experience of the contradictory character of the world
is based the prejudgement of Marx's historical materialism,
which grants priority of the economic basis of capitalistic
society over its cultural superstructure, including
religion. Habermas, like Hegel, Marx and Horkheimer
before him, does not accept the barbaric power with which
the economic conditions in capitalistic society hold a
determinate sway over all that is more sublime -- art,
religion, philosophy, including science -- as a sign of
the ontological structure of the world, which must remain
as it is forever. Instead, Habermas considers this power
of the material basis in advanced capitalistic and
socialistic society to be the sign of the governance of
nature over society. For Habermas this predominance is
historical and can therefore be overthrown in the course
of history as man's self-enlightening, self-emancipating
and self-formative process of becoming. For Habermas,
as for Lessing and Hegel before him, history is essentially
a learning process. Man is at least imperfectly
perfectible. Qualitative progress is possible. As long
as the governance of nature over society is not yet
broken in history as a learning process, the natural
condition subjects the system of social life to the joke
of the process of reproduction in its naked economic
form.

In Habermas's perspective, the egoistic relationship which
is established together with private property is interpreted
by Marx - following Hegel as the encapsulation within which
essenial human forces are concentrated and estranged from th
human beings themselves.[19] Marx considers private property
to be the dark focal point at which the eclipsing of the
world is concentrated, the knots in which all the threads
of compulsive social relationships are drawn together and
fastened. In Habermas's view, certainly such images can
only have a scientific bearing, insofar as concepts can
be developed out of them. But their coloration preserves

the wealth of meaning for the conceptual distinctions. For Habermas it is not otherwise with the concept of ideology. Of course, interests as well as ideas are but dialectical moments of the same totality. But this as totality is held together by the categories of a process of reproduction, which constitutes itself as a closed system and therefore can be constructed as such, as long as subjects do not recognize as their own the praxis that is severed from them within this context.

In Habermas's view, before any critique of ideology can be possible in the fields of religion, art and philosophy, this anticipatory conception must prove itself in terms of the relation between politics and economics.20 Political actions and institutions have to be derivable from conflicts of interests, which in turn necessarily have to emerge from the capitalistic process of production. This Marx sought to show empirically, especially in the example provided by the Civil War in France.21 In so doing Marx already presupposes, of course, as Hegel before, that the movements in the sphere of economic reproduction itself can be comprehended as a systematically coherent complex. According to Habermas, the proof for this must be furnished by political economy carried out as a critique, in that it derives all economic phenomena from the process of the accumulative utilization of capital, without any recourse to phenomena outside of this sphere, e.g., political, psychological or religious phenomena. Political economy cannot be permitted to transfer the real problems to the data. That which modern positive economics allows as given in the form of data series, it must also comprehend economically.

In Habermas's perspective, precisely because the late Ernst Bloch, a Marxian Schelling, or a Schellingian Marxist, in returning to Marx's theory of religion as contained in the latter's theses on Feuerbach, explicitly re-establishes the practical significance of ideology critique, he can go beyond the critique of religious ideology summarized in the Marxian theses.22 Marx states in the fourth thesis that Feuerbach proceeds from the fact of man's religious self-alienation, the doubling-up of the world into a sacred and a profane one. In Marx's view, Feuerbach's accomplishment consists in resolving the religious superstructure back into its secular basis. But in Marx's perspective, that this earthly basis elevates itself above itself and establishes itself as an independent realm above the daily verbal, instrumental and communicative practice of people in their immediate life world, can be explained only as the result of the internal ruptures and self-contradictions in this secular

basis. According to Marx, the worldly basis of civil
society must thus be understood both in its dialectical
contradictions and convulsions, which already Hegel
registers and predicts as superceding themselves
dialectically.23

But the religious world above, so Habermas argues together
with Bloch, is so intimately a part of its earthly basis,
the production and exchange system of organized capitalistic
society, that the idea of God is debased, distorted and
made use of as ideology by the inner antagonisms -- luxury
and misery, producer and consumer, owner and worker, rich
and poor classes, nations and hemispheres, which sunder the
late capitalistic world, yet without being entirely
dissolved into this ideology.24 Unlike Hegel and very
much like Marx and the early Horkheimer, Habermas has no
doubt that religion emerges as a product of
the dialectical contradictions in the secular world of
capitalistic society. But at the same time Horkheimer
knows like Hegel and very much unlike Marx, that religion
does indeed transcend the boundaries of civil society as
a specific social formation in the process of the evolution
of the human species. If this is correct, so Habermas
agrees with Bloch, then religion as the false consciousness
of a false world is not simply nothing. Religious ideas
are not merely fog formations, opiate, illusions. For,
as the negation of the negation of humanity in the
antagonistic capitalistic society, religion is still --
though not necessarily consciously so -- full of
encoded human experiences. Within the ideological shell
of religion, Habermas discovers more than Marx and like
Hegel as well as Horkheimer, Adorno, Marcuse, Fromm and
Bloch the concrete and real utopian core: Within the
false ideological consciousness the true consciousness,
within the opiate protest, within mere consolation the
courage to walk upright, within cold desperation, warm
hope, within conservativism revolution.25

According to Habermas, certainly the transparency of a
better world as respresented mythically or theologically
by positive religions, is refracted by hidden interests,
often class interests, even in those aspects, which being
utopian and as such subversive, point beyond the organized
capitalistic and even post-capitalistic socialistic
society.26 But while already for Marx religion includes
a protest potential and according to Horkheimer the
potential to become a critical productive force in
communicative practice, for Habermas the hopes, which the
transparency of a reconciled world in religious
consciousness awakens in people, the longing for justice,
which it justifies, contain energies, that at the same

time, once instructed about themselves by dialectical theory, turn into critical, if not revolutionary, impulses. According to Habermas, as for the early Horkheimer, and for Bloch before, something remains after religion is not only demythologized, but also deideologized. Reflecting on political systems on the Right and on the Left taught not only Horkheimer, Adorno, Marcuse, Benjamin and Fromm, but also Habermas, not to think of the claims to the Absolute as certain, and yet, not to deduct anything from the appeal to the emphatic concept of the truth contained not only in metaphysics, but also in the great world religions.27 In his critical theory of religion, Habermas is no less than Hegel, Horkheimer and Adorno, committed to this concept of the truth as the very opposite of ideology as the rationalization of irrational human action systems, be it the advanced capitalistic - or the bureaucratic - socialistic nation - or super-nation state.28 This is of greatest importance in the face of the present world wide identity crisis on the personal, collective and religious level. To the resolution of this identity crisis not only Habermas's theory of religion, but the very core of his whole philosophy of communicative praxis is devoted.29 Precisely this concern for the solution of the modern identity crisis constitutes Habermas's philosophy as Hegelian.

In his dialectical theory of religion the Hegelian Habermas
traces the relation of ego and group identity through four
stages of social and religious evolution.[1] According
to Habermas, on the first stage, in the archaic societies,
whose structure was determined by kinship ties, there
emerge mythical world views. Here the social relationships
of the family and the tribe serve as the interpretative
schema, according to which the mythical image forms
analogies between all the natural and cultural phenomena.
Here as elsewhere Habermas does not follow Hegel's
idealistic methodology constructing the history of religion
from above, the idea of God, but rather Marx's
materialistic methodology developing the history of
religion from below, the basis of the archaic society,
family, tribe and their verbal, instrumental and
communicative practice. Also for Habermas the model of Anselm
of Canterbury's ontological proof is broken once and for all.

In Habermas's view, for archaic man and society nothing
is so different as not to exist in universal interdependence. Everything depends on everything else in
the universe in an evident manner. The mythical world
image of archaic man assigns a meaningful place to every
perceptible element -- stone, plant, animal or man. In
so doing, the mythical world view absorbs the insecurities
threatening the archaic society, which due to its
underdeveloped productive forces, is barely able to
bring its natural or social environment under control.
Archaic man deals with almost every contingency through
the medium of interpretation. Every contingency of
nature, society and history can be interpreted away.

According to Habermas, the mythical world view comprehends
all its entities as analogues. Men are substances in the
same manner as are stones, plants, animals and gods. Thus
for archaic man his tribe does not stand out in contrast
to its individual members or to nature. Like Hegel,
Habermas compares the individual's identity in archaic
society to the natural identity of the child: The
immediate and hence non-spiritual, mere natural
unity of the individual with his species and with the
world as such.[2] In Habermas's as in Hegel's view, at

45

this archaic stage there cannot arise problems of identity.
The condition for this is the differentiation between the
singular identity of the individual, the particular
identity of the society and the universal identity of
religion. Habermas, equipped with Hegels' dialectical
notion, the differentiated unity of the singular, the
particular and the universal, can first discover this
differentiation among the three forms of identity only
in the world of the polytheistic religions of the early
civilization of the city state.

In Habermas's perspective on the second evolutionary
stage, in the ancient states, kingdoms or city states,
the early civilizations dispose of a form of centralized
political organization which requires authorization or
legitimation because of their inner class antagonism.3
Hence they must be assimilated into the religious
narratives, legends, myths and secured by cult and
rituals.

Following Hegel, Habermas observes that the gods of the
polytheistic religions in the ancient city states of the
Far and Near East, Greece and Rome assume human shape.
Here the anthropomorphism increases in religion, which
according to Hegel, comes to its peak in Christianity.4
These gods in human shape are conceived by the believers
as actively and sometimes arbitrarily controlling specific
realms of life and as themselves being subjected to the
necessity of an abstract destiny. This is the case
particularly in the Greek religion of beauty and fate.5

According to Habermas, the beginning of the desacralization
of the natural environment, sacralized by the previous
archaic nature religions, in e.g. Bablonian, Greek or Roman
city states, and the fact that the political institutions
for the first time get a certain autonomy relative to
the cosmic order, point to the emergence of a sphere of
contingencies, in which the individual can no longer deal
with the fortuitous by simply interpreting it away as
archaic societies had done in their nature religions,
but in which he or she must learn to bring contingency
under control by his own action.6 It is obvious that
Habermas emphasizes in his theory of religion the political
sphere much more and the economic sphere much less than
Marx and the early Horkheimer had done. The reason for
this is that for Habermas of the five potentialities
differentiated by Hegel in his *Jena System Fragments* as
so many media of man's humanization-language, work,
family, recognition, nation, the fourth one, communicative
action is more important than the first one, verbal practice,
the second one, instrumental action, the third one, familial

interaction or the fifth one, national cooperation.7 While for the mature Marx, Hegel's second potentiality -- work or instrumental practice -- becomes more important than all the other dimensions of human interaction, Habermas balances out the latter's one-sidedness by his own emphasis on verbal and mainly communicative action, understood to a large extent as political praxis.8

In Habermas's view on the evolutionary stage of the early civilizations new forms of religious action and thereby patterns of interactions between gods and men, are formed: prayer, sacrifice and worship.9 These indicate to Habermas the process of a single self emerging from the universal complex of the given order of substances and forces in nature and state and the forming of a single self-identity. Socrates would be the most outstanding example for the city state of Athens and beyond.10 For Habermas as for Hegel before, on the level of the city states and their positive religions, substance turns into subject on the theological as well as on the antrhopoligical level.11

In Habermas's view, since at this stage of evolution, the early civilizations, the adherence to the religion and the cult still coincides in a particularistic manner with the respective political community of the city state, a clear cut group identity becomes impossible.12 The concrete community, the city state, can be distinguished as the particular from the universality of the cosmic order on the one hand, and from the singular individual on the other hand. This can happen without endangering in any way the identity-preserving coherence of a world centered in the polity of the city state.

Habermas knows that this is precisely the reason, why the early Hegel exalts the mature form of Greek polytheism as a religion in which a free political morality finds exemplary expression.13 For Habermas as for Hegel, in Athens the singular individual seems to have found a particular identity which allows him to feel at one with the polis as a free singular person. Thus Hegel calls for some time the people of Greece the most human people. Although the deeper Hegel understands Christianity in the power of the dialectical notion the more he becomes aware of the fact that in Athens the infinite subjectivity of man, the absolute right of the individual himself, has not as yet been realized. The beautiful political morality of the citizens of Athens rested on the inhumanity of slavery. Only a few were free in Athens: freedom comprehended as the individual being at home with himself in solidarity with others.14 For Hegel

the person finds his or her infinite subjectivity
finally only in the love of the universal God of
Christianity.*15* In Christianity All are free.*16*

According to Habermas, as to Hegel before, it is only
the major universal religions on the evolutionary stage
of traditional society, of which Judaism and Christianity
are the most rationally structured, which raise a
universalistic truth claim.*17* The one, other-worldly,
universal, providential and wholly just, gracious and
loving God of Christianity leads to the formation of a
singular ego-identity in the believer, severed from all
particular identity to be gained in the concrete status
roles and through the norms of the specific family,
society, state or historical period, he or she belongs
to.   In Habermas's view, this singular "I" of the
believer can know itself as this completely singular
being in God's universal love.*18* The Christian idea of
the singular immortal soul in the face of the loving
universal God and sovereign in relation to any particular
family, society, state or historical period open up for
Habermas as for Horkheimer, the path to the idea, that,
as Hegel puts it, the singular individual has universal
and infinite value and is determined to the highest,
most liberated subjectivity.*19*

Here in Christianity, so Habermas - following Hegel - interp
the Christian system of interpretation and orientation, the
carrier of the religious structure is no longer the
particular family, tribe, village or city state as in
earlier mythical or polytheistic religions, but the
universal community of believers, to which potentially
all men and women can belong.*20* This is so, since the
commands of the one God are universal.

For Habermas, to be sure, the highly developed Eastern
and Western traditional, feudal civilizations are all
class societies with extreme inequalities in the
distribution of power and wealth.*21* On the one hand,
therefore, the political system of those civilizations
needs legitimation to a higher degree than the less
differentiated archaic societies or early civilizations.
On the other hand, the potential of monotheistic religions
to provide universalistic justification is not designed
to satisfy the particularistic demand of the particular
political system of the highly evolved traditional
civilizations.   At this stage of social evolution, the
traditional feudal society, the universal religious
semantic or meaning systems and the particular political
imperatives of self-maintenance in these highly
differentiated particular civilizations become

incompatible. Hence, according to Habermas, a counter-factual *nexus* must be formed between the legitimazing potential of the universal religions, especially Christianity, and the existing particular order in traditional-feudal society.

In Habermas's view this precisely is the function of ideology understood in the critical sense.22 Ideology functions as the counterweight to the structural dissimilarity between the specific collective identity tied to the concrete particular state on one hand, and the singular self-identities of individual persons formed within the framework of the universalistic religious associations, e.g., the Christian community on the other hand. This problem of identity inheres to all the developed traditional societies. But it becomes fully conscious only in the Modern Age with the arrival of the liberal capitalistic state, because until then a series of mediating mechanisms had been operative in traditional society, which concealed or postponed the identity crisis. Which precisely are these mediating mechanisms?

For Habermas in the first place, while it is true that those structures emerging with the monotheistic religions in traditional society made possible the forming of a not merely conventional, but of a highly individualistic ego-identity, nonetheless identity formations and conventional consciousness inherited from archaic societies and early civilizations remained widespread.23 This Habermas can see from the fact that all the monotheistic religions situated in the high civilizations of traditional societies incorporate symbols and practices from a pagan, i.e., of a mythical and magic origin in archaic societies and early civilizations -- e.g. Medieval Catholicism. Furthermore, according to Habermas, in the universal religions a distinction is made between the members of the community of believers and its addresses still held in the sway of pagan beliefs stemming from former archaic societies or early civilizations. Temporary demarcations established against external enemies can therefore be justified by the missionary function. Finally, and above all, in Habermas's view it was possible in traditional societies to put to use the dualism of divine transcendence and earthly immanence for an almost wholly secular world. Under the circumstances of the traditional feudal societies to preserve a sacramental dimension to the ruler or to his office was enough to legitimate the secularized realm of civil law and politics with its profane exercie of power. In the Western Medieval civilizations the two-empire-doctrine from St. Augustine to Martin Luther was to become the foundation of an however tension-charged but nevertheless long lasting coalition between the universal church and the particular worldly feudal regimes.

According to Habermas with the Modern Era, the fourth stage of social evolution, these mediating mechanisms which characterized the traditional societies have evidently become ineffective.24 Long before Habermas, Hegel saw himself confronted with the fact that these mechanisms had become non-functional in modernity. Hegel's social philosoph and philosophy of religion is to a large extent a response to precisely this challenge: the non-operativeness of the mediating mechanisms of traditional society in modern liberal capitalistic society.

In Habermas's perspective, those pre-Christian elements derived from archaic societies and ancient city states which were assimilated with a Catholic perspective in traditional Western feudal societies are discarded with the Protestant view in modern civil society. This in turn reinforces the demand for strongly universalistic commitments and the corresponding individualistic ego structures. We may add, that early Protestantism radically combines a universal religious identity with a singular ego-identity. But his combination was soon threatened by the Protestant commitment to the particular collective identity of specific states.

According to Habermas, as on the evolutionary stage of capitalistic society, the Catholic church split up into several confessions and a multiplicity of more or less Protestant denominations, sects and cults, the membership of the individual in a community of believers lost not only its exclusiveness but also its rigid institutional ties. The bourgeois principle of tolerance and of the voluntary nature of religious associations finally won general acceptance. Habermas forgets to mention that this development diminished considerably the importance of the truth claim of Christianity.

Habermas wants us to recognize that lately -- i.e., in the 1960's and 1970's -- there has taken place in advanced capitalistic society a significant shift in the direction of theological currents giving a radical this-worldly interpretation to the Christian message of salvation and tending to obliterate the traditional dualism, the dualistic theism of much of medieval Catholicism and modern Protestantism. Habermas criticizes that particularly for present-day avant guard theologians in organized capitalistic society God has come to signify little more than a structure of communication. It compels the participants in this structure of communicative the participants in this structure of communicative practice to rise above the contingency of a merely external existence in advanced capitalistic society on the basis of mutual recognition of each other's singular identity.

In Habermas's perspective, the repolitization of the biblical inheritance in contemporary theological discourse, particularly in the critical political theology of Wolfarth Pannenberg, Jurgen Moltmann, Dorothee Soelle, and Metz, and in the liberation theology of Gustavo Gutierrez, Rubem Alves, Enrique Dussel, etc., strongly committed to ideology critique, goes together with a levelling off of the this-worldly/other-worldly dichtomoy and so points toward the destruction of traditional dualistic theism.25 Habermas does admit that the repolitization of the Christian gospel of redemption, carried on in the critical theology, does not mean outright atheism in the sense of the liquidation of religion and theology without any trace of the idea of God. Such a liquidation does not even take place in the writings of the early Horkheimer or in the Frankfurt School in general.26 But Habermas seriously doubts that the idea of a *personal* God can be salvaged with consistency from the critical mass of thought involved in the political theology.27 In Habermas's view, in the critical theology the idea of God is transformed into the concept of a *logos* that determines the community of the believers and the real life-world of the self-enlightening and self-emancipating society. God, so Habermas argues, becomes for the political theologians the sign for little more than a communicative structure that forces men, on pain of the loss of their very humanity, to go beyond their accidental empirical subjectivity, to encounter one another indirectly, i.e., across an objective "something" that they themselves are not, a "wholly Other".

Habermas's critique of critical theology includes also at least indirectly Metz's and Peukert's new proposal of a fundamental theology as a basis theory for a critical political theology of subject, society and history.28 But more recently Habermas and Peukert have been in dicussion concerning the boundary questions of a theory of communicative practice.29 At the same time Habermas clarified for Peukert essential problems of interpretation of texts of the *Frankfurt School*, particularly of Walter Benjamin, whose latest writings on political theology are of greatest importance for the further development of a critical political or liberation theology.30

According to Habermas, in any case, the deideologized, demythologized, deidologized and deprivatized political theology characterizes a development in advanced capitalistic society in which whatever is left of universal religions, especially Christianity, is but the core of a universal moral systems.31 This happens to a greater proportion the more transparent the infrastructure of monotheistic belief systems -- the capitalistic production and exchange process -- has become. Here Habermas finds somewhat verified Marx's prediction in his theory of religion that religion could wither away only to that extent as men and women would understand and regulate their society as their own work and life process.32

In Habermas's view, long before Marx, Hegel has clearly seen the initial phase of this development of radical secularization going on in the evolutionary stage of modern society as well as its tremendous practical consequences: the inevitable cleavage between the self-identity of the single person derived from the universalistic meaning structure of Christianity and the special collective identity bound up with a particular nation - or supernation state.33 This is so for Habermas, since on the basis of universalistic norms no particular entity possessing an identity - forming power, such as the family, the tribe, the city state or nation can set up bounds to demarcate itself from alien groups. Rather, one's "own" ingroup is under the condition of universalistic norms replaced by the category of the "other", a central category of Hegel's logic.34 According to Habermas, the other is no longer conceived of as an outsider because of his non-membership. The other becomes for the ego two things in one: The other becomes absolutely identical with and absolutely different from the singular ego, the closest to and the most distant from the ego. The other becomes this double reality in one person.35

In Habermas's perspective, particular citizenship or national identity would have to be enlarged to become a cosmopolitan or universal identity.36 Yet, so Habermas asks, can this design of a new universal identity to replace the old religious universal identity of traditional and early modern society be conceived without contradiction? As much as Hegel, Habermas is aware of the fact that the whole of mankind is still an abstraction. It is not just another group which on a global scale could form its identity, similar as did tribes or states on earlier pre-modern stages of social evolution, until such a time as mankind were again to coalesce into a particular entity.

Habermas imagines futurologically, that mankind could coalesce into a particular identity, e.g., in defense against other populations in outer space. But what else, so Habermas asks, except the whole of mankind or a world society can take the place of an all-embracing collective identity from which singular ego identities could be formed? Habermas searches for a replacement for the universal God of Christianity in whose love the individual had found his singular identity once in the evolutionary stage of traditional society, and which is no longer available and plausible for more and more people living in the evolutionary stage of organized capitalistic or bureaucratic-socialistic society. Habermas is fully aware of the fact that if the place once taken by the universal God of the high religions is not filled by the whole of mankind or a world society, the universalistic morality, as well as the ego-structures consistent with it, would remain a mere postulate in the Kantian sense in that they could be actualized only occasionally and this only within the private sphere, without substantially grounding social or public life.

It is precisely at this point where the mature Horkheimer encounters an undesolvable aporia and despairs concerning the realization of a universalistic morality as described by Habermas.37 Horkheimer and Adorno still hold on in their book *The Dialectics of Enlightenment*, written cooperatively at the end of their American exile and published in Holland in 1947, like Marx before, to the idea of an inner-worldly reconciliation of man and nature and man and man, i.e., alternative Future III -- a reconciled society, including a universalistic morality.38 They do this up to the 1950's in their rebuilt *Institute for Social Research* in Frankfurt, a.M., Germany, in the face of the continuing self-destruction of the bourgeois enlightenment, its transition to positivism as the mythology of "that what is the case" described in *The Dialectics of Enlightenment*.39 Bourgeois enlightenment destroys itself by remaining captive to the capitalistic mode of production, on the basis of which it had once developed, but which in the meantime had become obsolete, regressive, irrational and anti-historical. At the time when they composed *The Dialectics of Enlightenment*, Horkheimer and Adorno still hoped that the enlightenment, the human spirit-nature which as alienated from itself can nevertheless perceive itself -- will be able to take back into itself the claim of man's dominion over nature and of man over man. Later on Habermas speaks of communication without domination.40

By 1970, the mature Horkheimer can no longer continue

the hope he once shared with Adorno and other members of the Frankfurt *Institute for Social Research* before, during and still shortly after World War II.*41* Since the end of World War II, Horkheimer informed himself thoroughly about the course of contemporary world history, particularly its trend toward alternative Future I - the totally administered technocratic and bureaucratic society.*42* So informed, Horkheimer refuses to think the "wholly Other", which before and during World War II he wanted to reserve for Future III, the concrete reconciled society and its universalistic morality, any longer as something to be achieved in this world.*43* While this turn in Horkheimer's critical theory of society and religion disappointed deeply Habermas and the whole New Left, it elicited from the positivistic Right the simple reaction: What is new?*44* In Horkheimer, Schopenhauer won the victory not so much over Hegel, but very much so over Marx. Horkheimer discovered positivistic elements not only in Eastern socialistic states, but even in Marx's work.*45* For Horkheimer the world is no longer an *Absolutum*, which it still is for Marxists and positivists, but rather a matter of appearance.*46* In Horkheimer's view, the world is a product conditioned through the qualities of our biologically and socially bound intellect and apparatus of perception.*47* According to Horkheimer, the dark "will to life" or "natural will" does not, as for Schopenhauer take the place of the Absolute, but rather remains as for Hegel part of the world as nature and history, which as appearance is not the ultimate truth.

For Horkheimer out of all this does not follow a positive theology.*48* According to Horkheimer, as to Kant and Voltaire, the word "God" indicates the impossibility of the thought, that the injustice and suffering which dominates the world could be the last word of history. Correspondingly, Horkheimer understood under theology, which today is fading away, not dogmatic statements about God, angels, etc., but the longing of finite beings to achieve an exodus out of the more and more administered world. Horkheimer moves toward a negative theology, which emphasizes more what God is not, than what he might be.*49*

The late phase of Horkheimer's intellectual development must in no way be misunderstood as a turning away from te real needs of people.*50* So it is misunderstood by the New Left.*51* In Horkheimer's view, the *malum metaphysicum*, the dark natural will in nature and history, exempts nobody from the task to fight against the *malum physicum*, the evils, which are produced by man and can be corrected by him.

Habermas does not follow the Schopenhauerian turn in Horkheimer's critical theory of society and religion, nor his way toward a negative theology.[52] Habermas remains faithful to the relative philosophical and sociological optimism of Marx and of the early Horkheimer. Habermas finds in Adorno, not in Horkheimer the real "atheist". Against Habermas we must insist, that also the mature Adorno shared his friend Horkheimer's pessimism in relation to society and history and that also he is not a clear-cut bourgeois or socialistic atheist, but rather committed to a negative theology which pushes the Jewish taboo against making images of the Absolute -- the second commandment of the Decalogue -- to its utmost extreme.[53]

But Habermas rightly holds that the problem of the dichotomy of singular, particular and universal identity, which constitutes the very core of his critical theory of religion, has been the actual impetus to Hegel's philosophy, not only to the dialectical notion as the very essence of his logic -- the concrete differentiated unity of universality, particularity and singularity -- but also and especially so to his philosophy of right, history and religion.[54] Habermas states correctly, that it is precisely because Hegel gave the impulse to reflections concerning the singular, particular and universal identity and its crisis in civil society, that he has been so far the philosopher of modernity par excellence and that he remains a relevant contemporary thinker in the present evolutionary stage of modern, i.e., organized capitalistic and post-capitalistic, socialistic society.

According to Habermas, Hegel evidently conceived the alienation of the subject from society in modern history as related to the subjects' estrangement from nature.[55] For Hegel there exists a threefold diremption of the modern "I": From external nature, from society and from internal nature. These dichotomies signalize for Habermas the context in which Hegel himself saw the motive force of philosophy. According to Hegel, the need for philosophy arises when the unifying power has disappeared from the life of man, when the contradictions have lost their living interrelation and interdependence and assumed an independent form. Habermas overlooks that Hegel was concerned with another diremption of the modern "I", namely that from the Absolute.[56] For Hegel, this latter diremption underlies the other three forms of modern man's alienation: from external and internal nature and from society. In Hegel's view the Absolute is not identical with nature or with society. Hegel is not

B. de Spinoza or Marx or Emile Durkheim.

But Habermas sees as clearly as Hegel that monotheism, particularly Christianity, was the last system of ideas, which provided a unifying interpretation acknowledged by more or less all the members of Western traditional and early modern society.[57] However, so Habermas states, once Christianity was confronted in modern society with the rival claims of positive science and profane personal and social morality, it could no longer satisfy the demand of modern enlightened men and women for a system of unifying interpretation and orientation. Here then, so Habermas argues, philosophy must step in the place of Christianity. While Hegel searches for a balance between divine and secular wisdom, Habermas pleads for the latter superceding, i.e., negating and abolishing the former.[58] But Habermas is fully aware of the fact that even if with the conceptual means at its disposal, philosophy were able to substitute itself for the unifying power of the universal religions, particularly Christianity, the identity problem itself remains unsolved.[59]

This is so for Habermas, since monotheism already had been an expression of the opposition between universalistic ego structures on the one hand, and the particularistic identity of the state on the other hand, on the evolutionary level of traditional society. This opposition resides in the fact that the state is the organizational form of a class society. The egalitarian character of such a class-state cannot find universalistic justification, authorization, legitimation from the universal religions. Furthermore, this opposition is rooted in the fact that precisely this class-state as the organizational form of a class-society opposes sovereign states to one another in the struggle for existence and survival, which again is not reconcilable with the universalistic principles of the universal religions, especially Christianity. In the modern age an Islamic or a Christian or a Jewish Republic is really not possible except if the religions are ideologically distorted in terms of the underlying class interests.

According to Habermas, if, then, philosophy is to accomplish the task of unification in modern society, which the religious systems of interpretation provided for in archaic society and city-state and even still to some extent in traditional society, it must prove capable of passing even beyond religion's claim to a unifactory interpretation of the world as nature and history and its contingencies. For Habermas this means that philosophy,

in Hegel's design, has to constitute the unity in modern
society which so far only the myth has been able to
provide in archaic society and in the city-state. This
explains to Habermas why Hegel, again and again, returned
to the example of the morality embodied in the Greek
Polis. This is so, since it is here within Greek
polytheism that in Hegel's opinion the individual could
find a singular identity of self that was in harmony
with the particular identity of the city-state. Stated
in the terms of Hegel, as Habermas understands them,
philosophy must create anew the same integration of the
individual beings with their particular political
community within the horizon of a universal cosmic
order, as was effected by the myth in archaic society
and the city-state, i.e., the concrete unity of the
universal, the particular and the singular identity. According
to Habermas, this time however, in modern society,
philosophy must accomplish this task of unification
under the extreme conditions meanwhile posited by the
modern ideas of the freedom and of the complete
individuality of the human subject -- free subjectivity
or subjective freedom as initiated mainly by Christianity
and only later secularized by the bourgeoisie.

Here Habermas is somewhat mistaken. Hegel did want to
reconstitute the unity of singular, particular and
universal identity, which so far only the myth has been
able to provide in the archaic society and in the city-
state. But only the young Hegel returns to the example
of the political morality embodied in the Greek city-
state, particularly in Athens.60 It is true that,
according to the young and mature Hegel, philosophy must
help to create a new integration of the individual beings
with their particular political community within a universal
religious horizon. But this was not to be done by the
myth of the archaic society or the city-state. Hegel is
not a conservative or revolutionary romantic. He is not
a proto-fascist. His philosophy is not a conceptualized,
rationalized mythology. Hegel warns the Germans against
any return to the mythology of the Germanic tribes.61
Hegel is fully aware of the fact that philosophy had to
accomplish the new concrete unity of universal, particular
and singular identity under the conditions of a modern
society determined by the principle of free subjectivity.
But since for Hegel this modern principle of subjectivity
was in its roots Christian, only a philosophy which
preserved Christianity in itself, a Christian philosophy,
could help to establish the concrete integration of
singular, particular and universal identity in modern
and post-modern history.62 Hegel understood his own
philosophy as a Christian philosophy. It was supposed

to solve the modern identity problem.

According to Hegel, the right of the singularity of the subject to find itself to be satisfied, or what is the same, the right of subjective freedom, constitutes the turning and centre point in the difference between Antiquity, the ancient city states and the Modern Era.63 In Hegel's view, this right has been expressed in its infinitude in Christianity and in Christianity it has been made into the general, real principle of a new form of the world, the modern world. To the more concrete formations of the Christian principle of subjective freedom belong romantic love, the purpose of the eternal happiness of the individual, as well as the individual morality and the conscience and furthermore the other forms, which partially later on assert themselves as the principle of bourgeois society and as moments of the political constitution of the liberal state, but partially in general in modern history, especially in the bourgeois history of art, the positive sciences and philosophy.

In Hegel's view, the principle of the independent, in itself infinite personality of the individual, the subjective freedom arose internally in the Christian religion and was therefore externally connected with abstract universality in the Roman world.64 According to Hegel, this Christian principle of free individuality could not come to its right in the merely substantial form of the real objective spirit of the ancient city states, which were built partially on the patriarchal and religious principle, partially on the principle of a more spiritual, but simpler social morality, in general on original natural perception. In Hegel's perspective, the Christian principle of free subjectivity is historically later than the Greek World. Likewise for Hegel, the philosophical reflection, which can descend to this depth of the Christian principle of subjective freedom is later than the substantial idea of Greek philosophy of a Plato or Aristotle. So in Hegel's view, particularly in the Christian religion, the right of free' subjectivity has arisen as well as the infinity of the individual's being-for-himself or herself. This Christian principle of subjective freedom demands, that the social totality receive at the same time the strength to posit the singularity of the individual in harmony with the moral unity of the state in the horizon of the universal, Absolute Reality.65

For Hegel this unity of singular, particular and universal identity is not a matter of the past or the present, but

rather of the future.66 In Hegel's view, the Greek epic
describes the triumph of the Occident over the Orient,
of the European measure, the individual beauty of self-
limiting reason over Asiatic splendor, the magnificence
of a patriarchal unity, which has not yet achieved
complete particularization and singularization, or as
abstract union disintegrates already.67 Hegel
anticipates a future American epic, which will present
the victory of a very distant, post-European, post-
modern, post-bourgeois living American rationality, i.e.,
concrete unity of universal, particular and singular
identity, over the imprisonment of the Late European
civilization in an infinitely continuing positivistic
measuring and particularization. Hegel has certainly
not yet happened in an America, which so far has been
characterized by the same positivistic civilization
which dominates old Europe up to today, and sometimes
even more so.

Nevertheless, Habermas understands Hegel rightly in his
theory of religion, when the latter's philosophical
attempt at the solution of the modern identity crisis
signifies to him that the modern problem of identity,
namely the problem of the diremption of the singular "I"
from the particular society, cannot be solved until the
absolute, universal identity of the ego or of the mind
with the whole of nature is rendered comprehensible.68
What must be made intelligible is that the world of
nature and the world of history are held together by an
unifying power which in unfolding itself produces these
diremptions, which it can also overcome. This unifying
power Hegel calls on the basis of the Judeo-Christian
tradition God's absolute Spirit.69

Habermas states that Hegel has undertaken the attempt of
producing for modern consciousness a system of knowledge
guaranteeing the concrete unity of singular, particular
and universal identity for modern man in a similar manner
as "the concrete science" of mythical thought must long
ago have created for the consciousness of archaic man.70
In principle Hegel is able to locate all the phenomena
of nature and history within the process of the self-
mediation of God's absolute Spirit -- his *exitus-reditus*
process.71 So each phenomenon in nature and history can
illuminate the point at which the singular "I" of modern
man finds its place. The universal structure of God's
Spirit as He moves outside of Himself into nature and
returns to Himself in history, which renders comprehensible
both nature and history in their essential manifoldness,
is at the same time the structure in which the ego can
find and preserve its singular identity. According to

Habermas, to comprehend means for Hegel to eradicate all
contingencies which threaten the singular identity of "I".
Habermas's view, this is so since it is through the very
acts of comprehension that the single ego identifies
itself with God's universal Spirit. Hegel says of God's
Spirit, that He in Himself produces the annihilation of
what is night and nothing and renders futile that which
is futile.72 This statement quoted by Habermas is a
generalization of the specific Christological statement
by Hegel, that God maintains himself in the process of
his death on the cross and that this is the death of
death, the negation of negation in God himself.73 At
the same time Hegel speaks energetically for a purified,
non-infantile realistic faith in universal, divine
Providence, in which the pain stemming from natural and
social contingencies remains very much pain, and
unhappiness continues very much to be unhappiness.74
According to Hegel, for pains there is no consolation.
Only the strength of the soul can be opposed to pains.
The only true consolation in suffering is a realistic
trust in the universal providence of God. Everything
else is idle talk, which glides off from the heart.

According to Habermas, this universal self-movement of
God's absolute Spirit in terms of an *exitus-reditus*
process Hegel makes intelligible precisely by the state,
not withstanding its particularity, in that the state
is the embodiment and the realization of the universal
ethical idea.75 In Hegel's view, modern society has
found its rational identity in the sovereign constitutional
state and it is the task of philosophy to show this
identity to be rational.

Approaching Hegel more from the outside than from the
inside, Habermas indicates some of the difficulties this
Hegelian thesis is confronted with in the light of
contemporary experience.76 Habermas mentions several
arguments against the assertion that the modern state
continues to be the plane on which societies form
their identities as Hegel has assumed: the unreality
of the existing class-conditioned nation- and super-
nation states; modern weapon technology; supra-state
organization of multi-national corporations; world public
opinion; coordination and steering problems of the
contemporary society and state; nationalism and
revolutionary parties. In Habermas's view, because of
these and other factors, modern society can no longer
find its rational identity in the bourgeoise or
socialistic sovereign constitutional state. Therefore,
it is the task of philosophy to find a new identity
beyond the state. But first of all, what precisely is

the old identity for which Hegel argues, and against
which Habermas poses his project of a new identity?
Habermas's proposal of a new identity can not be
comprehended, if Hegel's older concept of identity is
not completely clarified.

Hegel states in the socio-ethical part of his *Encyclopedia*
that the universal social morality is the particular
state, including family and society, insofar as it is
reduced to its substantial interiority.77 For Hegel,
the particular state is the development and the
realization of universal social morality. But the
substantiality of the universal morality of the
particular state is the universal religion. Furthermore,
while the state rests upon the universal socio-ethical
attitude of the single person, this attitude again is
based on the individual's universal religious conviction.
Since religion is the consciousness of the absolute
truth, that which ought to be valid as right and justice,
as duty and law, i.e., as true in the world of practical
reason and will and of intersubjective action can be
valid only insofar as it participates in the universal
religious truth and is subjected under it and follows
from it. But that true universal social morality can
at all be the consequence of religion, for that it is
required, that religion has the true content: The idea
of God which is known in religion must be the true one.
For Hegel that means the idea of the objective, universal
God with His internal and external *exitus* and *reditus*-
processes -- the living trinitarian God. Hegel
introduces the idea of the historicity of God.78 God's
history consists in his trinitarian movement in himself
as well as out of himself through the world as nature
and history and back into himself.

For Hegel, the true universal social morality is God's
universal Spirit as living in the human self-consciousness
as it exists in its real presence as a particular nation
and as singular individuals.79 The individual's self-
consciousness as it reflects back into itself from its
external empirical reality and as it lifts its universal
truth fully into its consciousness, has in its faith and
conscience only that what it poses in the certitude of
itself, in its spiritual reality. The empirical and
the spiritual reality of man's self-consciousness is
inseparable, identical. There cannot exist, in Hegel's
perspective, two different types of conscience, a
religious and a socio-ethical one, the latter of which
would be in its content different from the former when
directing communicative action in family, society, state
and history or church. But in terms of form, i.e., for

thought, the religious content of conscience as the pure truth in and for itself and therefore being the highest, absolute and universal truth, has the function to legitimate the social morality which stands in the empirical reality and guides the communicative praxis.

According to Hegel, it is the monstrous error of the Modern Age, to consider the inseparability or identity of religious and socio-ethical conscience to be separable and to understand the two consciences to be indifferent toward each other. Philosophers engaged in bourgeois enlightenment saw the relationship of universal religion to the particular state in such a way, that the latter with all its communicative interaction exists already for itself prior to universal religion and without any grounding in it, out of some kind of secular power or authority. For these philosophers, religion is merely a private subjective concern of the single individual, which to add as a stabilizing factor to an already in and for itself equilibrated particular state, may be desirable or merely a matter of indifference.

This is Hegel's description of the old identity of the singular individual, the particular state and the universal religion. What precisely is the new identity, by which Habermas wants to replace the insufficient old identity promoted by Hegel?

In Habermas's view, the difficulties of Hegel's thesis, as soon as it is confronted with the experience of contemporary society, state and history should not make us discard the concepts of group- and ego-identity themselves, which Hegel developed.[80] In a certain sense, Habermas remains a Hegelian. Certainly, for Habermas these difficulties are sufficient reason to recognize that an identity concept like that of Hegel, derived from the context of Western Civilization, centered around the modern constitutional state, and articulated as well as fixated in particular traditions and world-images -- i.e., the Judeo-Christian tradition, has become outdated and thereby irrelevant. Habermas outlines characteristics of a new identity, which he considers to be at least possible in complex, organized, capitalistic, post-capitalistic or post-modern, societies and at the same time compatible with universalistic ego structures.

In the perspective of Habermas the new identity of a society, which extends beyond state boundaries, can neither be related to a specific territory nor rest upon any specific organization. The distinguishing characteristic of this new identity can also no longer be that of association or membership. Against Hegel's thesis, Habermas advances his own thesis that collective identity can today only be grounded in the consciousness of universal and equal chances to participate in the kind of communication processes by which identity formation becomes a continuous learning process, which may or may not take the precise form of an institutionalized discourse as demanded by Hegel.81 Here, so Habermas argues, the individual is no longer confronted by collective identity as a traditional authority, as a fixed objectivity on the basis of which singular self-identity can be built. According to Habermas, rather individuals are the participants in the shaping of the collective will underlying the design of a common universal identity. Obviously, for Habermas the old identity of religious and socio-ethical conscience, Hegel was concerned with, has broken apart once and for all.82 Socio-ethical conscience replaces religious conscience. If Hegel was alive today he would very probably charge the socialist Habermas with the same error he found in contemporary bourgeois philosophers: Namely, that the identity of religious and socio-ethical conscience could be separated and that the singular identity of the individual and the particular identity of the state could be established *without* grounding them in the universal religious identity.83 This error which began with bourgeois thinkers, is continued by socialistic philosophers like Habermas even in a much more radical form.

In Habermas's view, the new universal identity of an as yet emergent global, i.e., universal society cannot find articulation in religious world images, although it must presuppose the validity of universalistic moral systems.84 How is that possible? Habermas trusts that the universalistic moral systems can be linked with the basic norms of philosophical discourse, instead of the traditional universal religious systems of interpretation. Here once more world wisdom is supposed to replace entirely divine wisdom.85 For Habermas rational discourse is in itself a step in the direction of a particular collective type of identity which is grounded in the consciousness of the universal and equal opportunity to participate in value- and norm-forming learning processes.86 Such an identity no longer requires fixed contents, as once the universal religious identity did.87 Those secular interpretations to be achieved in philosophical discourse, which make man's situation in today's world comprehensible are distinguished from the traditional religious or philosophical world images not so much in that they are less global and more limited in scope, but in that their status is open to counter-arguments and revisions at any time. Habermas overlooks here, that also the great religious traditions are not entirely unreflexive and that they are open to counter-arguments and revisions and that they are also able to learn and to correct inside of themselves ideological distortions.[88] Habermas thinks nevertheless that philosophical discourse as anticipation of a communication community and work toward it can achieve what the great religious traditions can no longer accomplish: the resolution of the modern identity problem. What precisely does such discourse toward a future communicative community look like?

CHAPTER VIII

COMMUNICATION COMMUNITY

For Habermas the limits of administrative interference
with tradition in advanced capitalistic or post-
capitalistic, socialistic society -- e.g., in case of
curricula formations on all levels of the public school
system -- and the compulsion to communicate mobilization
of tradition, reveal that very structure around which
alone a new collective identity -- if it ever comes into
existence at all -- could crystallize itself.1   Its form
would be an identity which is not prejudiced in its
content and which is independent of particular
organizational forms.   It would be an identity of the
community of individuals who engage in discursive and
experimental formation of an identity-related knowledge
on the basis of a critical appropriation of the truth
content of religious tradition -- its utopian content
-- as well as of the true, i.e., utopian inputs from
science, philosophy and the arts.

In Habermas's view, the temporal structure of a future-
oriented remembrance in the form of communicative action
as continuous learning process would allow the formation
of universalistic ego-structures on the basis of
partisanship for particular identity projections.2
Habermas trusts, that every particularistic position can
come to agreement with any other particularistic position
it is confronted with in the present, precisely in its
partisanship for a universality, i.e., a universal
communicative community, to be realized in the future.3
The communication community is the replacement of what
in the Jewish tradition was hoped for as the Messianic
Age, and in the Christian tradition as the Kingdom of
God.   It is the secular response to a protracted parousia
delay.

According to Habermas, we cannot explain the validity
claim of moral norms without recourse to rationally
motivated agreement or at least to the conviction that
consensus on a recommended norm could be brought about
with reasons.4   In that case, for Habermas the appropriate
model is the communication community of individuals
affected by the new norms, who as participants in a
practical philosophical discourse test the validity

claims of these norms. These individuals, to the extent to which they accept these norms with reasons arrive at the conviction that in the given circumstances the proposed norms are right.

In Habermas's perspective, the validity claim of norms is grounded not in the irrational volitional acts of contracting parties who need to know only what an ethical imperative means, but in the rationally motivated recognition of norms, which may be questioned at any time. The congitive component of norms is thus not limited to the propositional content of the normed behavioural expectations. The normative validity claim is itself cognitive in the sense of the supposition that it could be discursively redeemed -- i.e., grounded in the consensus of the participants through argumentation. Habermas admits that this supposition may very well be counterfactual. In any case, all particularistic positions are redeemable by universalization in philosophical discourse, no matter how much such particularism may so far have systematically distorted the communicative practice in a specific society.5

For Habermas, the problematic that arises with the introduction of new moral principles into a society through discourse is disposed of as soon as one sees that the expectation of discursive redemption of normative validity claims is already contained in the structure of subjectivity and inter-subjectivity and makes specially introduced maxims of universalization superfluous.6 Habermas sees, as the functionalist Luhmann discovered, the subject, just as the inter-subjectivity, which precedes it, primarily as a potential for foundations admitting of truth.7 The subjectivity of man consists for Habermas in the possibility of specifying rational grounds in inter-subjective communication, or of being able to accomodate oneself to such grounds or to the refutation of one's own grounds in terms of the self-liquidation of one's own position.

According to Habermas, in taking up practical philosophical discourse we unavoidably suppose an ideal speech situation.8 This ideal speech situation, on the strength of its formal properties, allows consensus only through generalizable interests. Habermas pleads for a cognitivist linguistic ethics. For Habermas such an ethics has no need of principles. It is as such based only on fundamental norms of rational speech. That, so Habermas argues, we must always presuppose, if we enter philosophical discourse at all. Habermas assumes the transcendental character of ordinary language. This transcendental character of ordinary language can be reconstructed in the framework of a universal pragmatic.9

In comparison with Hegel, Schopenhauer, Horkheimer and Adorno the Hegelian Habermas is certainly extremely optimistic concerning the effectiveness of a practical philosophical discourse on the basis of an ideal speech situation and in anticipation of the realization of the universal communicative community.10 He shares this optimism with Marcuse, Fromm and Bloch.11 This optimism makes Habermas's critical theory of society and religion attractive for a generation somewhat tired of Horkheimer's and Adorno's social and cultural pessimism.12 But the main question is, if Habermas's critical theory is true, or if it is a new form of ideology, i.e., false consciousness?13 Habermas's critical theory is reflexive and therefore fully aware of its own ideological potential. It's reflexivity enables the critical theory not only to recognize but also to correct its own ideological distortions to the point of self-liquidation in philosophical discourse. In any case, the critical theory developed in philosophical discourse on the basis of an ideal speech situation and in anticipation of the communication community is today a real hope for many men and women who have been disillusioned with the "divine wisdom" of religious traditions and who want to go beyond Hegel's reinterpretation of these traditions, but who at the same time do not want to fall into utter positivism and positivistic nihilism in the present world historical transition period, be it in advanced capitalistic or socialistic societies.14

Habermas initiates philosophical discourse in the bourgeois culture based on advanced capitalistic society. Habermas's critical theory of society and religion is itself part of bourgeois culture of organized capitalistic society. Orthodox Marxists do not get tired to point out this fact.15 Habermas distances himself not only from these critics but also from the bourgeois culture, with which they identify him.

Habermas knows that bourgeois culture as a whole was never able to reproduce itself out of itself.16 Bourgeois culture remained always dependent on motivationally effective supplementation by traditional world views. Certainly Hegel's philosophy makes this point perfectly clear.17 According to Habermas, religion having been privatized in the bourgeois culture of liberal and organized capitalistic society and having retreated into the regions of subjective belief can no longer satisfy neglected communicative needs, not even

in conjunction with the secular components of bourgeois
ideology, e.g., an empiricist or rationalist or positivist
theory of knowledge, the new quantum physics, or the
universalistic value systems of modern natural law and
utilitarianism.[18]

According to Habermas, genuine bourgeois ideologies,
which live only from their own substance, offer no
support in the face of the basic risks of existence --
guilt, sickness, death -- to religious systems of
interpretation that overcome contingency.[19] Bourgeois
ideologies are disconsolate in the face of individual
needs for wholeness. Bourgeois ideologies do not make
possible human relations with a fundamentally objectivated
nature -- with either outer nature or man's own body and
inner nature. Bourgeois ideologies permit no intuitive
access to relations of solidarity within groups or
between individuals. Bourgeois ideologies allow no real
political ethics. They accomodate in political and social
life an objectivistic self-interpretation of acting
subjects. An alliance between positive religion and
positivism or any other bougeois ideology is for Habermas,
as for Adorno before, very understandable, but also
hopeless.[20] Religion cannot rescue itself by an alliance
with bourgeois ideologies and the latter cannot save
themselves through support by the former.

In Habermas's view, the previous course of world history
confirms Hegel and the classical sociologists who always
conceived of society as a moral reality and who never
doubted that subjects capable of speaking and acting
could develop the unity or singular identity of their
person only in connection with universal, identity -
securing world views and moral systems.[21] The unity of
the person requires the identity-enhancing perspective
of a life-world, that guarantees order and has both
cognitive and moral-practical significance.

In Habermas's perspective, the fundamental function of
world-maintaining religious systems of interpretation
is the avoidance of chaos, i.e., the overcoming of
contingency.[22] Habermas understands the legitimation
of orders of authority and basic norms as a specialization
of the meaning-giving function of religious systems of
interpretation. Religious systems originally connected
the moral-practical task of constituting the singular
identity of individuals and the particular identity of
groups -- differentiation of the ego versus the social
reference group, city state, feudal society, on one hand,
and differentiation of the collective versus the natural
and social environment on the other hand -- with the

cognitive interpretation of the world-mastery of problems
of survival that arise in the confrontation of man with the
outer nature. They did that in such a way that the conting-
gencies of an imperfectly controlled environment could be process
simultaneously with the fundamental risks of human
existence, i.e., crises of the life cycle and the dangers
of socialization, injuries to physical and moral integrity,
guilt, meaninglessness, loneliness, sickness and death.
Religious systems mediated communicative praxis with
adaptive behaviour and vice versa.

In Habermas's as in Marx's view, the meaning promised by
religion on all levels of man's social evolution has
always been ambivalent.23 By promising meaning, religion
preserved the claim which until now has been constitutive
for the socio-cultural form of all human life in all
stages of evolution, that men ought not to be satisfied
with fictions, legends, myths, but only with truth, when
they wish to know why something happens in the way it
does, how it happens and how what they do and ought to
do can be justified. But religion's promise of meaning
has always implied a promise of consolation as well.
This is so since profered interpretations do not simply
bring the unsettling contingencies to consciousness but
make them bearable as well. This is the case even when,
and precisely when, these contingencies cannot be
removed as contingencies, e.g., terminal diseases, like terminal
cancer of the liver or the lung. Then in Marxian terms
religion is not only protest, but also opium.24

In Habermas's perspective, in the primitive stage of
social evolution, man's problems of survival -- and thus
his experiences of contingencies in dealing with outer
nature -- were so drastic that they had to be counter-
balanced by the narrative production of an illusion of
order.25 Habermas sees this clearly in the content of
myth.26 With increased control over outer nature in
the process of social evolution on the level of city
state, traditional and particularly modern society,
secular knowledge became independent from religious
world view, world wisdom from divine wisdom. Religious
systems of integration were more and more, most of all
on the evolutionary level of modern liberal and
advanced capitalistic society, restricted to functions
of social integration and equilibration.27

According to Habermas as to Hegel before, the positive
natural sciences eventually established a monopoly
concerning the interpretation of the outer nature.28
The natural sciences devalued inherited global religious
and philosophical interpretations. They transformed the

mode of faith into a scientistic attitude that permits only faith in the objectivating positive sciences. In the domain of the natural sciences, contingencies are recognized and, to a large extent technically mastered or their consequences made at least bearable, e.g., chemotherapy and radiation for cancer patients. Modern man defines natural catastrophies as world wide social events. The effects of these natural catastrophies are blunted by large scale administrative operations. The government declares emergency areas after a devastating flood, earthquake or snowstorm. Even the consequences of war, as if it was a merely natural catastroph belong into this category of administered humanity. In modernity rises the trend toward what Horkheimer and the Frankfurt School call the totally administered scientifized, technocratic, cybernetic society.29 Marcuse speaks of the one-dimensional society and Fromm of the dehumanized technological society.30 There is little doubt that alternative Future I - the administered society - will deal with many material injustices much better than the present capitalistic or socialistic society.31 The price is the loss of the individual's personal identity.32

In Habermas's view, with growing complexity in areas of social co-existence in advanced capitalistic and post-capitalistic, socialistic society, a number of new contingencies have been produced.33 This has happened without a proportionate growth in the ability of modern man to master contingencies. As a consequence the need for religious or social-scientific interpretations that ovecome contingency and divest not yet controlled accidents of their accidental character no longer arise in advanced capitalistic or socialistic society in relation to outer nature. It is rather generated in an intensified form by suffering from uncontrolled societal processes inside the modern human action systems. Some of the systemic diseases, like cancer, may originate not in the natural, but in the social environme They may be to a large extent civilization damages produced in the human organism by elements in the production and consumption process of organized capitalistic or socialistic society. They are therefore a matter of the accountability and responsibility of the dominating classes, the producer's, the owners.

According to Habermas, today the social sciences can no longer take on the functions of world views which overcome contingencies.34 Instead, at the same time that the social sciences dissolve the religious and meta-physical illusion of order, last produced by Hegel's objectivistic philosophy of history, they contribute to an increase in avoidable contingencies. This is so since in their present state the social sciences do not produce technical knowledge that society could use for mastering contingencies. This is also true for B.F. Skinner's behaviourism.35 Furthermore, the social sciences do not have confidence in the ability of strong theoretical strategies to penetrate the multiplicity of apparent, nominalistically produced contingencies and to make the objective context of social evolution accessible. For Habermas considering the risks to individual life that exist in advanced capitalistic and post-capitalistic society, a theory that could interpret away the facticities of loneliness, guilt, sickness and death is not even conceivable.

In Habermas's perspective, contingencies that are irremovably attached to the bodily and moral constitution of the individual can be raised to consciousness only as contingencies. The critical theorist Habermas must in principle live disconsolately with the contingencies of loneliness, guilt, death, etc. The critical theory is as disconsolate in the face of individual needs for wholeness as the genuine bourgeois ideologies. Habermas shares this desolation with all materialists, particularly with Marx, Horkheimer, Adorno and Marcuse. This desolation is the price to be paid for ideology critique. It is exactly at this point of desolation, where Kung's negative theology and Metz's and Peukert's new fundamental theology as basis theory for a critical political theology begins their own reflection and their own attempt at a non-ideological solution.36

In Habermas's view, to the extent that religious world views are impoverished, personal and social morality too is formalized.37 It is also detached from substantive interpretations. To the extent to which world views reach the extreme of impoverishment, practical reason can no longer be grounded, as Habermas intends to do, in the transcendental subject or inter-subjectivity or character of language. Habermas's communicative ethics appeals now only to fundamental norms of rational speech as an ultimate fact of reason. Habermas admits that if this is taken to be a simple fact, capable of no further explanation, it is not possible to see why there should still issue from it a normative force that organizes the self-understanding of men and women and gives orientation to their communicative actions.

At this point Habermas returns to the very basis of his whole theory of society and religion. If religious world views, so Habermas argues have foundered on the separation of cognitive from socially integrative components, if religious, world-maintaining interpretative systems today belong irretrievably to the past, then a long series of very difficult questions arises: What under the condition of the loss of universal religious systems of interpretation can fulfill the moral-practical task of constituting the singular identity of the

individual and the particular collective identity of the
group? Could a universalistic linguistic ethics, as
Habermas envisions it, as the very basis of an all-redeeming
philosophical discourse, no longer connected to cognitive
interpretations of nature and society, adequately stabilize
itself and could it structurally secure the singular
identities of individuals and the particular identities
of collectives in the framework of a universal world
society? Or is a universal morality, as Habermas presuppose
and intends it, without cognitive roots in religious systems
of interpretation condemned to shrink to a grandiose
tautology in which a claim to reason, overtaken by social
and cultural evolution, now merely opposes the empty
affirmation of itself to the objectivistic self-understandin
of modern man? Have changes in the mode of socialization,
that affect the socio-cultural form of modern life, perhaps
already come about under the rhetorical guise of a
universalistic morality that has lost its force? Does the
new universal language of systems theory, as proposed e.g.,
by Parsons and Luhmann and their many followers in America
and Europe, indicate that the intellectual avant-gard of
advanced capitalistic society has already begun the retreat
to particular identities of collectives, settling down in
the unplanned, nature-like system of world society like
the Indians on the reservations of contemporary America,
e.g., South and North Dakota? Would such a definitive
withdrawal mean the renunciation of the immanent relations
of motive-shaping norms to universal truth?

According to Habermas, an affirmative answer to these
questions cannot as yet sufficiently be justified with
a reference to the developmental logic of world views.38
One reason for this is the existence of the critical
political theology of subject, society and history as a
fundamentally religious system of interpretation able
to make possible the formation of the singular identity
of the individual and the particular identity of society
on the basis of the universal identity of God as the
Absolute Future and thereby to conquer contingencies in
relation to which natural and social sciences are
helpless, e.g., the death of the other and of oneself.39
Habermas does personally not agree with the critical
political theology, e.g., of Metz, Peukert, Jurgen
Moltmann or Soelle.40 But Habermas takes this new type
of theology, which to a large extent has grown out of
a Marxist-Christian dialogue, as serious as Horkheimer,
Adorno, Marcuse or Fromm.41 He is willing to speak
with the "right" kind of theologians, who search for the
truth *without* consolation.

For Habermas the other reason why an affirmative answer
to the above questions is not yet possible at this stage
of social and cultural evolution is the fact that it has
in no way been determined that the philosophical impulse
to conceive a demythologized unity of the world, intrinsic
to the critical theory of society, cannot also be retained
through scientific argumentation.42 Habermas admits that
science cannot take over the functions of religious world
views. But general theories, whether of social development,
like the critical theory, or of nature contradict
consistent scientific thought less than its positivistic
self-misunderstanding.43 According to Habermas, like the
irrecoverably criticized religious world views, such
general theories or theoretical strategies, like the
critical theory, also hold the promise of meaning -- the
overcoming of contingencies. But at the same time these
theoretical strategies aim at the methodological
removal of the ambivalence of religious systems of
interpretation and orientation between truth claim and
merely illusionary or superstitious fulfillment from this
promise of meaning. In Habermas's view, modern man can
no longer avert recognizable contingencies by producing
a rationalizing illusion or superstition. Here Habermas
presupposes, of course that the political theologian
Hegel's and contemporary critical political theologian's
eschatological expectation of the Kingdom of God is an
illusionary fulfillment and a rationalizing illusion,
while his own utopian anticipation of a communication
community or reconciled society is the truth.44 The
Christian's hope in the Kingdom of God must not exclude
the utopia of Future III - the rational society. Why
must the critical theorist's utopia exclude the
Christians Absolute Future?

Habermas finds comforting the fact that the developmental
logic of religious world views does not exclude the
continuance of a mode of socialization related to the
truth, like the critical political theology or the
critical theory of society.45 But in spite of this
comfort, Habermas foresees the possibility that the
steering imperatives of highly complex advanced
capitalistic, post-capitalistic or post-modern societies
could necessitate disconnecting the formation of motives
from norms, capable of justification and the setting
aside of the detached superstructure of norms. If this
happened, so Habermas predicts, legitimation problems
per se would cease to exist. Alternative Future I --
the totally administered technocratic, bureaucratic,
cybernetic society would be a reality.46 In such an
administered society, forms of socialization related to
the truth, like critical political theology or the

dialectical theory of society and religion may or may
not continue to exist and to develop.[47]

Habermas does not reproach the critical political
theologians with the charge that their theology is
nothing else than ethics or that it is merely this-
worldly and that it does not console anybody.[48] Such
charges against critical theology come rather from the
side of right-wing, i.e., bourgeois theology. Habermas
is aware of the fact that the critical political theology
is as liberating theory and practice very much contested
inside the churches as well as outside in advanced
capitalistic as well as in post-capitalistic society.[49]
Habermas does not want to see the effectiveness of a
radically this-worldly oriented political theology, for
which the concept this-worldliness has really no real
meaning any longer, merely in a functionalistic perspective.
But concerning some questions about critical theology a
functionalistic analysis may very well yield an adequate
answer.

Habermas's discussion with political theologians -- like
Soelle or Peukert -- centers around the concept of free
individuality or individuation, which already for Hegel
constituted the very essence of Christianity.[50] Habermas
agrees with the political theologians that the cognitive
structure, to which the concept of free personality
belongs -- the Christian system of interpretation -- is
a necessary presupposition for the living together and
an intercourse among people, which one can call truely
human, i.e., which fulfills the minimal conditions of
mutual respect.

Following Hegel, Habermas proposes the thesis to political
theologians that an objectivistic pre-enlightenment
notion of the transcendent God with the accompanying idea of
an immortal soul was necessary in the evolution of man,
not only in an external, contingent, but also in an
internal logical sense, in order to form an emphatic
concept of free human subjectivity. For Habermas the
idea of a soul, which is coextensive in the temporal
dimension with God, being eternal and temporal in one,
was necessary in order to conceive the idea of the
irreplacebility of an individual, who as an empirical
entity can very well be replaced in any social function.
According to Habermas, even in marriage, in highly
individualized relationships, one can speak in a trivial
sense of the replaceability of an individual. One may
think of the high divorce rate in the U.S.A. in 1978 or 1979
and of how many of the divorced partners will indeed be
replaced in the following two or three years. Against this

certainly superficial, but nevertheless massive evidence
the idea of individuality must be carried into effect, which
critical theorists and critical political theologians consider
to be necessary for a truly human life.

On the other hand, Habermas sees tendencies in the social as
well as in the intellectual traditions of advanced capitalistic
and socialistic society, which destroy such vitally necessary
cognitive foundation structures as individuality.51
Furthermore, these tendencies support and reinforce even
the consciousness that we are empirical entities of the kind,
as we perceive empirical entities in objectivating intercourse
with an external nature, and nothing else. Habermas calls
this consciousness positivistic and considers this positivistic
consciousness rightly to be outright pagan. The critical
theorist and the political theologian share the emphatic
opposition against pagan positivism.52 In Habermas's view,
in case this pagan positivistic consciousness would become
universal i.e., in the form of alternative Future I -- a
global, totally administered society -- the identity of
the human genus would certainly change.53 Maybe we would
also drop dead! The pagan positivistic consciousness could
lead mankind not only into alternative Future I -- the
totally administered society, but also beyond that into
alternative Future II -- the thermonuclear holocaust.54
Precisely contrary to this critical theory of society and
critical political theology aim at alternative Future III
-- the reconciled society, a humanistic world federation.55
According to Habermas, we cannot live with an extreme degree
of self-objectivation. Even a completely natural-science-
informed medical profession cannot transform patients into
pure objects, but must at least at the fringe recognize
them still as persons -- even in cancer wards or mental
institutions. Else the patient cries out in distress:
"I am not a thing, I am a person!"

While Habermas sees such tendencies which destroy the
cognitive foundation structure of personality in advanced
capitalistic and socialistic society, he does not want
to assert that political theologians could not oppose such
trends much more successfully than other theories or
strategies, e.g., the critical theory of society.56 Here
Habermas's doubts do not lie. But, according to Habermas,
in this case nothing would remain of theology except
practical theology. In Habermas's view in this case, in
a precise sense one would not even be allowed to speak
any longer of "theology" at all. But Habermas does not
have the impression that political theologians are much
bothered by this question. Thus Habermas does not want
to worry much about it either. Of course, in the long
run the political theologians cannot avoid the issue.

Küng, Metz or Peukert certainly do not, as we will see later

For Habermas there is the other question, under which
conditions young people in advanced capitalistic society
and its culture can carry through really in an action-
relevant manner cognitive structures, like individuality,
in which they have been socialized in a very externalized
way. 57 With the attempt to let universalistic principles,
like the irreplacebility of the individual, become
practical, great dissonances appear. These cognitive
dissonances can be transformed into motives of political
action only if people do not feel threatened; if they
are not afraid. Therefore, so Habermas argues, we must
really wish that this "damned" capitalism of organized
capitalistic society will function as well today and
tomorrow, as it did in the reconstruction period after
World War II. For Habermas it is very much possible that
precisely this is the necessary pre-condition under which
alone a sensible moral consciousness can become a
politically consequential fact and that it is not removed
into the realm of the "beautiful soul". This is so,
since economic compulsions produce an anxiety potential
which blocks the transformation of determinate cognitive
dissonances into political actions.

Habermas admits in his discussions with critical political
theologians that practical -- not technical -- questions
are, of course, always treated in a tradition-determined
language. 58 It can very well be that the essential or
fundamental predicates of such a language, i.e., a
language in which one can speak of redemption, in which
happiness as well as suffering can be related to
categories as salvation represent sections out of one
of the different traditional languages of the religious
heritage, e.g., Christianity. In this case what matters
is the question, if it appears still to be acceptable in
the speech related to a determinate life praxis in a
definite situation, that one speaks in a language, in
which such fundamental concepts as salvation or
redemption occur. Or if the listeners say: If you say
it this way, then I cannot express in your language the
experiences which I would like to articulate. I cannot
recognize myself in your language, or in your speech
act.

Therefore Habermas can understand the discursive speech
of the discourse as medium of the further formation of
tradition. The members of the discourse come discursively
to an understanding concerning the acceptability of such
traditional languages of a religious heritage. In
reality, such discourse takes place on very different

levels, beginning with the controversy between theologians, philosophers and sociologists among each other and reaching to the non-institutionalized formation of language, e.g., in a family or in a group or also in a pastor's practice of the care of the souls. Such a pastor may be faced with a new situation which he can no longer encounter with formulas of the traditional language of his religious heritage. Then he must transform the traditional language creatively in order to be effective. When a suffering creature asks for help, one will see, if the language rooted in a determinate religious tradition has a sufficient volume. Does the average priest, minister or rabbi speak a language in which he can adequately respond to a cancer patients cry for help in a year long dying process, or will his own honesty rather force him into silence because his message has no volume any longer? This is for Habermas such a process, in which one can see, if the fundamental predicates of a language, in which one can have practical discourse, are acceptable or if in reality they have become obsolete, since nobody can recognize himself in them, particularly not the suffering and the dying.

According to Habermas, when somebody who is in desperate need for consolation comes to a political theologian the latter must be very watchful concerning himself or herself that he or she does not exploit in a certain situation primitive anxieties, which all of us have.[59] This precisely Habermas means when he speaks of discourse. Habermas counsels the political theologians, that they see to it, that a communication situation is established, in which the other does not accept all interpretations only because he trembles. Otherwise the theologian would merely impose himself violently as authority. This every behaviouristic therapist can do better! Habermas hopes that the critical theologian will connect with his interpretation a truth claim. He hopes that the theologian does not want to give the suffering or dying person merely something which quiets him or her down. Otherwise the theologian could give a tranquilizer to the suffering man or woman. Habermas knows that such tranquilizers work nowadays quite well in many cases. A strong depressant may do better work "toward the end" than prayers of the priest or nun, who have become meaningless in the present historical situation. But it is not the function of the critical theologian to give any kind of tranquilizer - LSD or a form of morphine - to the people living or dying in advanced capitalistic society. At least Habermas does not think so.

Habermas can imagine that social scientists like himself

can maybe not dispense with theologians of the type of
the political theologians concerning their enlightenment
about the conditions which make our life truly human.60
According to Habermas, theologians still have a language
available which has appellant and meta-communicative qualitie
Social scientists can no longer afford such language.
Maybe, so Habermas argues, this theological language can
still put into motion the forces which must be put into
action in order to stop the encroachment of self-
objectivating natural and social scientific systems of
interpretation. For Habermas the other dimension in
which theologians cannot be replaced is the realm of
individual consolation. Habermas does not feel very
competent in this area. A third realm in which
theologians of the critical kind may remain necessary
is that of quasi-political praxis.

In Habermas's view, the traditional entrances to a
political practice, which is able to initiate qualitative
social change are not very encouraging in the advanced
capitalistic society of the middle and late 1970's, no
matter if it is practiced in political parties or in
worker groups in factories. But the alternatives, which
normally offer themselves, seem meaningful to Habermas.
Habermas finds competitive a political praxis which is
so strongly morally inspired as this is to be expected,
particularly from active religious groups. Habermas
thinks that the signal-effect of examples is not to be
under-estimated. He speaks of examples of life practice.
Habermas does not believe in the purpose-rationality of
enterprises like certain "new life styles". That would
be the tradition of the old utopian sectarian formations.
Habermas does not believe in the dissemination ability
of those regressive forms of the religious consciousness,
which today in the sign of Zen-Buddhism, Transcendental
Meditation, Jesus People, followers of Jacob Lorber and
other pseudo-scientific therapies, working with Yoga,
self-hypnosis and group dynamics, form a series of sub-
cultures in organized capitalistic society.61 Habermas
does not believe in the effectiveness of strongly morally
motivated citizen-initiatives.62

Nevertheless, Habermas must admit that signal effects
and the example character are important for social
movements intending structural change.63 They are not
only important in relation to the socialization effect
for the participants themselves. This still falls into
the moral sphere of the face to face willingness to help,
e.g., in case of the illness of a neighbour or a friend.
That means of course always that one wants to help
oneself as well at the same time. For Habermas that

signal effect is important which goes beyond the circle of the immediate participants. It means what traditionally was called witnessing. Not only as philosopher, but also as empirical sociologist Habermas can diagnose that social movements have not come into existence without exemplary action. Particularly the American resistance against the Vietnam War was rich in such exemplary political actions, especially in theological circles.

On the other hand, Habermas finds it risky to play the martyr, to expose oneself in an exemplary manner, to let oneself be imprisoned. Habermas thinks of the Berrigan brothers.[64] Habermas finds such martyr behaviour risky, because it can easily destroy the moral structure of the participating persons. For Habermas it seems to be at least very difficult for the persons engaged in such martyr behaviour to keep themselves free in the long run from an elitarian self-understanding. But this does not speak against the effectiveness of such behaviour. As a matter of fact, in case of the Berrigans, it was effective, at least to some extent. It evoked the conscience of other Catholics and Protestants. It produced followers. It served the honor of the Christians in American society at least to some degree.

Habermas's whole critical theory of society and religion is concentrated and can therefore be summed up in its core concept of legitimation faith.[65] Habermas proposes in one of his latest books, *The Legitimation Problem in Late Capitalism* to analyze the legitimation faith in terms of a factual recognition of criticizable validity claims.[66] "Criticizable" means for Habermas that the validity claim, which is connected with norms of action and valuation can be redeemed only through justifications which aim at consensus. A legitimation faith is put into question to that extent, to which the justifications lose plausibility among the participants. The disintegration of legitimation signifies the growing scarcity of disposable justification potential. This dwindling of a plausibility, which achieves consensus without compulsion, can be compensated by coercion. Maybe, so Habermas admits, a system of domination, like the advanced capitalistic system, can afford to live with somewhat less consensus and somewhat more forced compliance. But maybe also a longing for a new level of justification appears among the people living in the system of domination, which cannot be rendered harmless with inconspicuous, i.e., ideologically effective means. In such cases the system of domination can only then rely on legitimation faith again, when its basic norms have been brought into harmony with the now available justification potential. The respective niveau of justification depends on the structures of the accepted religious or secular world image.

Habermas, following Hegel, asserts that the world-image-structures are not arbitrarily variable, but that they follow a developmental logic which can be reconstructed. This happens in such a way that today in societies of our type -- organized capitalistic and post-capitalistic socialist societies -- validity claims of norms will be acknowledged with great probability only, if they have for themselves the supposition that they can hold their ground in relation to a universalistic mode of justification. For Habermas the ultimate mode of justification is the discursive formation of the will of the people affected by those validity claims and the norms, they justify. The mentioned suppositions can very often be secured only through systematically produced blockings of communication.

Habermas defends the assertion that the universalistic mode of justification does not mirror the accidental qualities of a particular culture or a determinate epoch in man's social evolution. The universalistic mode of justification rather corresponds to the sense of discursive redemption, which is always already contained implicitly in normative validity claims. Habermas tries to base this assertion on a discourse theory of truth, the beginnings of a universalistic linguistic ethics, the cognitivistic theory of development and proposals for a theory of the development of religious and secular world images. 67

Habermas considers legitimation claims and the possibility to criticize these claims to be a social fact. 68 Thus for Habermas legitimation problems appear as functional problems of the total social system, wherever the justification potential, accessible on the extant level, is exhausted, and wherever at the same time a new niveau of justification is already amenable. "Accessible" means that new ideas spread in a society, which are incompatible with the old decaying religious or secular world image structures. 69 Criticizable validity claims have a peculiar facticity, which shows itself particularly when they are shaken by critique. It would be naive as well as unnecessary to assume that critique of validity claims or the withdrawal of recognition could happen only or preponderantly in the form of philosophical discourse proper or even of institutionalized partial discourses. Habermas asserts merely that the implicit meaning of normative validity claims consists precisely in that they alone *could* possibly be redeemed discursively.

In Habermas's perspective it is possible to call a social system free of domination, when the possibility is institutionally secured, in principle to put into question the validity of all politically consequential norms and to make them dependent on discursive will-formation processes. In this case, of course, the elbow room for the institutional transformation of the democratic principle of organization depends on the developmental level of the respective social system. Habermas does not know if such a far reaching institutionalization of a domination-free political will-formation can ever be realized or made compatible with competing functional imperatives. Habermas does not even believe that this question can at all be decided with good reasons. But for Habermas, presupposed that such a far reaching institutionalization of domination-free political formation of will would be possible, then the discursive finding of decisions and the formation of compromising would also not in such a case not be superfluous. One can deny this only if one makes unprovable anthropological assumptions concerning the uniformity of human needs, the decline of human aggressiveness, the elimination of all other sources of conflict, etc.

Habermas does not reflect discursively upon fascist political contents.[70] But he presupposes that fascist contents cannot be universalized in discourse. Here his optimism concerning the universalization-power of discourse obviously ends.[71] That fascist contents cannot be universalized is for Habermas the result of the very premises of the philosophical discourse. Insofar as fascism, a phenomenon appearing in advanced capitalistic societies, is sytematically connected with racist, ethnicistic, nationalistic teachings, it can be shown, that its doctrines are not able to be discursively justified because of their essentially particularlistic character. Habermas asks rightly: How can possibly the respective minority groups, the oppression or physical annihilation of which the fascist doctrines intend and in Nazi Germany realized, be brought to consent concerning their own destruction by the dominant group without force? For Habermas the negative answer to this question does not at all mean that the partisanship *for* reasons which he, like Hegel before, recommends and practices throughout his critical philosophy, tacitly presupposes the partisanship *of* reason. According to Habermas, certainly the principle of universalization, which we, if we enter practical discourse, have thereby *eo ipso* accepted, since it results from the formal properties of discourse, is incompatible with all those proposals, which would like to bring particular interests to universal validity. This does not at all mean that the principle of universalization prejudges certain contents. Opponents of Habermas may argue that all interests are particular. If anybody asserts for any particular interest the ability to be universalized, he abuses rationality claims in order to mislead or to intimidate the antagonist. Habermas does not see how anybody can *a priori* exclude the possibility, that members of a given social system could have *common* interests -- even in an advanced capitalistic society with its infinite pluralism of often antagonistic interests.

In Habermas's perspective, the hypothetical attitude of a discourse participant allows very well, to thematize any given experience, just not to generate experiences.[72] Habermas admits the possibility, that discourse participants can come discursively to the agreement with each other concerning the statement of dissent. This way the discourse partners can prove the inability of a particular interest to be universalized. Habermas asserts a certain cultural invariance of a universal cognitive equipment of man on the basis of a cognitive developmental psychology. Particularistic value systems are already out of analytical reasons unable to receive universal justification. Habermas does not only take into consideration the affirmative meaning of a discursive examination of normative validity claims. To the contrary, under evolutionary perspective Habermas is interested in the criticizability of validity claims, which are designed for discursive redemption.

According to Habermas, legitimation-critical doubts can direct themselves against narrative explanations of mythical origin, against argumentative justifications of cosmological or religious derivation, against philosophical arguments of rationalistic theories of state and right, against justifications of a rationalistic ethics.[73] Historically critique occurs at fragile legitimation foundations, when thresholds of social evolution are reached, always in relation to the respective next level of justification, which is made accessible in the evolution of religious and secular world images. This new niveau of justification can then in the further development be put into question once more. The critique of extant legitimations is certainly always valid only in relation to the language-and concept-system which is accepted in the argumentation, i.e., relative to the theory language. But well-founded legitimation-critical assertions do not lose their validity through the fact that the theory language, in which they are formulated, is superceded historically by the next following theory

language. The relative right of the original theory
language must let itself be reconstructed in the new
relational system in a similar way as this happens in the
framework of quantum mechanics concerning the validity
claim of classical mechanics. But in no way does
Habermas want to confuse with this comparison the
structural differences between the development of the
sciences and of social morality or religion.

In Habermas's view, in this sense Marx tries, for instance,
in the framework of his historical materialism at the
same time to relativize and to substantiate the right
of the bourgeois revolution-rhetoric, i.e., the right
of that critique which has been exercised in the name of
the bourgeois ideals of freedom, equality and brotherhood
against the foundations of traditional, i.e., feudal
class societies. Shortly, in the perspective of the
historical materialist Habermas, the discourse concept
of the ability of particular interests to be universalized
can serve the purpose to clarify legitimation-critical
processes.

According to Habermas, the discursive mode of justification
takes on an affirmative function, of course, only to the
extent to which a social system approaches the condition
which he calls hypothetically domination-free.74   For
Habermas this expression does not necessarily signify
the absence of social force, but rather a determinate
form to legitimate binding decisions. In Habermas's
view, if we should call the exercise of social coercion,
which is coupled back with discursive will-formation
processes, still dominion or power, depends on the way
we regulate the use of these terms. If one defines
dominion so narrowly that the expression is used
synonymously with class domination, then a discursive
justification of dominion is not possible out of
analytical reasons. But also in the case of this use of
language the discourse-related concept of legitimation
is a proper instrument for the examination of legitimation-
critical processes and thereby initiated transformations
of systems of domination. Communication without
domination in a communication community is the ultimate
practical intent of Habermas's critical theory of society
and religion.75 It shows its critical power particularly
in confrontation with Talcott Parson's and Niklas Luhmann's
functional sociology, especially their analytical theory
of religion.

CHAPTER IX

ULTIMATE REALITY

Parsons is one of the main architects of the detente
between religion and the positive sciences of man which
has lasted over the past two generations in advanced
capitalistic society.[1] At present this detente is no
longer operative. Once more as before in liberal
capitalistic society, a cold war has broken out between
theology and science. B.F. Skinner's *Beyond Freedom
and Dignity* challenges the place of religion in organized
capitalistic society. Skinner's work is in fact an
opening cannonade for the new conflict between faith and
reason. More recently 250 American scholars, including
Skinner, issued the *Humanist Manifesto* which further
marks the rupture of the relationship between revelation
and scientific enlightenment. Despite these signs of a
new strain and struggle between religion and secular
science, the link between the thological community and its
focus on ultimate concern and ultimate reality on one hand
and a positive social and behavioural science that cannot
possibly avoid recourse to ethical norms legitimated by
religious values and symbols on the other hand is irrevocable.

The Parsonian accommodation between social science and
religion in advanced capitalistic society in the last
four decades depended in part on the widespread conviction
that there is no scientific basis for determining whether
religious beliefs are true and whether religious practices
are good. This conviction is based on the dubious
fundamental rules of all forms of positivism from Comté's
historical positivism over the logical positivism of the
Vienna School to K. Popper's reform positivism: phenonenalism,
nominalism, value freedom and unity of a quasi-natural
science methodology.[2] These assumptions have blinded
sociologists in organized capitalistic society to the
judgements concerning religious beliefs and practices
that are implicit in their analytical theories. In
advanced capitalistic society, general sociological
theory, bound more or less to one or the other or several
of the positivistic rules has implied that although there
is much in religion that is good, religious beliefs are
not true. But in recent years, an increasing number of
particularly Parsonian sociologists have become aware of
these judgements. In particular, these sociologists

have perceived that the negative judgement concerning religious truth claims jeopardizes the accommodation between social science and religion in organized capitalistic society. Much of the newest theoretical work in sociology of religion in advanced capitalistic societies is an effort to restore this accommodation by devising some way in which positive social science might affirm religious truth. Parsons' own recent concern with ultimate reality, the Parsonian R. Bellah's symbolic realism, D. Anthony's and Th. Robbin's search for religious deep structures and P. Berger's search for signals of transcendence are not only signs of the intense legitimation crisis of advanced capitalistic society, but also serious attempts to deal with it by being open for religious truth claims. Whatever the scientific merits of these new approaches, the fact that they have clear implications for theology means they cannot form the basis for an accommodation between social science and religion that is as broad as the one built by Parsons and his many disciples in America and Europe earlier, which is now destroyed by militantly anti-religious and anti-metaphysical humanists. Our central question is: does Parsons in the newest form of his functional analysis of religion show to advanced modern society an adequate way to reconcile anew the religious and the secular and in connection with it the individual and the collective or does it lead into an *a-poria*, i.e., no-way.

Parsons' analytical theory of religion as his whole functional analysis of action and evolution has many intellectual roots: Hobbes, Locke, Darwin, A. Marshall, V. Pareto, Durkheim, etc.3 But, the most influential source of Parsons' structural functionalism, as before of Habermas's critical theory -- is German idealism as it passed from Hegel through Marx to Max Weber. In Parsons' view, the movement of German idealistic philosophy was intimately associated with protestant theological concerns and also brought such traditions into close contact with the bourgeois enlightenment and its romantic counterpart. In Parsons' perspective although it is fashionable today, particularly in the Anglo Saxon world, to ridicule Hegel's alleged glorification of the Prussian state, he did nevertheless develop a very sophisticated theory of human action and of general societal evolution and its culmination in the modern West. Hegel is indeed not only the last great old-European Christian and humanistic philosopher, but also the philosopher of modernity par excellence. According to Parsons, the theological philosophy of Hegel involved the philosophical grounding of Marxism, which is more central European than western European in its main cultural foundation, although it linked with the bourgeoise enlightenment in being strongly anti-Christian. Parsons criticizes Hegel's as well as Marx's theory of action and societal evolution for having too definite a temporal closure. Parsons overlooks that Hegel's time perspective does not only embrace thousands of years of primitive, archaic, historic, intermediate and modern evolution of politics, art, religion and philosophy but also anticipates thousands of years of post-bourgeoise, post-European, post-modern history, including in a very distant future a reconciled American or Slavic world in which the individual and the collective as well as the secular and the religious will be in balance.4 Parsons admits that Marx did indeed recognize that feudalism was not confined to Europe, but felt that the emergence of capitalism had enabled Europe to take the lead in general societal development, so that the final phase of socialism, i.e., communism, had to originate there, rather than in Russia or in China.

Why did Parsons, similar to Habermas, develop his functional analysis of society and religion not only out of but also against Hegel's philosophy? The reasons are at least partially methodological. According to Parsons, the independence that components of action gain through differentiation and its relation to variation has a time perspective.5 A differentiated cultural, social, or psychological component of an action system need not be bound to one concrete territory-and-population-instance, nor to any particular period in evolution. Above all, culture, particularly religion, through documents and otherwise, can become relatively independent of particular bearer societies or their individual members. Thus a cultural system's consequences for subsequent societies cannot be inferred very directly from its mode of involvement in the societal structure of its origin, but must be analyzed in a much more complex framework -- that of the societal evolution of the human species. Parsons discusses the case of Israel and Greece as particularly striking examples of this cultural-temporal independence. Parsons suggests that this independence presents a peculiarly difficult problem for a naive Marxist-type sociological analysis to demonstrate how the enormous religious, philosophical, scientific and artistic influence of these two cultural seedbed societies was really or in the last analysis based on the particular economic interests of either their originators of the adopters of these cultural patterns, i.e., Hebrew religion and Greek philosophy, science and art. While the critical theorist Habermas has intensely studied the functional analysis of Parsons

and his German disciple Luhmann, there is no indication
throughout the total work of Parsons since the 1930's
that he ever took into consideration the critical theory
of the Frankfurt School and its highly differentiated
and sophisticated basis and superstructure theory, which
emphasizes cultural-temporal independence at least as
much as he himself.6

In Parsons' view, great confusion over issues such as the
Marxian basis-superstructure theory has arisen from the
dogma, often left implicit, that evolutionary theory must
be historical in the sense of Hegelian and Marxian
"historicism". Whether following Hegel, Marx or later
Germans such as Dilthey, historicism has characteristically
denied the possibility or relevance of generalized
analytical theory. In Parsons' view, such theory
systematically treats the interdependence of independently
variable factors, e.g., the economical and religious
variable of action, in explaining temporally sequential
socio-cultural phenomena. Particularly in challenging
this idea, so Parsons argues, Durkheim and Weber introduced
a new era in the history of sociological science, quite
different from the one initiated earlier by Hegel and
Marx. Parsons, following Durkheim and still more so
Weber assures us, that once the problem of causal
imputation is formulated *analytically* the old chicken
and egg problem about the priorities of ideal and
material factors, e.g., religion and modes of production,
in action and evolution simply loses its significance.
Hegel and Marx become obsolete in advanced capitalistic
society. Parsons hopes that his analytical treatment of
the problems of action and evolution in his most recent
works *Societies* and *The System of Modern Societies* will
overcome the differentiation between idealism and realism
and thus will help to lay to rest once and for all this
ghost of our 19th century intellectual past, i.e., Hegel's
idealistic and Marx's materialistic "historicism". Parsons
forgets, that long before Weber, Hegel discovered the
mutual causation between the state, including civil
society and family, and religion and precisely thereby
superceded the contradiction between historical materialsim
and historical idealism.7

Parsons theory of action is indeed an analytical mutation
of Hegel's dialectical philosophy of law, his theory of
evolution an analytical transformation of Hegel's
dialectical philosophy of history and his theory of
religion an analytical metamorphosis of Hegel's
dialectical philosophy of religion.8 Through his
analytical method, Parsons understands societal evolution
not like Hegel or Habermas as self-constitutive learning

process of the human species, but rather as a process of
differentiation of action systems, which happens very
much behind the backs of the individuals and groups
involved.9 By his analytical approach, Parsons fixes
the differentiated components of action systems once and
for all. Parsons excludes by his analytical method
negative dialectics.10 This makes it difficult, if not
impossible for Parsons to see that in action and evolution
the difference between the religious and the secular as
well as between the individual and the collective can
turn into opposition and even contradiction and has
indeed done so in advanced modernity. Furthermore, by
his analytical approach Parsons excludes positive
dialectics. Thus he is not aware of the fact, that out
of the differentiation, opposition, and contradiction of
faith and reason, person and society, can arise the need
and the longing for their reunion in a qualitative new
post-modern society. The exclusion of positive dialectics
prevents Parsons from seeing action and evolution not
only as processes of quantitatively more and more
differentiation, but also of qualitative transformations
and thus blocks his view of a qualitatively different
post-modern development. Parsons exclusion of negative
and positive dialectics is the methodological reason for
the well known conservativism of functional analysis.11
Dialectical reason presupposes and includes analytical
understanding, not vice versa. Therefore, the dialectician
Habermas can learn from the analytical theorist Parsons
but not vice versa. We turn to Parsons analytical paradigm
of action which is the very basis of his theory of
evolution, particularly the religious development.

Parsons' theory of action systems presupposes a theory
of action.12 According to Parsons the social system,
be it Canada, the U.S.A., West Germany, Yugoslavia, etc.,
is made up of the interaction of human individuals.
Therefore each member is both actor, having goals, ideas,
values, attitudes, etc., and object of orientation for
both other actors and himself or herself. The social
interaction system then is an analytical aspect
abstractable from the total action process of its
participants. At the same time these individuals are
also natural and behavioural organisms, personalities
and participants in cultural systems. Thus Parsons
differentiated in the total human action system four
particular subsystems of action: culture, social system,
personality, behavioural organism. Each of these
subsystems has all the others for its environments.
According to Parsons' analytical interpretation beyond
the total action system, including the four subsystems,
are the environments of action itself, standing above

and below the general hierarchy of cultural, social, psychological and behavioural factors that control action in the world of life. Below action in the hierarchy of the total action system stands the physical-organic environment including not only phenomena understandable in terms of physics and chemistry, but also in terms of the subhuman species of organisms and the non-behavioural components of the human organism, the natural organism of man, not exposed to learning. Here Parsons speaks of the world of living organisms so far as they are not integrated into human action systems. For Parsons this boundary between nature and action is particularly important, because as humans we know the physical world only through our organism. Our minds have no direct experience of an external physical object unless we perceive it through physical processes and the brain processes information about it. In their psychologically known sense, however, physical objects are aspects of action. Relations with the physical-organic environment are mediated through the behavioural organism.

In Parsons' view, in principle similar considerations apply to the environment above the total action system. It is not only open downward to the cosmos, but also upward to the ultimate reality. Parsons conceives the ultimate reality to be independent of the physical environment as well as of action systems. Parsons speaks of the ultimate reality in a sense derived from traditions of Christian philosophy and theology reaching from Thomas Aquinas over Hegel to Paul Tillich.13 For Parsons, as for Tillich, ultimate reality is interchangeable with being itself, with the power of being in opposition to non-being. For Parsons, men are ultimately concerned with ultimate reality in grappling with what Leibnitz and Hegel called the theodicy problem and Weber the problem of meaning, e.g., contingencies like natural and social evil, suffering, the temporal limitations of human life, illness, death, war, hunger, oppression, ecological destruction, alientation, injustices, etc.14

In Parsons' perspective, ideas in this area, as cultural objects, are in some sense symbolic representations, e.g., conceptions of God or gods, totems, the supernatural, the ultimate realities, but are not themselves such realities. The ultimate reality which concerns the problem of meaning for human action is mediated into action primarily by the cultural system structuring meaningful orientations that include, but are not exhausted by cognitive answers to the theodicy question. More precisely relations with the action environment ultimate reality are mediated through the constitutive symbol systems, i.e., the

religious components of the cultural system. The system
of ultimate reality is like the cosmic system, entirely
environmental to human action in general and not a
constitutive element of it in the analytical sense. Individuals
know of the ultimate reality only through their participation
in a particular culture. People have no direct experience
of the ultimate reality unless they perceive it through
the constitutive symbols of the action system of which
they are a part.

Parsons' ultimate reality is definitely Judeo-Christian
heritage in the sense that it is neither identical with
society, as Durkheim asserted, nor with nature as the
pantheistic tradition has it from Hinduism and Buddhism
over Sufism to Spinoza. Furthermore, one must admit that
Parsons' ultimate reality or being itself constitutes
a manifest ontological and theological residual in the
allegedly non-metaphysical logic of functionalism and
that precisely thereby, as the descendent of several
generations of Presbyterian ministers, he does indeed
what he intends to do, namely to go beyond the positivism
of his predecessors, the positivistic organizists from
August Comte over Herbert Spencer and Leslie Waard to
Durkheim.15 But at the same time, Parsons by positing
not unlike traditional dualistic theologians ultimate
reality entirely external to action system and nature
limits it, and thus makes finite what he intends to be
infinite. There is a manichaic tendency present in the
analytical method as such. Beyond that Parsons is
committed, knowingly or not, to a methodological atheism
in so far as he, while the theistic world religions are
mainly concerned with *God's work* in the world, speaks
merely of *human action*. To be sure, Parsons is aware
of the fact that all traditional cultures report narratively of
divine actions in nature and society, but such glories
cannot be analytically verified or falsified. Functional
analysis does not accept the truth claims of the world
religions which is their very rationale. While Parsons
takes very serious the corectness of positive science,
he considers religious truth to be negligible. Fundamentally,
Parsons is no less pagan than his positivistic predecessors
in spite of all the Christian vocabulary he uses.

For Parsons, the criterion of the Aristotelian self-
sufficiency of a society as subsystem of the total action
system can be divided into five subcriteria, each relating
to one of the five environments of the social system:
ultimate reality, cultural system, personality system,
behavioural organism, and the physical-organic environment.
In Parsons' view, the self-sufficiency of a society is
the function of the balanced combination of its controls

over its relations with these five environments, particularly the ultimate reality, and of its own state of internal intergration of its social identity. Parsons identifies a hierarchy of controls which organizes the inter-relations of the analytically distinguished subsystems of the total action system. This includes the cybernetic aspect of control by which subsystems of total action high in information but low in energy regulate other systems higher in energy, but lower in information as well as the cybernetic aspect of conditioning by which subsystems high in energy but low in information carry other systems higher in information, but lower in energy. Thus a programmed sequence of mechanical operations, e.g., a washing machine can be controlled by a timing switch using very little energy compared with the energy actually operating the machine's moving parts or heating its water. Another example Parsons uses is the gene and its control over the protein synthesis and other aspects of cell metabolism. Parsons vascillates between mechanistic and organizistic understanding of cybernetic action systems. But, originally coming from biology, he shows particularly recently a greater inclination toward the latter. While for Parsons, religion does as cultural component range high in the hierarchy of cybernetic control, he has, over his conern with action systems, either as mega-machines or as mega-organisms entirely forgotten Hegel's central concern with spirit. For Parsons, ultimate reality means no longer, as for Hegel, absolute spirit. Parsons reifies Hegel's absolute spirit into the culture system, his objective spirit into the social system, his subjective spirit into the system of personality and behavioural organism.16

Parsons classification of four highly general subsystems of action is an application of the general structural-functional paradigm which he is using to analyze not only total action systems, but cultural, social and personality systems as well. Through this paradigm, Parsons analyzes any action system in terms of the four functional categories: pattern maintenance, concerned with the maintenance of the highest governing or controlling patterns of the system; integration, dealing with the internal unity or identity of the system; goal attainment, concerned with the systems orientation to the attainment of goals in relation to its environment; adaptation, dealing with the system's more generalized adaptation to the conditions of its environment. In Parsons' view within the total action system, cultural systems, including religion, are specialized around the function of pattern maintenance, social systems around the

function of goal attainment and the behavioural organism
around the function of adaptation. These functions can
be latent or manifest for the people involved. On the
proper functioning of these subsystems depends the
equilibrium and survival of the total action system.
Equilibrium and survival is the highest value of functional
analysis. It is also in that sense no longer entirely
positivistic, that even manifestly it does not follow the
positivistic rule of value freedom. Each subsystem of
action must reach a certain optimal value of functional
achievement, if the total action system is to survive.
A subsystem is eu-functional, if it serves the survival
of the total action system; dysfunctional, if it hinders
such survival; and non-function, if it is without
consequence for such survival. While Parsons is little
concerned with the truth claim of religion, its functionality
for the realization of the optimal value of pattern
maintenance and therby for the survival of the total
action system is of utmost significance to him. What
Hegel warns of, the functionalization of religion, is
almost complete reality in Parsons' functional analysis.17
Parsons' analytical theory signifies the almost complete
triumph of instrumental understanding over substantial
reason in the old European sense, as it was comprehended
from Plato to Hegel and still continues in the Frankfurt
School up to Habermas.18 Adaptive behaviour dominates
almost completely communicative praxis.

According to his four-function-scheme, Parsons treats a
society as analytically divisible into four primary
subsystems: societal community, pattern maintenance
system, polity, and economy. The societal community,
the core of the social system, contains norms as structural
component and as such integrates culture with personality.
The pattern maintenance system, containing values is
particularly concerned with the relations of society to
the cultural system and through it, with the ultimate
reality. The polity or the goal attainment system is
characterized by collectivities and is, as such, concerned
with the relations between society and the personalities
of individual members. The economy or the adaptive system
is determined by the structural component of roles and as
such is concerned with relations of society to the
behavioural organism and through it with the physical
world. The main aspect of developmental process is for
the societal community inclusion, for the pattern
maintenance system value universalization, for the polity
differentiation and for the economy adaptive upgrading.
To each of the four subsystems of society is related a
regulating medium of communication: love to the societal
community, faith to the pattern maintenance system, power

to the polity, money to the economy.

In Parsons' perspective, these functional divisions are
clearest and most important for advanced modern societies.
But Parsons admits that the complexity of the relationship
both among subsystems of action and of society prevent
these functional divisions from ever being very neat.
Thus religion must be located in the pattern maintenance
system of society, but is, even in modern social systems,
still present in the integrative societal community and
in premodern societies functions in the goal attaining
polity as well as in the adaptive economy.

Not only culture, including religion, is environmental
to the social system, but also the individuals with their
concrete impulses and motivations. The individuals as
personalities and behavioural organisms are cybernetically
controlled from above by society and culture and conditioned
from below by the physical-organic environment, including
their own non-behavioural organisms. In order to survive,
not only religion, but also the individuals must fulfill
to an optimal value the four functional requirements.
According to Parsons, in modern society the religious and
the secular as well as the collective and the individual
are sharply differentiated from each other.

Parsons does not like Habermas borrow from Hegel and Marx
the concept of the unity of theory and practice as well
as the related idea of the self-constitution of the human
species or society. The analytical theory per se, excludes
the appropriation of these concepts. But Habermas is
right when he states that Parsons' theory of action
systems is, as it helps to reduce the complexity of these
systems, as practical as these systems which it explores.
Thus, Parsons' theoretical work stands, probably latently
so, in an objective connection which is determined through
the progress in the complexity of action systems, in such
a way that the social evolution rises out of the
achievements of the social systems themselves. The
theory is the organ, which in society's process of self-
constitution, often today begins to take leadership instead
of religion, as the system of science gains functional
primacy in the cultural system of advanced modern action
systems. As such, theory is immediately practical.
Parsons overlooks the reflexivity of his own functional
analysis of action systems: that his own theory is part
of the cultural system of the organized capitalistic
action systems and, as such, it participates in the
solution of their pattern maintenance problems and thus
serves their survival. Here lies the material reason
for the conservatism of structural functionalism and

Parsons' apologetic posture concerning advanced
capitalistic societies. Parsons' theory of Action is
particularly vulnerable in the dimension of meaning as
the critique of his German follower Luhmann and even more
so of Habermas can show very clearly.

CHAPTER X

MEANING

While Luhmann who carries Parsonian functionalism to its
last conclusions, confirms that Parsons has indeed
overcome the purely behaviouristic position and defines
action, following Weber, through intended meaning, he
criticizes him nevertheless for not asking behind the
notion of meaning as it is connected with ultimate
reality.1 Parsons sees meaning as a property of action
and not like Luhmann and his many followers in Europe
as a selection from a universe of other possibilities
for the purpose of the reduction of environmental
complexity and the conquering of contingencies. Parsons
does no longer posit the problem of order, as Hobbes
did, in respect to political instrumentalities, but from
the perspective of subjectively intended meaning. Thus
Parsons does not identify order with domination, but
determines it as normative structure, which overcomes this
contingency of domination and guarantees the complementarity
of behavioural expectations. But Parsons does not as
Luhmann functionalize the concept of meaning or of its
correlate, the ultimate reality. According to Luhmann
precisely therefore Parsons comes only to statements
like: If there should be order at all, there must be
structures, norms, commonly accepted values, institutions,
roles, etc. But all these structures, roles, values,
norms, institutions remain entirely empty and formal and
are only subdivided by an analytical classificatory
system-theory constructed besides them. While Parsons
can from this starting point apply the technique of
functional analysis inside of given system structures,
he can not as Luhmann does, ask for the function of
systems and structures in general.

According to Luhmann, action systems can under certain
circumstances vary their environmental horizons. They
can through escalation of their own complexity lower
the complexity pattern of their environments. They can
defer the solution limitation of their functional
problems. They can also draw relatively improbable
issues into the sphere of their reaction. To this the
consequences of the modern positive sciences give ample
witness.

In Luhmann's view transverse to this there is for every
individual the possibility to know that there are in his
or her own environment systems-in-an environment. In the
18th century begins with the bourgeois enlighteners the
discovery of the milieu and the milieu-dependence. From
this follows finally the self-reflection of the action
system as sytems-and-part-of-the-environment-of other
systems. In Luhmann's view both transformations lead to
a crisis of religion, particularly Christianity, and
metaphysics, which were used to look idealistically from
inside of systems toward their environment rather than
like the bourgeois and then socialist materialists from
the milieu into the system. The two transformations
remain nevertheless inside the framework of system-
relative environmental perspectives. They change the
reality definition which is used for the probing and
scanning and normalization of the environment. They
also change for the social system, not necessarily for
the individuals, the stabilizable grade by rising the
complexity of the system and of the relevant environment
correlatively.

For Luhmann most importantly the two transformations
change the meaning of ultimate reality or being itself
as the aggregation formula for all system environments.
Thereby they change the foundations of the possibility
to decompose being, i.e., the table of fundamental
categories. Modern philosophy reacts promptly, e.g.,
in the form of Hegel's new dialectical logic. Then
also the theologians take over the quest for ultimate
reality or being as reference point of their aporetic
situation. In Luhmann's view, according to sociologists
of religion informed by Tillich through Parsons concerning
the ultimate reality the task of religion is the
thematization of the deep structure of the world. For
Luhmann it is not clear at all, why the depth of the
world has a structure and why it should not be possible
to ask behind even being itself or the ultimate reality
instead of accepting it aporetically. In any case,
according to Luhmann, the problem of the reductivity of
penetrable system environments as such is not resolvable
by Tillich or by Parsons. They do not resolve this
problem better, nor do they even come close to its
resolution, but merely postpone it. Luhmann warns that
precisely thereby Tillich and Parsons endanger the
possibility, and there is no other for him, of the use
of the typography of the immediate lifeworld for the
very transcending of its horizons. For Luhmann the
concept of ultimate reality, being or God, has become the
mere contingency formula of the total action system and its
environment. Not with Parsons, who still preserves Luhmann ar

Presbyterian heritage in the concept of ultimate reality, but with Luhmann the long history of the positivistic self-destruction of Western metaphysics and theology comes to its final conclusion. Parsons nevertheless helped to prepare the way. According to Habermas, Parsons', still more so Luhmann's theory of religion means indeed the end of religion.

In the perspective of Habermas obviously social spheres of organization can be understood as Parsons does, like living organisms as self-regulating cybernetic systems and can be analyzed as such.2 If the logic of system research agrees concerning social organizations and biological organisms and if the functionalistic assumption of their similarity is correct, then Parsons has indeed demonstrated the conditions of the possibility of general theories of social action. But this is rejected not only by positivists on the Right, but also by critical theorists on the Left. Habermas's main objection is, that the control values of pattern maintenance, integration, goal attainment and adaptation, which Parsons introduces for total action and social systems in order to determine their equilibrium and their survival possibility, are related not to factual, but to possible functional conditions. They depend on rules of evaluation, which must constitute themselves first in a hypothetically identifiable procedure of the formation of will, in a discourse of some kind. Without these standards we do not have the reference system inside of which we can measure the factually found optimal values for pattern maintenance, integration, goal attainment and adaption as control values for an equilibrium condition of total action systems, social systems, cultural systems or personality systems in their respective environments.

According to Habermas we are not able to grasp descriptively in boundary maintaining social systems a condition of equilibrium. At best we can determine control values for such a system condition under pragmatic perspective -- is has been said -- in discourse. Habermas rejects the descriptive claim of Parsons' functional analysis as it moves from organisms to social organizations, which are not in the same way established and fixed as the former. But thereby that what Parsons presupposes in empirical-analytical intent, goes over into system research, which explores the functioning of social institutions in relation to a pragmatically presupposed system purpose. Technical imperatives appear at the logical locations, which are occupied in the theories of strategic action by the hypothetical maxims. The status of the statements which have the greater an information

content, the more empirically discovered data enter into
the calculation, is the same in both cases. Also the
system research generates as the decision theory
prescriptively usable informations, i.e., a form of
technical knowledge. Habermas recommends against Parsons
to differentiate sharply the system research, which is
spreading in the biological sciences in empirical-analytical
intent, from the system research which in relation to its
realm of objects deals with the issue of meaning and as
such must procede normative-analytically, no matter if
this is manifest as in the case of Luhmann or latent as
in the case of Parsons.

Habermas suggests a way out of the dilemma of the
Parsonian theory of action systems: a re-historization
of social analysis. But Habermas sees difficulties
in this. One difficulty is the result of the fact
that the Parsonian functional analysis of role systems
presupposes the grasping of so-called cultural value
systems, including religious values. The action-orienting
meaning of social norms stems from a cultural, often
religious tradition, which belongs to it. It is indeed
true, that Parsons as a sociologist, is concerned with
traditional contents of meaning only insofar as they
enter the institutions of society. But the problematic
of the understanding of meaning can therefore not be
pushed, in terms of a division of labour, into the area
of the historical-heremeneutical sciences. The
hermeneutical problematic is thereby not resolved, but
at best repressed into non-reflected starting stages.

According to Habermas, value systems constitute, when
they are grasped descriptively as facts and are not
constructed as pure maxims of behaviour, for the social
scientist methodologically the same problem as for the
historian the meaning of documents and the philologist
the meaning of texts. Also the institutionalized values
belong to an, in colloquial language handed down, more or
less articulated, always historically concrete, mostly
religious world view of social groups. Parsons strips
the conception of handed down meaning of its problematic
by the simplifying presupposition of a value universalism.
According to Parsons the contents of meaning which are
objectivated in value systems are not part of unique
cultures and traditions, they rather build themselves
atomistically up out of elementary value parts which
remain the same in different cultures and evolutionary
periods and appear only in different combinations.

In Habermas's view, this elementary presupposition
connected with the imputation of the autonomy of the

value system of institutionalized sciences, like sociological structural-functionalism, cuts off the important question: Are the theories of action and the system theories not forced in the unavoidable dimension of a hermeneutical appropriation of handed down meaning to confront themselves with the problematic to which Weber paid at least attention under the name of value interpretation. On the value interpretation, which must direct itself out of the value relations of ones own situation, behind which one can not go, toward historically objectivated cultural meanings, depends the reccupleing to the hermeneutical starting point.

According to Habermas a social science, which not simply turns its back to the hermeneutical question, which imposes itself upon it, can not deceive itself about the fact that unavoidably a preunderstanding of historical situations enters the fundamental assumptions of its theories. That may make easier the identification of social systems. But for the identification of an equilibrium or survival condition not much is gained yet thereby. This is so, since the cultural values do not only serve the steering of the social system. They also function inside the system for goals which are not reflected in these values. Only if it was possible, so Habermas argues, to differentiate in the value system the utopian, under pragmatic perspective purpose-rational and the ideological contents, we could identify for a given system the objectively possible conditions of an equilibrium. The difficulty with Parsons is that the categorical framework, which he proposes, does not allow for such differentiation. Nowhere does Parsons or is he even able to differentiate, like Hegel, Marx, Horkheimer, Benjamin or Habermas between good, utopian religion, which is the impulse that society must become just, and evil ideological religion, which is the tendency to gild social conditions no matter how corrupt they may be.[3]

In Habermas's view, in the framework of Parsons action theory, motives of action are harmonized with institutional values, i.e., with the intersubjectively valid meaning of the normatively binding behaviour expectations. Not integrated driving forces, which do not find in the role system a legitimated chance of satisfaction are analytically not grasped. Habermas starts from the assumption that these repressed needs, which are not absorbed by the social roles and transformed into motivations and sanctioned, do nevertheless have their interpretations, sometimes in utopian religious traditions. Either these interpretations shoot beyond the status quo of the given action system and signify as utopian anticipations a not yet achieved

social identity, a reconciled society, or these
interpretations serve, transformed into ideologies, as
much the justification of the drive repressing authorities,
often religious, as the projective compensative satisfaction.
Thus they reinforce the legitimation of domination and the
non-functional compensation of socially undesirable, i.e.,
for the collective self-preservation useless impulses.

In Habermas's critical perspective, a condition of
equilibrium can be determined in terms of such criteria,
depending on the question, if the system of domination
of a society realizes the utopian contents, religious or
secular, in such a measure in which the given level of
productive forces and of technical progress allows it
objectively. At any rate, society can then no longer be
comprehended exclusively, as Parsons does, as a system
of self-preservation. The objective-intentional connection
is then no longer determined by the purpose-rational
adequacy of instrumental action or adaptive behaviour,
i.e., through technical or instrumental rationality.
Rather the meaning by which the functionality of societal
processes is measured, is anchored in the idea of
communication without domination. The functionalism of
the artisan model, to which Parsons is committed is
replaced by the theatrical stage model, which Hegel used
in his philosophy of history.4

According to Habermas, functional analysis and critical
theory are in a certain sense complementary. In the
context of functionalism the level of adaptive behaviour
is posited too low. In the framework of critical theory
the level of communicative action is posited too high.
Social action has always been, as far as our historical
remembrance reaches, adaptive behaviour *and* communicative
action. That must be comprehended by functionalists and
critical theorists alike. The reduction to externally
stimulated behaviour, as we find it not only with Skinner,
but to some extent also with Parsons, encounters the
limitation of linguistically mediated communication. It
is not possible to liquidate intentionality without any
trace. But the projection of behaviour to the level of
intentional action shows itself to be an anticipation
of a future communicative community which needs correction.
Man is neither merely animal, nor God. It is not possible
to derive action completely out of the subjectively
intended meaning. The empirical connection of actions
directed through societal norms transcends the manifest
meaning of the intentions and demands of an objective
system of reference in which the latent meaning of
functions can be grasped. This is so, since the
orientation of the actors is in the last analysis anyhow

not identical with their motives.

According to Parsons -- as Habermas understands him -- handed down contents of meaning gain their normative binding power for social action in any case not at all from the ultimate reality but from their institutionalization in society. The institutionalization, as Parsons describes it, binds to the until then, so to speak, freely suspended intentions or behavioural expectations a sufficient portion of energy or needs, the interpretation of which agrees with the content of the role definition. The institutionalization of values is equivalent with a corresponding canalization of instinctive energies.

But for Habermas, who does not start like Parsons from ungrounded harmonistic presuppositions, the binding of drive energies to rules and roles is always also coupled with the respression of the interpreted needs, often religious, which cannot be integrated into the offered roles. The reflection-inhibiting hardness of institutions, so Habermas argues, can be measured by the relationship between the integrated and the repressed needs, be they religious or profane. But if integrated and repressed needs do likewise motivate behaviour, then it is demonstrated that Habermas is right, when he, unlike Parsons, does not understand the institutionalization of values analytically, but rather comprehends it dialectically. While the institutionalization gives to the intentional expectations of behaviour intersubjective validity and thereby motivating power, it reshapes the repressed part of the needs into stimuli of non-intentional modes of behaviour and coded actions as well as into a potential of dreams, many of them religious, which inundates the conscious intentions. Thus the social action is the result of reactive compulsions as well as of meaningful interaction. The relationship in which action is behind the back of the actor merely stimulated by the split off motives or is on the other hand guided intentionally by the communication of meaning determines degrees of freedom of social action, degrees of the loosening up of the institutions and of the individuation of the individuals. The degrees of freedom can be read from the respective aggregate condition of history. In this aggregate condition is mirrored the emancipation of the human species from the compulsion of nature as well as from its reproduction in human action systems and social systems.

Habermas predicts that only if the split off motives and deeply internalized rules are comprehended out of their objective connection with the rational compulsions of

the collective self-assertion on one hand and with the
irrational compulsion of authorities, which have become
obsolete, on the other hand, and only if they would be
reconciled in the heads of the actors themselves with
the subjectively meaningful motives, social action could
enfold itself into truely communicative action. But
Parsons' analytical theory, which from the very start does
not even take into itself this dimension of the enfolding
of social action into communicative action, makes an
unreflected predecision in a matter of which the critical
theorist can at least not be certain of apriori: namely
a methodological decision concerning the question, if we
are more similar to the animals or to the gods?

According to Habermas those theoreticians, who have decided
too fast for the similarity with the gods, afterwards
introduce nevertheless their heroes through the backdoor
again into the animal realm. Unexpectedly the actors,
to whom the theoreticians have left their intentions,
find themselves together with the cultural values
harnessed into systems which obey alone the biological
foundation values of survival and efficient adaptation.
As Marx makes this charge against Hegel, so Habermas
against Parsons, in whose cultural determinism is
present more idealism than even in Hegel's philogophy
of society and history and certainly more than he is
willing to admit.   This is true not only for his theory
of action, but also for his theory of evolution built
on the former.

CHAPTER XI

EVOLUTION OF RELIGION

According to Parsons the high complexity of modern action
systems, including culture, social system, personality
and behavioural organism, and of its relationship to its
environments, nature, other action systems and ultimate
reality is the result of the social evolution of the
human species as process of differentiation.[1] Parsons
divides social evolution into four stages: primitive
societies, including the society of aboriginal Australia
and the Shilluk society; archaic society, including
ancient Egypt and the Mesopotamian Empires; the historic-
intermediate empires, including China, India, the Islamic
Empires, the Roman Empire, the Western Medieval societies;
and the modern society, including modern England, Holland,
France, Germany, Japan, the U.S.A., Russia, etc. While
in primitive society the religious system is dominant
together with the kinship group, and in archaic and historic-
intermediate societies the political system gains
importance, in modern societies the economic system is
of greatest significance. From the primitive over the
archaic and historic-intermediate stage of evolution the
religious and the secular, as well as the collective and
the individual are more and more differentiated. This
differentiation process reaches its culmination in the
secularism and individualism of early and advanced
modern society.

In Parsons' view Weber provides a more subtle theoretical
justification than Hegel or Marx and their followers on
the Left, for distinguishing modernity from the highest
evolutionary level attained by other principle civilizations
particularly, the historic-intermediate societies of
China, India, Rome, etc. Even those, so Parsons argues
who question Weber's propositions about the central role
of religion, i.e., Christianity, in bringing about the
high evolutionary level of modernity, must agree
nevertheless that long after the process of modernization
had begun in the West, no comparable developments had
occurred elsewhere. Indeed, so Parsons states, the
system of modern societies has extended beyond Europe
only by colonization or, as in Japan, by processes in
which the model of the modern West has been indispensible.

With Weber, Parsons raises the question of whether or
not the modern West has universal significance? Citing
Christianity, science based on experiment, the fine arts,
rational systems of law and administration, the modern
constitutional state, and rational bourgeois capitalism,
Parsons, like Weber before, concludes that the combination
of such factors constitutes a unique socio-cultural
system with unparalleled adaptive capacities, superior
in evolutionistic terms to all previous primitive, archaic
and historic-intermediate societies.

In Parsons perspective elements derived from classical
Hebrew and Greek sources, after undergoing further basic
development and combination comprised some of the main
cultural components of modern society. Their focus was
Christianity. As a cultural system Christianity proved
in the long run able both to absorb major components of
the secular culture of Antiquity and to form a matrix
from which a new order of secular culture could be
differentiated.

According to Parsons, Christian culture, including its
secular components, was able to maintain clearer and
more consistent differentiation from the social system
with which it was interdependent than either of its
forebearers -- the primitive religion of the Australian
aborigines and of the Shilluk, the archaic Egyptian and
Mesopotamian religions, the historical-intermediate
religions of China, India, Rome and Islam - had been able
to. Christian culture came to serve as a more effective
innovative force in the development of the total socio-
cultural system than had any other cultural complex that
had yet evolved up to the modern stage of evolution.

In Parsons view, Christianity originated as a sectarian
movement within Palestinian Judaism. It soon broke with
this religio-ethnic community, however. The decisive
event was St. Paul's decision that a gentile might become
a Christian without joining the Jewish community and
observing Jewish law. The early Christian church then
evolved into an associational religious group independent
of any ascriptive societal community, either ethnic or
territorial. Its focus was specifically religious: The
salvation of the individual soul. In this respect
Christianity became especially differentiated from any
secular organization. It was thus gradually spread
throughout the historic-intermediate Roman society
by the proselytizing of the apostles and other
missionaries. Its main early success was among the
humbler "non-responsible" urban population-craftsmen,
small merchants and the like -- who were bound neither

by the traditionalism of the peasant group nor by the "responsible" upper classes vested interests in the status quo. While Parsons' emphasizes the petite bourgeois character of the early Christian community, he is remarkably silent on its proletarian components usually stressed by critical theorists.2

According to Parsons, in terms of religious content the crucial elements of continuity with Judaism were transcendental monotheism and the concept of a covenant with the ultimate reality, i.e., God. A sense of having been chosen by God for a special divine mission thus continued. In classical Judaism the people of Israel had enjoyed this status. In Christianity it adhered to the company of the professing individuals, who gained access through their adoption of the faith. Salvation was to be found in and through the church, especially after the sacraments had been crystallized by the end of Antiquity. The early church was a voluntary association however, quite antithetical to a people in the sociological sense. The individual could only be a Jew as a total social personality, as one of the people. But one could be both a Christian and an Athenian or a Roman on the level of societal participation, a member of both the Church and an ethnic-territorial community.

In Parsons' view this step was crucial in differentiating both role- and collectivity-structures. This new definition of the basis for the religious collectivity and its relation to secular society had to be legitimated theologically. The new element was "Christ", who was more than simply another prophet or the messiah in the Jewish tradition. Such figures had always been purely human, with no claim to divinity. Christ was both, divine and human, the only begotten son of God, the Father, but also a man of flesh and blood. In this dual aspect, his mission was to offer salvation to mankind.

In Parsons perspective the transcendence of God, the Father, was the essential source of the sharp differentiation between what were later called the spiritual and the temporal sphere. The basis of their integration was the relation of individual souls to God through and in Christ and his church. It was defined theologically as the mystical body of Christ and partook of the divinity of Christ through the Holy Spirit. Christ not only offered salvation to souls but also freed the religious community from previous territorial and ethnic ascriptions. The relations among the three persons of the Christian trinity and of each to man and the other aspects of creation were highly complex. A stable theological ordering of these relations required intellectual resources not present in prophetic Judaism. It was here that late Greek culture furnished its crucial contribution.

In Parsons view, when after the radical decline from the highest historic-intermediate level of civilization by imperial Rome, gradual revival and consolidation began in the historic-intermediate early Middle Ages, a significant new relation between the universal church and the particular secular authority and society emerged. The legitimation of Charlemagnes' regime revolved around its relation to the church, as symbolized by his coronation by Pope Leo III in AD 800. This ceremony provided the model for the later Holy Roman Empire of the German Nation, which, though never a highly integrated polity, served as a legitimating framework for a unified Christian secular society.

In Parsons analytical perspective, within this institutional framework, the great medieval synthesis was characterized by the differentiation between the universal church and the particular state, in the special medieval sense of the word. This differentiation came to be defined as that between the spiritual and the temporal arms of the Christian mission. The special mode of differentiation and integration formed the core of what Parsons, following Troeltsch, considers to be the first version of the conception of a Christian society.

According to Parsons the Renaissance gave rise to a highly developed secular culture that was differentiated from the primarily religious, i.e., Christian matrix which had evolved through the historic-intermediate late Roman and western medieval society. Originating in Italy the Renaissance movement laid the foundations of the modern arts and intellectual disciplines. Indeed theology itself was affected through feedback from the new elements of secular culture that later crystallized in philosophy.

For Parsons the Reformation was an even more radical movement of cultural change than the Renaissance. It profoundly affected the relations between the cultural system and society. Its major cultural innovation was theological, the doctrine that salvation comes, in the Lutheran version, by faith alone, or, in the Calvinist predestinarian version, through the direct communion of the individual human soul with a sovereign universal God without any particular human intervention. This innovation deprived any Protestant church and its clergy of the power of the keyes, the capacity to mediate salvation through sacraments. Furthermore, the universal visible church, the concrete collectivity of human believers and their clerical leaders, was conceived as a purely human association. The attribute of divinity, the status of the universal church as the mystical body of Christ, belonged only to the invisible church, the company of individual souls in Christ.

On this protestant basis, so Parsons argues, the world could not consist, as Thomism had held, of two layers with profoundly different religious statuses: the universal church, divine and human, and purely human particular secular society. Rather by Protestants the world was believed to consist of one society, all members of which were both, bodies as secular beings and souls in their relation to God. This view represented a much more radical institutionalization of the individualistic components of Christianity than had Roman Catholocism. It also had profound egalitarian implications. Parsons admits, that this egalitarianism has indeed taken long to develop, however, and has done so very unevenly. Parsons is fully aware of the fact that this major change in the relations between the church and secular society brought about by Protestantism has often been interpreted as a major loss of religious rigor in favour of worldly indulgence. Parsons considers this view a major misinterpretation. According to Parsons the reformation was much more a movement to upgrade secular society to the highest religious level. Every single man was obligated to behave as a monk in his religious devotion, though -- to be sure -- not in his daily life, i.e., he was to be guided mainly by religious considerations. Parsons knows, of course, that the reformation did indeed shatter the religious unity of Western Christendom and by this fact alone reinforced the secularization tendencies originating from the Renaissance.

According to Parsons the outcome of the struggle between Reformation and Counter-Reformation was a double step toward pluralization and differentiation. Development within the Holy Roman Empire of the German Nation posed the crucial problem of integration across the Protestant-Roman Catholic line. Parsons criticizes the many historians and sociologists of modern Europe who have recognized only stalemated conflict here. But in Parsons' view religious toleration has been extended to Roman Catholics in Protestant polities and "even" to Protestants in Roman Catholic polities, though generally without radical sacrifices of the establishment principle. For Parsons religious pluralization was part of a process of differentiation between the cultural and the societal system in early modern action systems that reduced the

rigidity and diffuseness of their interpretation. In
Parsons' perspective it is of greatent importance that
religious legitimation of secular society was retained
without committing governmental authority to the direct
implementation or inforcement of religious goals.

In Parsons' view the industrial and democratic revolutions
were aspects of the great transformation by which the
institutional bulwarks of the early modern system-monarchy,
aristocracy and church - were progressively weakened.
Today there are still established churches. But only at the
less modern peripheries of the European civilization, like S
and Portugal, is there severe restriction of religious freed
The broad trend in advanced modern societies is toward
denominational pluralism and the separation of church
and state.

In Parsons' perspective as far as America is concerned,
religious pluralism rapidly spread from differences among
the original colonies to pluralism within each state,
in contrast to the old European pattern of *cuius regio,
cujus religio*, established in 1648, after the thirty
years religious war. This pluralism formed the basis
for bourgeois toleration, and eventually for full inclusion
of non-protestant elements, especially a very large Roman
Catholic minority. For Parsons this inclusion has been
symbolized in the 1960's by the election of a Roman
Catholic, John F. Kennedy, to the Presidency. Thus
according to Parsons American society went beyond England
and Holland in differentiating organized religion from
societal community, a process that had many important
consequences. In particular, publicly sponsored and
supported education as it developed in the 19th century
was secular education. Parsons' has no difficulties to
state that there was never, as in France, a major
political struggle over that educational problem in the
U.S.A. In Parsons' view, the American societal community
that emerged from these and other developments was
primarily associational. This characteristic was rooted
in certain components of the American value system.
American universalism, which had its purest early modern
expression in the ethics of ascetic Protestantism, has
exerted strong and continuing value pressure toward
inclusion, now reaching to the whole of the Judeo-
Christian religious community and beginning to extend
beyond it to Muslims, Hindus, Buddhists, etc. Parsons
admits that, of course, the inclusion component alone
could lead to a static universalistic tolerance.
According to Parsons this inclusion is however, complemented
by an activist commitment to building a good society in
accordance with divine will, that underlies the drive

toward mastery of the various social environments through
expansion in territory, economic productivity, knowledge
and so on. The combination of these two components has
much to do with the associational emphasis in advanced
modern social structure, economic and political democracy
being conscious aspects.

Parsons admits that the pluralization of the American
religious complex, culminating in the inclusion of large
non-protestant groups, has in a sense been a process of
secularization, especially in contrast to the functioning
of the older established churches. Also Parsons knows,
that since the values of society are rooted in religion,
one possible consequence of the pluralization of religion
is the destruction of the moral- or value-consensus in
society. But Parsons consoles his American readers,
that this destruction has by and large not occurred in
the United States. Value universalization has been much
more important. The underlying universal moral consensus
has persisted, but is now defined at a higher level of
universality than in the modern European societies, that
have institutionalized internal religious uniformity.
These highly universal moral values, are, through
specification, made applicable to the numerous structural
contexts necessary in highly complex advanced modern
societies. Thus Parsons insists that American society
and in somewhat different ways other advanced modern
societies, maintain strong universal moral commitments
that have survived through, and have even been strengthened
by religious pluralism and secularization.

In Parsons view the newest phase of advanced modern society
returns to primary concern with cultural elements. But
the focus is no longer religion. The emphasis is rather
on secular intellectual disciplines and the arts. Whereas
philosophy was in the ascendence in early modern society,
e.g., German idealism, positive science overtook it in
advanced modern society of the 20th century particularly
in America. This happened above all through extending
the scope of positive science to the social and behavioural
fields and even to the humanities. Parsons own functional
sociology is paradigmatic for this development.

In Parsons perspective the educational revolution has
introduced mechanisms by which the new cultural standards,
especially those embodied in the intellectual disciplines,
are institutionalized in ways that partly replace
traditional religion. Unlike a century ago when the
religious implications of Darwinisms stimulated bitter
controversies, Parsons notices relatively little recent
theological agitation about science in advanced modern

society. There has been much concern with culture however, especially the arts and some aspects of philosophy, one being an aristocratic disdain of mass culture by such figures as T.S. Eliot, Dwight MacDonald and Ortega Y Gasset. Here Parsons fails, as usual to take into consideration besides this conservative critique the much sharper ideology critique of the Frankfurt School against mass culture in advanced capitalistic and socialistic society.3

According to Parsons even concern within the religious context has a different flavour in advanced modern society from that of the 19th century conflict with science. One aspect of this concern is ecumenism, so widely heralded by liberals, especially in the Roman Catholic shift since the papacy of John XXIII and Vatican II. Another is the new scepticism about all traditional and organized religion, as in the atheistic branch of existentialism, e.g., that of Jean P. Sartre, and the specifically American God-is-dead-movement within Protestantism. Parsons ignores the Protestant and Catholic critical political theology of Jurgen Moltmann, Metz, Peukert, etc., as completely as the critical theory of society.4 What Parsons is really looking for in his theory of evolution is a *secular religion*, which would be able to provide for the legitimation of organized capitalistic society *together* with structural-functional social science.

To Parsons intellectual alienation in advanced modern society seems to be primarily a manifestation of strains involved in the universalization of moral values. The moral value specifity of certain older religious symbolic systems has hindered the establishment of a universal moral consensus that, at the level of total societal values of particular advanced modern societies, could have more integrative than divisive effects. Parsons calls resistance to the universalization of moral values fundamentalism. Fundamentalism has been conspicuous in religious contexts often closely linked with extreme societal conservatism, as among the dutch Calvinists in South Africa. In Parsons view, indeed, the fascist movements in advanced modern societies have on the whole been fundamentalist in this sense. Parsons also speaks of the fundamentalism on the extreme Left, from certain phases of the Communist Party to the current New Left. Parsons forgets to mention that for the critical theory, the very foundation of much of the New Left in Europe and America, value universalization is at least as important as for the functional analysis.5

For Parsons the widespread pessimism over the survival of modern societies is closely linked to doubts, especially among intellectuals, about the actual viability of advanced modern societies and their moral right to survive without the most radical, i.e., qualitative changes. Indeed, so Parsons complains, it is often alleged that modern society is totally corrupt, can be cleansed only by total revolution, and is ripe for it.

Parsons knows, of course, that such pessimism is by no means new. He cites the famous example of Christian pessimism about the society of the Roman Empire. While for Hegel the extremely secularized late Roman and the modern society are equally entirely corrupt, by Parsonian standards neither of them is totally corrupt.6 Parsons also recognizes a similar pessimism during the Reformation. For Parsons a most interesting and suggestive comparison is with Colonial New England. Here under the stress of misfortune, whatever its source, a jeremiade often took place, a kind of orgy of guilty self-accusation by colonists, who insisted that they failed to live up to their obligations in their errand into the wilderness. It suggests to Parsons, that a highly activist this-worldly value pattern makes people especially sensitive to the gaps between expectation and performance. At the extreme they attribute all such gaps to the short-comings of the current generation.

In his apologetics for bourgeois modernity and his general ahistoricity, Parsons does not appreciate the fact that there are no contingencies present in the late Roman Empire, in the Reformation or in Colonial New England which are even comparable with those which are the reasons for e.g., the Frankfurt School's pessimism: two bourgeois World Wars, the great depression, fascism, Auschwitz, Hiroshima, the cancer epidemic, etc. In his general optimism Parsons expects that anything like a culminating phase of modern development is a good way off -- very likely a century or more. any talk of post-modern society is thus decidedly premature. Taking into account the undeniable possibility of overwhelming destruction -- alternative Future II -- Parsons' expectation is nevertheless that the main trend of the next century or more will be toward completion of the secular modern cybernetic type of society -- alternative Future I. While Parsons certainly hopes that alternative Future II -- ABC wars -- will not occur in the system of modern societies in the next two hundred years, and while he helps prepare at least latently through his functional analysis as an integral part of the pattern maintenance system of advanced capitalistic society alternative Future II -- the totally cybernetically controlled signal society which makes all practical reason superfluous by substitution for it instrumental understanding, he seems to be in no way interested, like Kant, Hegel, Marx, Horkheimer, Benjamin, Habermas, Metz, et., in the desirability,

possibility or probability of alternative Future III --
a post-modern free and solidary society in which the
religious and the secular, the individual and the collective
will no longer be merely environmental and external to each
other but will dialectically reproduce each other and as
such will be truely reconciled.7 What Parsons' theory of
action and evolution, reinforcing the already powerful trend
toward a totally cyberneticized society, including a secular
religion, renders most problematic is the inter-subjectivity
and subjectivity of man and women living in the modern syster
of advanced capitalistic and socialist states.

CHAPTER XII

INTERSUBJECTIVITY

Luhmann affirms that Parsons has undertaken the most
important attempt in his theory of evolution of religion
to relate the problem of secularization to the conditions
of enhancement as well as of the structural risks of
modern society.1 But Luhmann criticizes Parsons rightly
for doing this in such a way, that in perspective of
functional theory-design he overemphasizes the enhancement
and de-emphasizes the risks produced by secularization in
modern society. Therefore Parsons functional analysis
of the evolution of religion ends up with the conception
of secular religion. Our main concern is: Can this
secular religion be the foundation for the highly
differentiated intersubjectivity and subjectivity which
once developed out of primitive, Catholic and Protestant
Christianity? What risks does secularization involve
concerning intersubjectivity and subjectivity?

According to Luhmann, Parsons differentiates in his
analytical theory of evolution four aspects of enhancement
of the societal development: Adaptive upgrading in
relation to resources, differentiation in relation to
system goals, inclusion in relation to the comprising
of persons and universalization in relation to values.
With the help of these fundamental categories Parsons
is able to characterize secularization as mobilization
of resources, e.g., attention, time of presence, readiness
to give support, for functionally stronger specified goals
of a differentiated system of religion. At the same
time this system of religion must represent to society
higher, more universalized values, since they must
overreach differentiation. Thereby this system of
religion is dependent on inclusion of always larger
circles of persons. Luhmann is particularly interested
in Parsons new concept of inclusion. According to
Parsons the differentiation demands besides a corresponding
mobilization of resources and universalization of values
the full inclusion of all persons as possible participants
in all functional realms of the social system and the
action system. In the religious dimension this explodes
the differentiation between clerics and laymen, and
demands a purely organizational or cybernetic, in
religious terms irrelevant reconstruction of this

difference. This happened during the reformation.
Furthermore, inclusion means that the entrance to religion
must not be limited through other roles and likewise the
entrance to religion must not limit the entrance to other
roles. Under this perspective Luhmann finds celebacy
connected to the clerical office problematic. To the
postulate of inclusion correspond indeed central demands
of the bourgeois revolution. Furthermore, to this
postulate corresponds the reconstruction of the notion
of bourgeois society from a society of independent heads
of households into a society, in which man participates
as man.

According to Luhmann, carrying further the Parsonian
position, the broadening of the inclusion to everybody
came into existence in two stages during the evolution
of the system of modern societies, the Reformation and
the bourgeois revolution. In the first stage the
reformers tried to upgrade the role of the layman as
that role which everybody can occupy in the system of
religion without particular status and without further
consequences and to adjust the role of the clergyman
accordingly. Laymen and clergymen have according to the
concept of the reformers equally immediate access to the
ultimate reality or to God and the same probability of
salvation. This program of the Reformation could in the
face of an already organized church not be realized
without schism. In Luhmann's view this was in hindsight
a lucky chance, in any case an important circumstance in
evolutionary terms. This is so, since out of it resulted
the possibility of a second developmental stage -- politica
revolution.

In Luhmann's view, independently from the meaningful
upgrading of the role of the layman by the reformers
everybody through the schism and the complete formulation
of the confessions gained the possibility to chose his
faith. Now in this point, all members of society had
equal access to religion. There was no need for a
religious, dogmatically unified solution of the problem
of inclusion. This resulted from the segmentation of
the religious system into a plurality of denominations
automatically and needed merely the recognition by law.
Only thereby it could be formulated, that inclusion
signifies at the same time differentiation: that namely
the membership in one or the other denomination must not
have any effects concerning the access to public offices,
on the participation in political elections, on the
choice of the marriage partner in terms of civil marriage,
on the acquisition of scientific reputation, etc. In
Luhmann's view these demands have been formulated by the

value postulates of freedom and equality proposed by the
bourgeois revolutionaries. Luhmann leaves out the wisest
bourgeois revolutionaries' postulate of brotherhood, which
alone can mediate between the otherwise exclusive demands
of freedom and equality.2

According to Luhmann the value postulates of freedom and
equality have at the same time misled socialistic critics
of bourgeois society, whom he opposes as much as Parsons
does. The critical theorists, e.g., Horkheimer, Adorno, Marcuse
Benjamin or Habermas, concentrating on the proof that not
all members of civil society are free and equal, have
overlooked the function of the inclusion-postulates of
freedom and equality and have dismissed them as ideology,
i.e., false consciousness or untruth. In the wake of
realized postulates of inclusion, which had served the
realization of functional differentiation, then appear
political-bureaucratic programs of the welfare state,
which are directed toward contemporaneous, all-sided
growth.

In Luhmann's view from this starting point religion
stayed, inspite of the fact that it is structurally
in the same problematic situation, outside of critique
and realization. The critique of religion remained
fundamentally that of the 18th centure. Luhmann wants to correc
this culture-lag by going not only beyond Adorno, Marcuse,
Horkheimer, Benjamin and Habermas, but even his own great
model Parsons: by throwing sharper light on the connections
between functional societal differentiation, inclusion
and privatization of decision making. In Luhmann's
perspective the privatization of the decision making
process has resulted in the consequence of functional
differentiation as correlate to the demands of inclusion.
Through privatization of decision making a statistical
neutralization of those role connections is aspired to,
which can result in the complementary roles: they should
have validity only for the individual person and his
micro-motives.

Luhmann criticizes Parsons for not seeing the relationship
of inclusion to functional differentiation. Parsons has
simply not argued historically enough! But according to
Luhmann Parsons has certainly grasped the connection
between inclusion and the privatization of decision making.
This connection carries Parsons further analysis of
evolution, including the evolution of religion.

Habermas agrees with Luhmann against Parsons, that complex
modern societies can no longer constitute an identity
through the consciousness of the individual members of

the social system.3 The reconciliation of universal,
religious identity and singular, personal identity in the
particular, collective identity, so characteristic for
primitive, archaic and still to some extent historic-
intermediate societies is no longer possible in advanced
modernity. According to Luhmann, as Habermas understands
him, the intersubjectivity of knowledge, experience and
action in a social life world, generated through universal
religious symbolical systems of interpretation, orientation
and value has too small a capacity or volume in order to
harmonize the steering needs of the highly differentiated
partial systems of advanced-modern societies, not to
speak of post-modern societies. The cover of the normative
structured life world, which in the high cultures had been
formed and held together through religion, right and
political institutions, in the advanced modern age is
exploded by growing systematic problems. Luhmann supposes,
that the specific combination of right and politics was
precisely in its particular achievement ability a wrong
specialization of the human evolution. This combination
can not be transferred to the system of the world society,
which Luhmann envisions as much as Parsons or Habermas. The
world society has constituted itself mainly in dimensions of
interaction, which like the economy, technology and
positive sciences pose cognitive problems. The risks
arising here cannot be overcome by new normative
regulations, but only by learning processes, which
conquer contingencies. These learning processes are of
the kind which fall outside of the dimension in which one
makes oneself understood in relation to personal, collective
and religious identity.

According to Luhmann's thesis -- as Habermas interprets
it -- the identity of the modern world society can only
come into existence on the level of system integration,
i.e., in such a way, that a highly differentiated partial
system constitutes suitable environments for each other.
The identity of the world society can no longer be
established on the level of social integration. Therefore
the system reality of society emigrates, so to speak, out
of the inter-subjectivity of the lifeworld inhabited by soci
individuals. This is equally true for Parsons as for Luhman

Habermas points out, that for Luhmann as for Parsons, the
individuals belong merely to the environment of their own
social systems. The society gains an objectivity in
opposition to the individuals, which can no longer be
brought back into an inter-subjective life connection,
since it is no longer related to subjectivity at all.
The objectivity of society means not merely any longer
its independence from the individuals. It is no longer

merely a symptom of a reified identity. Luhmann is of
the opinion, that the social evolution, including the
evolution of Christianity has led beyond a situation, in
which it was still meaningful, to relate social relations
to concrete human beings out of flesh and blood. This is
the secret and the truth of the Parsonian mechanisms
supposed to produce a new unity of personal, social and
religious itentity. It is the end of all hope for any
real reconciliation of these three forms of identity in
particular modern action systems or in the action system of
the modern world. As Parsons before, Luhmann not only
recognizes, but also reinforces theoretically and practically th
tendency in advanced capitalistic society toward alternative
Future I -- the totally administered, scientificized,
technocratic and bureaucratic society.

In his theory of evolution, including the evolution of
religion, Habermas shows how in the process of the
demythologization of the religious images of the world
-- including the Christian world image -- the dimension
of nature is desocialized and thereby is set free as
subject matter for objectivating analytical and instrumental
understanding. Habermas sees Parsons and Luhmann extending
this process of demythologization and scientification in
the form of the dehumanization of society. As a consequence
the society is alienated from the intelligible world of
concrete human beings in a second process of objectification.
This happens not in order for society to become the subject
matter for objectivating understanding, but in order to
relegate the individual human subjects on their part into
the position of controllable system environments. But
as soon as the individuals and their society, so Habermas
argues against Parsons and Luhmann, stand in the relationship
of mutual system-environment-relations to each other, the
inter-connection of ego-identity and group-identity, in
which indeed complementary inter-subjectivity structures
express themselves, has lost, so to speak, its foundation.
The same is true for the universal religious identity.
No unity of personal, social and religious identity can
any longer be constituted.

In Habermas's view, Luhmann believes that this inter-
connection between ego - and group identity has not only
become impossible, but also unnecessary. This is so
since the proper achievement of identity -- the being-
reflected-into-oneself of a subject, which in his or her
turn toward the world is at the same time with himself
or herself -- can very well be taken over by social
systems. Reflection is no longer the essential property
of persons, but rather the quality of social systems.
The unity of a system can be made accessible through

thematization, without it having any need for a human subject. While the system directs itself through adaptation in conformity with the changing situations of an over-complex environment, in its reflection a partial system relates itself to the embracing system, to which it belongs. With these fundamental concepts the question concerning the rational identity of a highly complex society can be reformulated in the context of Parsons or Luhmann's system theory. The incompletely formed identity of the world society is introduced as deficit of reflection. It can thereby be balanced, so that the functionally differentiated subsystems learn to identify themselves at the same time as adequate

According to Habermas, this learning process demands a radical orientation toward the future. The renunciation of a system unity produced through a normative integration means that the cultural, particularly religious traditions, can be manipulated in accordance with steering needs. History can be neutralized. The partial systems can decide arbitrarily from case to case, in which connections it is regarding to have a past, and in which it is not. Beyond that the partial systems project their developmental possibilities into a contingent future. This is so, since in the horizon of planning the present appears merely as the past of today pre-selected future contingent presents. Historical consciousness has been arrested in favour of a self-objectification, in which the anticipated futures determine a memory-less present.

In Habermas's perspective, the main objection of Luhmann or Parsons against this chain of assertions is simple. In the language of Parsons' or Luhmann's system theory this objection says: A sufficient system integration of society is not a functional equivalent for a necessary measure of social integration. In Habermas's view this means: The preservation of a societal system is not possible if the conditions of the self-preservation of the members of the system are not fulfilled. The rising world society may escalate its steering capacity as much as possible. But if this is only possible for the price of the human substance of the individuals, then every further step of evolution as learning process must mean the self-destruction of the socialized individuals and their life world.

Habermas reminds us, that Horkheimer and Adorno have proven in their common book *Dialectics of Enlightenment* for the history of the human species a similar perversion

of the progress in the rationality of the self-preservation.4
The rational penetration and the growing technical
disposition over a demythologized external nature must
be paid at the end, so Horkheimer and Adorno diagnose and
prognosticate, with the denial and repression of man's
own nature: the subjects themselves are crippled. The
subjects, for whom after all the subjugation, reification,
disenchantment of nature had been begun in the first
place, are finally so oppressed and alienated from their
own nature, that progress and regression can no longer
be differentiated from each other. The objectivism in
relation to a desocialized nature, which Horkheimer and
Adorno trace in *The Dialectics of Enlightenment*, is
overtaken by the self-objectification of a dehumanized
society, which as social system makes itself not only
independent in relation to the individuals, but which
also establishes itself outside the life world which can
be inhabited by concrete individuals. According to
Habermas, Horkheimer's critique of instrumental
understanding does, of course, not overcome through the
uncovering of an objectivistic appearance the autonomy
of a nature which cannot be dissolved into subjectivity.
Habermas is fully aware of the fact that likewise also
his own critique of Parsons' and Luhmann's functionalistic
understanding must not deny the relative autonomy of
system structures, which remain external to the structures
of inter subjectivity and subjectivity.

In Habermas's view, Marx undertook this attempt in the
first volume of the *Capital*.5 Marx has constructed in
his genial research into the double character of the
commodity the exchange relationship and thereby the
steering mechanism of the market, as a relationship of
reflection. Marx did this in order to be able not only
to explain functionalistically the whole capitalistic
economic process under the perspective of the steering
problem, but at the same time to make it intelligible
as class antagonism, i.e., as a dichotomous moral totality.
In a research-strategic perspective Marx's value theory
has the meaning to allow the representation of problems
of the system integration on the level of social integration.
Habermas has serious doubts, if today an analogous attempt
to that of Marx to reach through system-theoretical
connections into inter subjectivity- and subjectivity-
structures, could really still be successful.

On the other hand, Habermas has no doubt whatsoever,
that the structures of the life world in which inter-
subjectivity and subjectivity are located, must be taken
into consideration as constitutive elements of the system
of society and that they must enter the system analysis

of steering problems as limitations. A system theory, which has run wild, like that of Luhmann more so than that of Parsons, and which therefore neglects to consider the structures of the lifeworld, of intersubjectivity and subjectivity, will become the victim of the dialectics of the escalation of system complexity. This dialectics will not only enfold the life of the society in evolutionary terms, but will also kill it as the same time. In Habermas' view a society which is separated by system-environment-relations from its members, their inter-subjectivity and subjectivity and their concrete life world, is dead in terms of the notion of a social life, which individuates the individuals and subjectivizes the subjects through socialization and social universalization.

Habermas agrees with Parsons and Luhmann when they admit that the modern level of reflection and secularization does indeed exclude the possibility to seal off world problems under the perspective of the reality perfection or God problems under the theodicy perspective of compensation against possibilities of negation.6 Habermas also agrees with Parsons and Luhmann, when they have serious doubts that for the time being the function of religion can be adequately defined as design and administration of a societal-structurally adequate and therefore sacralized world view. But while these doubts make it plausible to Habermas to accept communicative competence or linguistically mediated, universal, pragmatic, moral discourse as a function equivalent of religion, Parsons and Luhmann shy away from such a possibility. They do this in spite of the fact that they admit that science, including their own, has already to a large extent replaced religion in secularized advanced-modern societies.

At the same time it seems to be very improbably that the mechanisms which Parsons and Luhmann recommend in order to reconcile religious, social and personal identity -- inclusio differentiation, value universalization, privatization of decision-making -- will be more effective in advanced capitalistic or socialistic society than those which collapsed already in early capitalistic society -- preservati of conventional consciousness, differentiation between believers and pagans, dualism between world immanence and transcendence. How little effective the mechanisms proposed by Parsons and Luhmann are, shows particularly the example of such outstanding scholars as Paul Tillich or Teilhard de Chardin, who have spent their lives in the attempt to reconcile the religious and the secular as well as the individual and the collective in a way that intersubjectivity and subjectivity would not only be preserved but even enhanced. Both men are up to the present under attack by secular scientists for being too religious and too individualistic, and by religious proponents for being too secular and collectivistic. The cold war against religion recently initiated anew by scientists and humanists in advanced capitalistic society demonstrates that Parsons' and Luhmann's architecture of detente between the religious and the secular, the personal and the collective is much less than their true reconciliation. Whoever today lives as a member of a religious or political minority group in the midst of organized capitalistic or socialistic society can daily experience that the mechanisms recommended by Parsons and Luhmann do not really reconcile religion and secular society and culture, or the individual and society. Like many others the brothers Berrigan, being faithful to their universal, religious and singular, personal identity came in conflict with their particular national identity during the Vietnam War and later. The mutual accusations of advanced capitalistic and socialistic societies concerning the continual violation of human and civil rights of their own citizens speaks for itself.

Habermas's critical theory of society and religion does not aim as Parsons' and Luhmann's functional theory of society and religion at alternative Future I -- the administered society for which intersubjectivity and subjectivity remain entirely external and merely objects of social control, but at alternative Future III -- the rational reconciled society, in which individual and community are mediated through each other and reproduce each other.7 But what happens, when intersubjectivity and subjectivity continue to move into boundary situations and to be threatened by contingencies intrinsic to alternative Future I and II: war, hunger, oppression, environmental destruction, alienation, injustice, illness, death? This aporetic question points not only beyond Parsons' and Luhmann's functional system theory, but also beyond Horkheimer's, Benjamin's and Habermas's dialectical theory of society to Kung's negative theology and to Metz's and Peukert's political theology of intersubjectivity and subjectivity.8

CHAPTER XIII

NEGATIVE THEOLOGY

In January 1978, Küng entered an official colloquium with
three German bishops and a few theologians.1   During the
colloquium the chairman of the German Bishops Conference,
Archbishop Cardinal Höffner, accused Küng again and again
of curtailing in his book *Being Christian* the church's
teaching on Jesus the Christ.2   Küng, so the Cardinal
argued, delivers only statements about the functions of
the son of God, but not about his "essence".   Küng recommended
to the Cardinal and the other members of the colloquium to
await patiently his next book *Does God Exist?* before they
come to a final conclusion and possibly rejection of his
Christology.3   The communication was dominated by the
Cardinal.   It remained rather fruitless.

In the meantime, Küng's new book *Does God Exist?* has indeed
appeared.   But the book does not, as a central matter,
treat the Christ problem, but rather the God-question, as
its title indicates.   Only a very small section, about 14
pages, in the last part of the book, dealing with the
Christian concept of the trinity, is devoted to the
Christological complex, at which the urging questions of
Cardinal Höffner aimed during the colloquium.4   Concerning
this small Christological part in Küng's huge book, embracing
875 pages, the critical German journal, *Der Spiegel* and some
critical theologians suggested, that Küng has capitulated
before the church's traditional authority.   Has Küng
indeed capitulated?   Is his theology "positive" in an
eclesiastical sense?

It is true that Küng expresses himself very carefully in
the Christological section of *Does God Exist?* which is
otherwise mainly a summary of the large Christological
part of *Being Christian*.   Küng is, of course, completely
in his right to do so.   But there are several sentences,
which are particularly weak and can easily be construed
by critical theorists of society or critical political
theologians as capitulation before irrational tendencies
in Catholic tradition and authority.   One of these
sentences says: "In general, whether we describe this
relationship between God and Jesus theologically more
in functional or more in ontological terms, whether we
start more from abstract "essential" statements or from

concrete salvivic expressions, that may very well be a
secondary matter and it must certainly not be a
contradiction."5 At this point we are not concerned
merely with scholastic subtleties without any further
significance, but rather with the total case and cause
of Küng himself and in a certain sense even with the
whole further evolution of Christian kerygma. We must
admit that in the above quotation Küng's language is at
least very vague and indefinite, if not even ambiguous.

But in spite of this weakness in Küng's new book, he has
not become captive of irrational dogmatic and authoritarian
elements in the Catholic tradition. This becomes clear
by the very fact that Küng does in general not fall
behind the dialectical philosophy and theology of Hegel,
which he reached in his Hegel book *The Incarnation of
God.6* The very core of *Does God Exist?* is a summary of
The Incarnation of God.7 According to Horkheimer,
Hegel's whole philosophy aims at a negative theology.8
It lies in the dialectical Hegelian logic of *Does God
Exist?* that Küng considers "essential" statements about
God and thus also about the relationship of Jesus to
God to be illegitimate at the present point in history
as process of learning, reflection and emancipation.
Thus Küng develops further consequentially Hegel's
negative, i.e. functional theology.9 What precisely is
negative theology?

G. Sczesny, the founder of the Humanistic Union in Europe,
confessed once to be as an atheist nevertheless, also
a kind of "believer".*10* He experiences himself as being
carried by an original trust in "something" of which we
cannot dispose, which embraces us, which demands from
us absolutely, which poses life tasks for us unconditionally
Sczesny was not able to call this something "God" especially
he could not understand this something as "person".   There
are Christian intellectuals today, who can sympathize
with Sczeny's original trust in an indisposable,
incomprehensible, all embracing ultimate reality to a
high degree. Küng is one of them.

When these Christian humanists call this ultimate as
well as primordial reality, which transcends everything
in nature and history 'God', they do so in the understanding
of negative theology. According to the Christian negative
theologians, the mystery which at the same time carries
us and demands from us, and in which we trust, cannot be
grasped by any human representation or conceptualization.
In contradiction to the "godlessness" of humanists a la
Sczeny, which remains rather empty, the faith of the
negative theologian, as much as it must miss its object,

aims nevertheless at least in the direction of the absolute and ultimate truth. The same is true for the problematic concept of God's "personality". The application of this concept is for the negative theologian merely the legitimate attempt to ascribe to the indisposable ultimate reality and ground of being, from which we come and toward which we move, what we consider the very peak of all evolution so far, from original matter over the animal life and the animal-human transition period to pre-history and the history of contemporary man: namely, freedom, dignity, self-knowledge, self-determination, reflection, autonomy, shortly, personality. This is the legitimate anthropomorphism of negative theology, which Hegel stressed like nobody else in Modernity. According to the negative theologian, this rational interpretation of his original trust in an ultimate reality would remain without power, if there was not at least in a few, very good hours the experience of something like a dialogue: a speaking and a listening God. This dialogue is not easy and therefore also not frequent. It is not simply a religious talk with one's self. In the view of the negative theologian real personal prayers are more like a stroke of lightening or like the dew on the grass in the morning, than the usual human exchange of thoughts and communication called a dialogue or discourse. But negative theologians do assert, that people can and do have such experiences.

It is plausible to the negative theologian, that the God whom he trusts, revealed and opened himself up to the Neanderthaler or the Cromagnon man. It is understandable for the negative theologian, that in a fullness of time, during the archaic stage of evolution, in the first oriental high cultures, God approached a group of persons in a special manner, who otherwise were not at all standing at the evolutionary front of their time: the people of Israel. Finally, it seems to be plausible to the negative theologian, that God in a second fullness of time, when the people of Israel as well as their intermediate-historical surroundings, had become relatively receptive for such an event, filled a singular man -- Jesus of Nazareth -- completely with his spirit. The encounter with this man decides over everything: salvation or damnation!

The negative theologian, if need be, can accept the formula of Chalcedon: Jesus Christ is true man and true God. If Jesus' divinity should not swallow up pantheistically his finite humanity and if there should not appear a human-divine monstrosity, then the negative theologian can not represent the divinity of Jesus, including his

"pre-existence" in God's "eternity" in any other way than
in the perfection of his humanity. Jesus was divine in
the sense of being the truely human man per se, i.e., as
transcending himself absolutely. To be radically Christian
means precisely to be radically human. Jesus does not only
appeal to our humanity and something which transcends it,
the Kingdom of God, but he is an event in the history of
mankind. This history should be more human, not only
through the mutations Jesus set in motion in social structu
concerning women, children, slaves, the sick and the dying,
the oppressed, the poor, but also through what happens
by people's faith.

In the terrible hours of doubt in God and his work in
nature and history, Jesus is, for the negative theologian
as the most human man merely "historical" and "factual".
In hours of faith Jesus is for the negative theologian
the most human man in an extraordinary and for all future
binding meaning. In both cases the negative theologian
holds firmly onto Jesus. In the first case the negative
theologian holds on to the Jesus, who has been more human
than Hammurabi, Aneknathon, Moses, Buddha, Socrates or
Mohammed. In the second case, the negative theologian
is committed to Jesus as the God-man. This then, and
the decision of Chalcedon, appears to the negative
theologian as the ingenious emergency-formula, which
tries to resolve the awesome Christological contradiction
in the simplest way possible, namely, by calling it by
its name and therby expressing it and thus bringing it
closer to its possible resolution.

The negative theology, as described here is precisely
Küng's position in *Does God Exist?* and has been his
position in *The Incarnation of God* and in *Being Christian*.1
Küng has not compromised his negative theological position
by exchanging it for a positive or even positivistic
traditional theology. The progressive thinker has not
become a traditionalist. Küng has not fallen into sterile
resignation in the new conservative and even reactionary
atmosphere of advanced capitalistic society and in a
church depending on the latter. According to Küng, what
we can say of God, we can only express on the precondition
that he has revealed himself to humans. God reveals
himself always only in the measure of the acceptance of
this revelation, as human speech act, about that aspect
of himself which he has shown to human beings as humans,
and that in their relative measure. In this process
truly only functional statements can come into existence,
the word "functional" taken in all those meanings it can
possibly have: relationship, consequence, special task,
purpose, plan, service, etc. Ontological expressions are

really excluded.

According to Küng and other Catholic and Protestant theologians, we owe the 1500 year old positive and even positivistic boundary transgressions in the church's traditional teaching on God and Jesus, to the hellenistic and thereby to the Greek thinking in general. When Christians in the fifth century made the effort to understand the many titles, which in the *Acts*, the *Letters of the Apostles*, and in the *Gospels* were attributed to the pre-Easter Jesus and the post-Easter Christ, then for these hellenistically educated people remained nothing else to do than the rather adventurous attempt to make statements about the "essence" of God and Christ and this not even in the dynamic Heraclitean, but in the static Parmenidean and Platonic tradition. The "tools" of thought. the categories, of these hellenistically trained Christians were fundamentally different from the traditions of the Jews, who thought *historically* from the perspective of their experiences of the actions of God *in history* and society.

In the perspective of negative theology, Küng has aimed somewhat too short in his controversy with the German bishops, when he gave to them merely pastoral reasons for the demand, that the Christian message must be dehellenized and the Christian truth must be expressed in another form, in order to make it intelligible to modern man, be he a bourgeoise or a socialist. This is correct, but it is not enough in the present stage of evolution, learning, reflection, and decision. From the parts of *Does God Exist?* in which Küng analyzes critically the present philosophy of science, its logic and the closely related theory of language, his real position -- negative theology -- can be easily concluded.[12] On the level of present knowledge the sentences of Chalcedon, which rest on the logic, language and sentence-understanding of Antiquity, can be interpreted in terms of the Christian truth-message intended in them, but they can no longer in Modernity be subscribed to as sentences, which claim to be true as such.

In the Christological chapter of *Does God Exist?* Küng does not want to call Jesus "God" any longer. He is more careful with the title "son of God". Without analyzing the mythological or analogue-biological meaning of the concepts "procreation" or "sonship", Küng describes the relationship of Jesus to Jahve, whom the former calls his father, in several determinations in such a way, that he is able to confess to the title "son of God" as a statement about a relationship, i.e.

129

functionally.

For the negative theologian the question is whether the church authorities in Germany, or in Rome will be satisfied with Küng's functional interpretation of the understanding of Christ, or if they will at least grant validity to it as King's private theological opinion. Will they respect Küng's religious freedom? We may assume from past controversies between Küng and the authorities of the church, that Cardinal Höffner will, in the last analysis, insist on Küng's acceptance of the sacred formulas of Chalcedon. What then? Will a split occur between positive and negative, ontological and functional theology?

The common believers will probably hold on to the fundamental formula-Christ is true man and true God -- with a slight monophysitic assymetry. They will care little how the theologians of Chalcedon, or their successors in modern Germany, America, Yugoslavia, Poland or Rome, or elsewhere interpret this most ingenious and most tortured "and" in intellectual history. They are not interested in the two natures and the one person of Christ, the "hypostatical union", together with all derivations. At least the people are not yet interested.

At present the little man and even some highly educated bishop can still live in advanced capitalistic and even in socialistic society on two different stories: on the first floor, where he learns to think in terms of worldly wisdom, which enables him to adapt and to survive; and on the second floor, in the chapel, so to speak, where he is devoted to divine wisdom and where he expresses his religious needs or his honest Christian faith in categories, which really belong into the second, fourth, fifth, thirteenth or nineteenth century. This is what Ernst Bloch has called the contemporaneity of the non-contemporeneous, which he tried to correct with and against Hegel by a negative philosophy of hope in an atheistic form.13

This is the modern spiritual schizophrenia between the religious and the secular consciousness which Hegel analyzed thoroughly long before it developed to the present extreme and for which he recommended reconciliation in the framework of a negative theology.14 Hegel maintains that, if in the development of modern society, the opposition between religious and secular consciousness has moved to the point of formation, where upon approaching one another, they repulse each other as enemies, the need for a new balance arises. Horkheimer, Benjamin and

Habermas on one hand and Parsons and Luhmann on the other
hand register precisely such a situation as anticipated
by Hegel on the basis of his dialectical method and his
wide and deep knowledge of the history of religions.
More than a century before Küng, Hegel proposes a unified
comprehension of reality, where neither the world is
godless or God is worldless, but the Infinite is in the
finite and the finite in the Infinite. God is conceived
as being in this world as nature and society and history,
and this world is thought of as being in God. Hegel as
later Küng thinks of a God who repeatedly withdraws from
all finalizing determinations of human representation and
understanding.15 This God is not to be understood as
supreme being in terms of bourgeois enlightenment or as
ultimate reality above, outside or beyond this world,
and then, after all, once more beside and opposite this
world as nature and human action systems, as mere
environment of action and evolution, in order to exist
as a mere part of the total reality, as finite reality
beside finite reality, as an addition in competition with
the world, as it was the case in pre-Hegelian traditional
dualistic theology.

Hegel, as Küng later on comprehends God as the Absolute in
the relative, as the Ultimate Reality in the heart of
all things, in man himself, in world history, rather than
above all human action systems and evolution. Already
for Hegel, God is the inexplorable and inexhaustible
ground, origin and meaning of all beings, the This-Wordly-
Other-Wordly, the Transcendence in the immanence. For
Hegel neither the Infinite nor the finite forms an entirely
separate realm for itself. There is difference, but also
identity. This dialectical comprehension, in Hegel's
view, would constitute the true reconciliation of religious
faith with knowledge and intelligence. In this reconciliation
the highest demand of knowledge and the dialectical notion,
as the differentiated unity of the universal, the particular
and the singular, must be fulfilled, since reason cannot
and should not give up its dignity. But neither can any
part of the absolute content of religion, the Absolute
Reality be sacrificed. The Ultimate Reality must never
be drawn down into finitude, be it nature or human action
systems or evolution, or degraded into the mere environment
of action as it happens in the functional theories of
Parsons and more so even of Luhmann. In Hegelian
perspective such degradation is outright idolatry and
blasphemy. In relation to the absolute content of faith,
the finite form of knowledge-analytical, instrumental,
functional understanding as it triumphs in Parsons' and
Luhmann's system theories, must be superceded in dialectical
reason if any reconciliation between faith and reasons is

to come about. To reach the level of Hegel's program of reconciliation, Parsons and Luhmann would have to broaden the methodological limitations of their sociology from the phenomenological level of analytical understanding to that of dialectical reason. The dialecticians Horkheimer, Benjamin and Habermas are closer to Hegel than Parsons or Luhmann.

In the view of the present day negative theologian, who depends on Hegel, but also intends to go beyond him, this dichotomy between the religious and the secular, which Hegel described and analyzed first adequately, can go on for quite some time in organized capitalistic as well as in socialistic society, but certainly not forever. Insofar as the contemporary level of reflection -- whatever this may include in terms of truth and ideology or at least of truth chances -- is the condition of survival for the individual and the group, for all classes and for all societies, the religious world view and the faith traditions can stay alive in the long run only if the believer is not forced by them into a continuous dangerous schizophrenia. The therapy for this spiritual disease may influence the relationship which exists between the two entrances to reality, that of reason and that of faith. But it does not supercede the difference of these starting points: the confidence in the power of reason and the trust in the ultimate reality and ground of being who transcends infinitely human reason and the possibilities of experience, which are given to humans immediately. These are the fundamental insights not only of Küng's recent book *Does God Exist?*. They determine Küng's whole life work. Küng is devoted to realize fully Hegel's program of reconciliation of the religious and the secular consciousness, of faith and reason, of revelation and enlightenment, of salvation and emancipation, divine and worldly wisdom, in the context of a negative theology.16

The weakest point in Küng's negative theology is his treatment of the theodicy problem: the justification of God in the face of the terror of nature and history. It is the real test case of any theology, negative or positive Kung does indeed treat the question concerning evil, guilt, suffering and death particularly of the innocent and just others before the all-mighty and at the same time infinitel good God in the Christological part of *Does God Exist?*, as elsewhere.17 His deepest statement concerning the theodicy problem is his faithful assertion that God justified himself by justifying the innocent victim Jesus through his resurrection before the establishment, which murdered him. Thus, ultimately, God does not allow injustice to have the last word and the murderer to triumph over the innocent victim.

But Küng does not develop this core-theodicy in such a
way that it would really convince critical theorists like Marx,
Horkheimer, Adorno, Benjamin, or Habermas, more than the
theodicy of Leibnitz or Haecker.18   Horkheimer has posed
the theodicy problem in a sharpness as this had never been
done before in Modernity, not even by Voltaire.19   While
Horkheimer recognized that Hegel had faced the negative
in nature and particularly in history with as much
truthfulness and radicality as his most passionate
opponent, Schopenhauer, the father of "metaphysical
pessimism" who accused his philosophy, quite falsely of
a "cursed optimism", it may very well be asked, if Küng
has not fallen back, specifically in his theodicy attempt,
behind Hegel and Schopenhauer and Horkheimer?20

In any case, Küng does not sufficiently appreciate, that
in relation to the experience of evil since Auschwitz,
and all the horror it stands for in the twentieth century,
a turnover has taken place from quantity to a new quality,
a qualitative jump in evilness.   The SS man who in 1943
sleeps with a Jewish woman and then leads her to a gas
chamber and then plays Chopin for the rest of the night
is in relation to evilness qualitatively different from
the British soldier who watched concentration camps in
South Africa around 1900.   Today the question "Does God
exist?" has become for millions of more or less maltreated
and degraded men and women on all continents, and for
those who are able to identify with them in solidarity,
primarily a question concerning the meaning of suffering.
How can Küng's loving God possibly embrace and permeate
a world characterized by wars, hunger, oppression,
environmental destruction, alienation, prisons,
slaughterhouses, mental institutions and cancer wards?
For all men and women who have raised their consciousness
to the modern level of reflection, the answer to this
theodicy question is decisive for their affirmation or
refusal of the truth claim of any of the world religions,
be it Buddhism or Hinduism, Judaism, Islam or Christianity.
Today too many terminal cancer patients ask in their great
pain: "I know God is in this world -- but really --
where is he at times?"

When the outstanding convert to Catholicism, the historian
and theologian Reinhold Schneider was in the last stage
of his life he observed through the microscope the
merciless struggle of the living organisms: Life as
eating and being eaten.21   All depends on the individual
organism, also the human organism, where it is situated
in the universal food chain!   Schneider did not have to

wait until his 55th year and his approaching death in order to know this Darwinian truth. He could have known it earlier. But obviously Schneider was only then disposed in his mind to see a darkness, which he could no longer harmonize with his faith in the all-mighty creator and the all loving heavenly father. Schneider, feeling continually the nearness of death, had to confess that he arrived again at the doubts of his pre-Catholic youth. Schneider no longer knew what to do with the spirit of hope inside or outside of Christianity. But against all laws of apologetical logic Schneider held on to Jesus Christ as the one who suffers and who is abandoned and who is crucified. In him Schneider trusted in the last months of his life. Schneider belonged to those tempted Christians who do not see, but still have faith; who in their anxiety and desperation do not refuse to accept the most extreme offer of the God who has become a riddle for them; and who get ready to die with their eyes directed toward the crucified.

The great theologian Romano Guardini as an old man on his death bed told his friend Walter Dirks, that he will not only let himself be asked in the Last Judgement, but that he will also ask questions himself.22 Guardini hoped in confidence that the angel will then not deny him the true answer to the question, which no dogma and no papal teaching office, no theodicy and no theology, also not his own phenomenological theology was able to answer: Why, God, for salvation sake, these terrible detours, the suffering of the innocent others, the guilt? There is the guilt of the murderers as they triumph over their innocent victims. We can rephrase this more concretely and radically: God may be able to forgive the murderers, but who will be able to forgive God for abandoning the innocent victims of history, who had faith and confidence in Him, who trusted in Him, who hoped for Him, who loved Him, in their most extreme need, distress, pain and desperation in the process of their destruction. Believers -- except mystics like Master Eckehardt -- often   to repress this question with an authoritarian gesture, if they allow it to surface at all. It is remarkable that dialectical and functional sociologists see the importance of religion precisely in that dimension, where it seems to be most problematic, in the sphere of the contingencies -- injustice, sickness and death.

In the perspective of the negative theologian, Küng's theodicy arguments transcend through their intellectual quality, but not by their substance, the classical scholastic and neo-scholastic theodicy attempts. In reality, Küng's theodicy is as little communicable to differentiated modern people as the classical theodicy. In Habermas's terms: It has no volume! One may, of course, argue that no adequate theodicy can possibly be developed in the context of organized capitalistic society, the ability of which to cause suffering and death -- colonialism, imperialism, world wars, slums, profitable production of carcinogenic foods, economic depressions, facism, Dachau, Hiroshima, Vietnam, clean neutron bombs which "merely" kill life but leave dead productive goods in tact, etc. -- is so out of proportion to its capacity truely to heal. Does not the necrophilous character of organized capitalistic society mock any theodicy attempt?

We know only too well the over and over repeated fundamental pattern of the old Catholic theodicy: God is incomprehensible in his creation of evil, or as the apologist says rather weakly, "admission" of evil; God gives and God takes; something good always accompanies something evil; evil is only the absence of the good where God closes a door, there he opens a window; evil is the price for freedom; evil is the resultant consequence of sin; in the end evil will be superceded in perfect salvation. The believer, who can still believe this classical theodicy may tell it to himself and to other human beings who are likewise priviledged. He fundamentally, if also unconsciously the Christian God into a concentration camp director.

For the others, who are not blessed with such naivete, the theodicy remains stuck in their throats in the face of the innocent victims of history, e.g., the victims of the five chronical, terminal, systemic civilization diseases one of which alone, cancer, with its two hundred different forms, kills 35% of the population of advanced capitalistic societies.23 This theodicy can obviously today not be announced anywhere outside sheltered religious groups, located in niches of evolution, without turning into utter scorn and disdain. "You cannot put us into hell" say the men of Brecht's *City of Mahagony*, symbol of capitalistic society, to God, who approaches them at dawn in order to judge them. "You cannot put us into hell,since we have always been in hell! We have always been in hell!"

Küng admits at the end of *Does God Exist?* that the resolution of the theodicy problem depends on ortho-praxis rather than on orthodoxie: that one practices the imitation of Christ at the risk of one's own life. But Küng does not make it entirely clear that only either active reformers or revolutionaries, like Martin Luther

King Jr., Che Guevarra, the priest Torres, Dr. Alende, Mahatma Ghandi, or saints like Mother Theresa and others of the same spirit, have the right and the possibility to announce the God of Abraham, Isaak and Jacob and the Father of Jesus Christ, to the innocent victims.

But if there is any possibility at all to approach the theodicy problem effectively in theory as well as in practice in organized capitalistic or socialistic society, then it must and can only happen in the framework of a negative theology. The greatness of Kung's *Does God Exist?* as well as of his whole life work as apologist of Christianity in an almost impossible situation, lies in his successful attempt to prepare the way toward a negative, functional theology for Catholics and Protestants alike. In the view of the negative theologian therefore Chr at least, should feel solidary with Kung, who as theologian our time works hard and creatively between the conceputally bishops and many arrogant theologians. The latter often behave rather distantly toward their all too robust and energetic colleague, whose books have so suspiciously quickly climbed up the best seller list. Today the Christian truth, insofar as it falls under the competency of theology at all, can be found only in the cooperative work of the theologians. That at present outstanding theologians like Karl Rahner and Kung cannot cooperate in the struggle for truth saddens the negative theologian, who has good reasons to respect both of them highly, if not without critique, and also to take seriously their much more radical colleagues -- the critical political theologians of the subject - Metz and Peukert.24

CHAPTER XIV

UNIVERSAL SOLIDARITY

Peukert following Metz explores in discourse with Habermas
theological proposals which can claim to develop a basis theory
for theology.1 In Peukert's view paradigmatic for such
theological proposals are the works of Rudolf Bultmann,
Rahner and Metz.2 Furthermore, Peukert inquires like
Kung, into the development of the philosophy of science
in recent decades.3 He starts from the radical denial
of the possibility of theology by the early Wittgenstein
and, empirically radicalized, by the neo-positivistic
Vienna School. Peukert presents the consequent development
of positivism as the always further radicalized return
of the theory of science to intersubjectivity, communicative
action as the basis of scientific rationality. Peukert
traces this positivistic development through the general
science-theoretical research as well as through the
foundation problematic of linguistics and sociology.

Finally, Peukert makes the attempt, against the background
of the theological as well as the science-theoretical
considerations to open up the problem dimension, in which
it is possible once more to speak theologically in a
plausible and accountable manner. Following Horkheimer,
Benjamin and Habermas, Peukert proves that the normative
postulates, which in elementary human interaction are
posited as necessary and binding for all participants,
have the character of anticipating fundamental actions
which make freedom possible and open up new reality.
Peukert discovers that Habermas's normative theory of
intersubjectivity and sommunicative practice comes to
its limits, where the concern is the experience of the death
of the innocent other. Influenced by Benjamin, Peukert speaks
of the paradox of anamnetic solidarity: the solidarity
with the just other, who has been destroyed and who is
nevertheless remembered in the intersubjective praxis
of the survivers.4 According to Peukert this paradox
or this dialectics of anamnetic solidarity explodes
once and for all not only Parsons' and Luhmann's
functional system theories, but also Marx's, Horkheimer's,
Benjamin's and Habermas's critical theories of society
and religion. In Peukert's view the main concern in the
fundamental experiences of the Judeo-Christian tradition
is the determination of the reality of God in relation

to this experience of the annihilation of the innocent
other. So Peukert understands fundamental theology as
the theory of universal, therefore also anamnetic solidarity
solidary, communicative action, and as a theory of the
Absolute Reality which is experienced in this action and
becomes termable in it. If a proposal for a fundamental
theology on the way over Horkheimer's, Benjamin's and
Habermas's theory of communicative action is developed,
the question arises necessarily concerning the relationship
to practical theology. Habermas was aware of this.5
Peukert considers the foundation of practical theology
as an explicit theological theory of communicative
action best possible from the basis of Habermas's
practical philosophy, his theory of intersubjectivity,
subjectivity and communicative praxis.

The study of the Judeo-Christian tradition shows Peukert
that its main concerns are the extreme limit situations
of communicative action and thereby the extreme boundary
experiences of subjects and their communicability.6
Peukert poses the question: Can there be such a thing
as a theological theory of this communicative interaction
and of these boundary experiences? Can theology be
understood as science? Can theology as science be
grounded in a kind of basis theory, i.e., in a fundamental
theology. Peukert's answer is affirmative.

For Peukert, as for Hegel before, God is the central
subject matter of any theology.7 Peukert makes the attempt
in his fundamental theology to enfold the question of
God., i.e., the question concerning the determinability,
identificability and finally the linguistic termability
of the reality meant by the question, in such a way, that
he analyzes the extreme boundary situations of communicative
praxis, its inner contradictions and the experience of
reality and the reality assertion implicated in the
carried-through communicative practice.8

In Peukert's as in Habermas's view, both following Hegel,
communicative action is, according to its very structure,
directed toward the mutual equal recognition and   .
unconditional solidarity of the participants.9 The
possibility of the partner's finding their singular,
personal identity depends on this reciprocal solidarity,
their common identity, which in principle embraces
all dimensions of existence in intersubjectivity and
in principle draws into itself all possible subjects
of communicative action. This solidarity is universal.
The universal solidarity realizes itself in
temporal, innovative communicative action, which opens

up and makes room for the action possibilities of the other. So the fundamental law of action posited *a priori* in this action is universal solidarity in historical freedom.*10* Ultimately this solidarity could not be universal if it was not besides being anamnetic in relation to the past victims also anticipatory in relation to the life chances of future generations.

For Peukert, as for Habermas, Benjamin and Horkheimer before, there are boundary experiences which put radically into question this normative structure, this law of action, this universal solidarity in freedom, as well as the possibility of its theoretical comprehension in social philosophy or theology.*11* Peukert characterizes the most extreme of these boundary experiences in the following way: It happens factually, that men and women who have tried to act in solidarity with others, particularly with the oppressed, i.e., to whom others owe their own possibilities to live, speak, love, and to act, have been destroyed without their own fault, in the context of the systematically distorted communication in alienated action systems and periods of history.

For Peukert this experience of the death of the innocent other is analytically significant insofar as it contains other aporetic experiences in itself and even goes beyond them. It contains the experience that one man or woman in intersubjectivity can give to or take from the other lifetime and life possibilities, and that therefore the one man or woman can owe something to the other and can become guilty in relation to the other. It includes the experience of the factual contingency of existence -- pain, sickness. It contains finally the experience of the ultimate contingency of death in such a mode, that the other is irrevocably removed and that in relation to him or to her there is no possibility any longer to make good his or her suffering. The possibility of the mutal presence of the one and the other in intersubjectivity and in communicative action is destroyed.

For Peukert this experience is heuristically significant, insofar as it as an extremely negative experience reveals dimensions of action which remain concealed in the every-day interaction of the one and the other in their usual life world. The experience of the death of the other is systematically significant, insofar as the normative foundation-structure of interaction, namely the reciprocity and solidarity, is destroyed as possibility of action. But with this structure is, according to Peukert, as well as to Habermas, connected the singular identity of the subject. Thus the surviving subject is threatened to be destroyed in his or her innermost centre by the death of the other. Indirectly the death of the other causes the identity crisis or even the identity loss of the surviving subject. That happened to the old Marx when first his wife and then his daughter died.

At this point Peukert asks for the possibilities of action which still remain for the surviving subject after the experience of the death of the other. Peukert thinks of the attempt to cut out completely the memory of the other. Ultimately this would fall together with the attempt no longer to acknowledge reality at all, but simply to repress it completely. One could furthermore draw cynically out of the experience of the annihilation of the solidary actor the consequence that everybody must utilize optimally all possibilities of action only for himself or herself. In this case universal solidarity as fundamental principle also of the finding of one's own singular identity would then be abandoned. Communicativ action would degenerate into purely instrumental, strategic and tactical action in one's own singular or particular interest. There is finally the more naive and more resigned attempt to let oneself as a limited nature-being fall back into a cruel process of mutual annihilation and to go back once more behind the evolutionary threshold of the achievement of the fundamental norm of communication -- universal solidarity. Peukert, of course, rejects all these attempts to deal with the experience of the death of the innocent other. What then remains to be done after the death of the just other, which modern man experiences with a finality unknown to generations living in primitive, archaic, historic-intermediate or even early modern society?

Peukert asks, if there is a behaviour thinkable which holds on to the principle of unconditional universal solidarity and does not repress in any way out of consciousn the fate of the annihilation of the just and loving person, but preserves it rather in consciousness, i.e., re-members it. How can such remembrance be thought of? According to Peukert, when the other has come into view as reciprocally recognized and recognizing subject of speech and action, of work and love, then his or her death cannot simply be held on to as a mere *factum brutum* in the external natural world, in the sense of the complete objectification, as e.g., practiced by the present medical profession. The remembrance of the other as the one who has acted for the remembering subject and toward him, is possible only in such a way that one reaches back to the action possibilities opened up by the dead person; that the dead person is present, remembered and affirmed in the praxis of the communicative action of the surviving others as actors. But Peukert knows only too well that against this presence and affirmation in communicative praxis stands the statement that the innocent other has indeed been destroyed definitively and conclusively and that oneself is simply the usufructuary of his or her destruction. The inner contradiction of this aporetic situation is not solved by directing the solidarity simply toward others and finally toward future generations.

For Peukert neither the natural nor the social sciences bring adequately into focus the temporality of inter-subjectivity. Not even the existential philosophy is able to do this, since in its analysis death is the cause for the radical singularization of the subject. But the biographical time of an existence matures and ripens particularly in communicative interaction. Communicative praxis, which posits the other as an autonomous and innovative actor, who reaches not only back into the past but also foreward into the future, opens up the possibility that the communicative, reciprocal, reflexive temporal action appears in its temporal genesis itself for the partners as their genesis and becomes presence. In communicative practice finite free persons experience themselves in time provoked to greater, conceded and received freedom and become perspicuous for each other in the presence of the moment.

According to Peukert, the becoming-present-for-each-other in the moment has as becoming-present of the reciprocal-reflexive genesis of communicative action the character of the transcendence of time: the moment of free mutual recognition becomes the origin of the maturation of time and explodes the continuum of time. Therefore, it is possible that the moment can become biographically and historically significant in an epochal sense. In this way the moment of the ecstasis into the finality of death can be comprehended not only subjectively, as in the existential philosophical analysis, but also inter-subjectively. This argument is based, as Habermas's whole theory of communicative action, on Hegel's analysis of the potential of the struggle for recognition in his *Jena System Fragments*.12 More than Habermas, Peukert excludes from his analysis the other potentials of language, work, family and nation.

In Peukert's view, the death of the innocent other takes from one's own existence, first of all, the reciprocal reflexivity and produces assymetry. The other has been withdrawn from me once and for all and is destroyed!

But can the relationship toward the other in his or her
death, so Peukert asks, be thought of in such a way that
his or her annihilation is simply stated as a fact? Does
this not contradict the fundamental structure of human
interaction? But how should an action be structured,
which does not eliminate the memory of the innocent
victim of history and tries to carry through the
unconditional, universal solidarity with him or her concrete
Does not the praxis of a communicative actor who continues
to make the unconditional recognition of the other the
condition of the possibility of his own singular identity,
contain the factual refusal to accept the destruction of
the other? Is not in such a praxis the fate of the
annihilation of the other posited as superceded or at
least as an event which can be annulled? How is such
an assertion through praxis at all thinkable, and how
can it all be practiced in the face of the absolute
irreversiblity of the suffering and death of the innocent
other? He or she has reached the point of no return.

On the basis of Habermas's critical theory of religion
and of the analysis of the Judeo-Christian tradition,
Peukert defends the thesis that in solidary, temporal,
communicative action moving toward death, the actors
anticipate a reality, of which they assert through their
own practical process, that it can save the other and
that it actually rescues the other. The realization
of the actor's own existence in communicative action is
then factually, in practice, the assertion of a reality,
which does not let the other become simply a $factum$ of
the past, which is already overtaken by time and history.
This is to be further explained in the framework of
Peukert's fundamental theology.

According to Peukert, the ideology suspicion of Marx,
Freud, Horkheimer, Adorno, Marcuse, Benjamin, Wilhelm,
Reich, Habermas and other modern critics of religion is
directed against the assumption that the reality
assertions of the religious consciousness are illusionary
projections.[13] Their only purpose is to secure and
stabilize the factual realization of one's own existence.
Thus ultimately they aim only at one's own realization
of existence. Peukert asks: To what extent is in the
analyzed praxis a reality asserted, which does not simply
exhaust itself in the praxis of communicative action,
but proves itself as independent acting reality in and
for itself. According to Peukert, this must be shown
out of the very structure of this praxis itself.

In Peukert's view, the death of the just other certainly
has the character of a $factum$. The other's physical

destruction is in the realm of accessible experience
precisely the paradigma of an irreversible process.   The
assertion of a reality, posited in carried-through solidary
action, which does not let the other simply be destroyed,
must continually let itself be measured in its intention
in relation to the facticity of the death of the other.
This assertion of reality aims according to its structure
beyond the surviving subject's own communicative action.
If the possibility of the remembrance of the other would
lie only in the surviving subject's own factual achievement
of consciousness, then at least the insight that also the
remembering subject moves irrevocably toward death would
destroy the experience of the indestructable presence of
the other in communicative interaction.

In Peukert's perspective the analysis of death from
Kierkegaard to Martin Heidegger has asserted that the
experience of the death of the other is secondary in
relation to the existential execution of the anticipation
of one's own death.   In Peukert's view, this assertion
is proven wrong.   For Peukert the anticipation of one's
own death opens up existential-dialectically the possibility
of the impossibility of existence.   So far the
existentialists are correct.   But that, so Peukert argues
rightly, toward which the anticipation anticipates, one's
own death, opens itself up as reality in the solidary
expereince of the death of the other.

Communicative action in remembering solidarity with the
destroyed innocent person, appears then to Peukert as
the assertion of a reality who rescues the just other as
the one, who has acted historically, from the annihilation.
Only in this kind of interaction and from the reality
opened up in it, man receives the possibility for his
own single identity in an existence moving toward death.
Peukert reaches behind the beginning of Marxist ideology
critique and tries to do once more, with the help of the
Marxist critique of religion and against it, what Hegel
tried to do before: to prove that God is not only the
God of the feeling of the private individual -- the
product of his fear, joy, misery, will to power or
possessions -- but that God is an independent reality in
and for himself. 14 Like Hegel in his logic, his philosophy
of history and religion, Peukert makes the attempt in his
fundamental theology to develop a political proof of God,
politically understood in the broad Aristotolian,
Thomistic and Hegelian sense of the word. 15

According to Peukert, this reality, revealed in communicative
action, who is asserted as the saving reality for the just
other, who has been destroyed, and at the same time, as

the reality, who through this rescuing of the other makes
possible one's own temporal existence, which moves toward
death, must be called "God". So the reality of God becomes
identifiable and thereby termable out of a boundary situation
of communicative action, which is ultimately unavoidable,
through communicative practice itself. In this way, Peukert
has pointed to the fundamental situation of the manifestation
of the reality of God and its identificability, and thereby
at the same time to the origin of a possible, plausible
speech of God after Marx, Freud, Horkheimer, Benjamin
and Habermas.16 Peukert aims at a new God-language after
the development of the theory of science and the theory of
action, the functional as well as the critical theory of
subject, society and history.17

Peukert admits that such an analysis of communicative
action as he has made on the basis of Horkheimer's,
Benjamin's and Habermas's critical theory of society and
religion and of the experiences made in communicative
practice is not thinkable without the Old Testament
traditions and their extreme further development in the
New Testament traditions, in the appearance of Jesus of
Nazareth. For Peukert, the talk of concrete freedom in
solidarity is not possible without reaching back to
historically experienced and realized dangerous freedom.18
The paradox negative dialectical boundary situation -- the
annihilation of the innocent other who has attempted to
enter into undistorted communicative practice and to act
in solidarity with the oppressed in the midst of alienated
action systems - leads Peukert at the same time to the
thesis, that at this limit of human experience not theoretical
projects mark the front of what can be experienced and
known. For Peukert the innovative character of these
boundary experiences and modes of behaviour is the real
reason, why their narrative representation is first of all
the original mode of their communication and their presence.
In spite of this, Peukert considers it possible to make the
attempt to reconstruct such experiences and to comprehend
them theoretically. Peukert relates his previous reflections
concerning the anamnetic solidarity and the reconstruction
of the God question to Christiology, especially a Christology
from below.20

According to Peukert, his previous considerations of the
practical, paradoxical, anamnetic solidarity and the God
question throws light on the fact that in the New Testament
texts, on the one hand, the reports about the death of
Jesus, and on the other hand, only much later again, the
witnesses of the disciples and the early Christian
community concerning the resurrection of Jesus can be
historically grasped.21 From this New Testament

scholars have constructed the alternative, that the resurrection of Jesus is either merely an interpretation of his claim or a real experience. Peukert understands his previous considerations on paradoxical anamnetic solidarity and the reality of God also as a contribution to the hermeneutics of the resurrection. In Peukert's view, in the light of his previous considerations this alternative of the New Testament scholars must be judged as mistaken from its roots because it falls outside of an analysis of a communicative interaction moving toward death. But only such an analysis can open up the dimension in which the death of the other and his rescue in death can be constitutive for one's own life possibility. Peukert examines the presently made proposals of a hermeneutic of the resurrection reality -- be they by Bultmann or Rahner -- concerning the question how far they take into view the intersubjective dimension of the experience of death. In Peukert's perspective, only considerations concerning the ontology of the resurrection reality, which strictly start from communicative interaction moving toward death, can contribute to the clarification of the meaning of the New Testament texts. Proposals concerning a hermeneutic of the resurrection, which constitute the test case for the understanding of any theology, must also be examined, in relation to the question to what extent they break out of the horizon of communicative action and thereby put themselves in an objectivating manner above the subject matter of theology and thus cease to be theology in the proper sense.

In Peukert's view, the hermeneutical start from an analysis of communicative action, as he recommends it, opens up the possibility to explain in what precisely consists the eschatological escalation in the experience of the death of Jesus and in the witness of his resurrection.22 According to Peukert, Jesus has through the assertion of the saving reality of God for the others posited practically in his existence, provoked and opened up the possibility for his followers to assert God as the rescuing actor also in the case of his own death.

In Peukert's perspective from now on -- the Christ event -- the assertation of the presence of the saving God for others*can no longer be limited. Also, the experience of the Kingdom of God, the reality of God for All, can no longer in its universality be historically separated from this singular person, Jesus of Nazareth. Only as practiced solidarity with All is the assertion of the resurrection of Jesus real. Peukert's teacher, Metz, has emphasized the inseparable connection between the hope of resurrection and universal solidarity, i.e., the

eschatological horizon of solidarity.23 For Metz as for
Peukert, the word of the resurrection of the dead is a word
of justice, a word of resistance against the attempt to
simply cut into half the always longed for and searched
for meaning of human existence and to reserve it at best for
the generations to come, for those who have made it, the
happy victors and unsufructuaries of our history. According
to Peukert the confrontation with the Judeo-Christian
tradition forces a theory of universally solidary communicat
action, like that of Habermas, to manifest the reality,
which is presupposed and experienced in human interaction.
According to Peukert, out of this communicative action the
reality of God becomes determinable.

Peukert is aware of the fact that Habermas has denied in
his article on Benjamin *Conscious-making and Saving Critique*
that out of the experience of anamnetic solidarity, which
affirms the innocent other in his annihilation and so
anticipates his or her rescue -- the very core of the
critical political theology -- an orientation for social
action can be gained.24 According to Peukert in Habermas's
argument at least that much is true, that a theological
theory of historical experience of this kind must be
connected with an empirical and at the same time normative
theory of communicative action, a theory of the subject
and a theory of society, which try to comprehend the inner
correlation of these dimensions and their respective
historical genesis. Metz and Peukert can develop their
theology of communication only in cooperation with Habermas
and other members of the Frankfurt School. But in Peukert's
view, only an *unconditional* theologically grounded universal
solidarity, which includes the innocent victims of history,
can gain from the past the potential for the resistance
against the totalitarian claim of social systems which
overplay the subject -- i.e., against alternative Future
I -- the totally administered and cybernetically controlled
society.25 Peukert predicts that the concept of history
will in the future gain even more significance for the
orientation of political action than it had already in the
past since the start of Hegel's philosophy of history.

For Peukert the critical political theology, as a theory
of communicative action, which is developed out of the
paradox of anamnetic solidarity with the innocent other
who is destroyed but has nevertheless been rescued from
total annihilation, has the task to develop a hermeneutic
of the history of religions, which is connected to a
theory of the development of human consciousness and
action in general.26 Peukert discovers behind the modern
attempts to develop theories of intersubjectivity and
subjectivity of society and history, like that of

Horkheimer, Benjamin and Habermas, or that of Parsons and Luhmann, an elementary experience. It is the self-experience of a mankind, which sees itself emerge out of natural and social evolution to consciousness and reflection. The universal communication community of beings who rise out of the evolution and come to an understanding with each other demands its own new solidarity. This universal solidarity or identity shows itself as the condition for the possibility of the individual person's singular identity and of the particular identity of societies. For Peukert the sicence-theoretical insight of the convergence of the problem positions in a theory of communicative action contains thus also the insight, that one can break out of the universal solidarity of all finite beings only for the price of the loss of one's own singular identity and of the particular identity of societies.

According to Peukert, this is also true for theologians. In the face of the biblical tradition the theologian must ask the question concerning the universal, particular and singular identity even more radically than the philosopher of science or of communicative action. Then, it becomes the question for a reality, which makes this universal, particular and singular solidarity possible even in the face of the destruction of the innocent other in death. A critical political theology which points to this reality, for which traditionally the name of God is reserved and to this universal solidarity can together with the philosophy of science and the philosophy of communicative action prepare alternative Future III -- the reconciled society. What does all this mean in terms of concrete practice under world conditions in which the trend toward the administered society or toward war powerfully prevails? What heroism or saintliness is necessary to resist the temptation of total administration or total war? A simple paradigm may at least clarify the question further and maybe even point toward an answer.

CHAPTER XI

Horkheimer and Benjamin emigrated too early from Germany and
Habermas was too young to follow the immediate effect-history
(Wirkungsgeschichte) of the theologian Haecker's work in the
Christian community of fascist Germany. Thus neither Benjamin
not Horkheimer or Habermas could know of the many anonymous
Catholics who, in national-socialist Germany, decided for
Haecker's theology of history and on its basis, resisted fascisı
the first form of total administration and total war - more or
less heroically. One of these anonymous followers of Haecker's
Christian theory of history was George W. Rudolphi, a Catholic
parish priest in Frankfurt a.M., Germany.*1* Rudolphi's life,
work, suffering and death is paradigmatic for Haecker's impact
upon Catholic practice in Nazi Germany and in the following
Adenauer restoration. Haecker's theory of history can be
adequately judged only together with the praxis it was able
to motivate, to inform, to sustain and to direct under most
inhuman circumstances. Rudolphi's theoretical and practical
work anticipates Kung's negative theology and Metz' and Peukert
theology of communicative practice. His life work, suffering
and death is exemplary for the universal practical solidarity
promoted by Haecker, Kung, Metz and Peukert as well as by
Horkheimer, Adorno, Habermas and other members of the
Frankfurt School.*2*

From 1931 on through the early 1960's, Rudolphi built
and worked in two churches, only a short distance away
from Horkheimer's *Institute for Social Research* at the
Johann Wolfgang Goethe Universitat, Frankfurt. One of
the churches is dedicated to the progressive German
scholastic Albertus Magnus. Throughout the Naxi period,
Rudolphi preached sermons, wrote and practiced the care
of the souls in the spirit of Haecker's theology of history.
He had to bear the political consequences. Masons,
belonging to the National Socialistic Labour Party and
the connected Labour Union, mocked the critical pastor
by building a huge swastika with red stones right into
one of the walls of his newly built St. Albertus Church.
Since it could not be removed without taking the whole
wall out, it remained there throughout the whole Nazi era.
Hitler youth groups beat up the leaders of Rudolphi's
Catholic youth groups. The pastor was finally forced --
in spite of the *Concordat* between Hitler and Pius XII --
to dissolve his youth groups in public. He reconstituted

them again in the underground. Hitler youth disturbed his
services by marching up and down before his churches.
Once they threw huge stones through a large window of
Rudolphi's St. Familia Church during the Sunday morning
service. The pastor picked up one of the stones and carrie
it to the pulpit and swore with his loud, prophetic voice
that it would fly back some day. Once Rudolphi defended
his parish house with a shot-gun against penetrating party
members. The courage of the pastor, who had been wounded
four times in World War I and had been decorated for braver
impressed the fascists inspite of his "Jewish teachings" an
they withdrew. After one of his Haecker-sermons during the
war, the Frankfurt gestapo took Rudolphi into remanding
custody for a week. The harassment of the Haecker-follower
Rudolphi by members of the Nazi party never ceased througho
the twelve years of Hitler's regime. Haecker himself was
forbidden by Hitler's government to give public speeches
and to publish later in the war. Rudolphi was to use Benja
expression, a man of great messianic intensity.3

During the war, Rudolphi preached from Haecker's *The Tempta-*
*of Christ.*4 His audience, which came from all over Frankfu
in search of strength, direction and consolation, listened
to him in utter amazement. People were often in fear for t
pastor's and their own security, freedom and life. Every
second sentence of Rudolphi's sermons, based on Haecker's
theology of history, was an anathema against National Socia
and against all similar pagan movements in Europe or elsewh
then and later. According to Rudolphi, Haecker's theology
was an indictment against a whole age, against late bourgeo
society, the contradictions of which made fascist tendencie
possible in the first place. According to Rudolphi, he who
does not understand the temptations of Christ in the late
Western Civilization, has yielded to them already long ago.
With Haecker, Rudolphi finds the meaning of the temptations
of Christ not in the hypocritical speeches of the *diabolos*,
but rather in the answers of Christ. The lies of Satan
are: Man lives by bread alone! Man lives by God alone!
Man lives by power alone!

For Rudolphi, following Haecker, the biblical "bread
alone" means the absolute immanence of the world, man's
imprisonment in its limitations. The first temptation
does not only signify the materialism of the palate or
of the eyes, so wide-spread in bourgeois society. Idealists
can say proudly and arrogantly, that they do not live at
all from the bread alone, but also from the notions of
Immanuel Kant and Friedrich Neitzsche, two "very haughty
men". They live from the bread and the sp irit of *this*
world alone. So do the nations and states who succumb
to such tempters and temptations.

While Rudolphi condemns Kant's subjective idealism, he is silent about Hegel's objective and absolute idealism. The latter contains so much crypto-Catholicism, that Rudolphi's attack against it would have boomeranged back.5 While Rudolphi argues against Nietzsche's theory of the superman, which was very popular in Nazi Germany, he says nothing against Marx's dialectical materialism, which he derived from Hegel's dialectical idealism and which was even more hated by the fascist party than the "Jewish" bible. Communists who had survived the concentration camp, lived in Rudolphi's overwhelmingly proletarian parish of St. Familia. At that time, they studied the Christian Hegel again: From Marx to Hegel!6

To live by "God alone" means for Rudolphi, as for Haecker, that man ignores the orders which God has given to him as a mandate. A man lives by God alone, when he refuses to step down the staircases carefully, which lead from the pinnacle of the temple to the plain earth. God should dispense man from this descent. God should send his angels to carry man down to earth. God should produce miracles!

Rudolphi asks himself: Is this really the temptation of Western civilization? Is this not rather the temptation of the Orient, the temptation of oriental pietism and mysticism? Rudolphi answers this question to the negative. In Western civilization, this arrogant "God alone" was perverted into a gruelling petrification. Rudolphi and his parishoners had in their ears the rude shout, by which Hitler innumerable times profanes one of the most sublime words of Christ: providence.7 Hitler shouted: "Providence" is "our Father!" According to Rudolphi, in those Hitlerian blasphemies "providence" was an impersonal, hollow, and ghostly fate, *fatum, kismet*. Hitler's official propagandist, Dr. Joseph Goebels, demasked the desolate contentlessness of the high name when, in the last weeks of the war, he spoke instead of "providence" of the "godess of history". At the same time, Goebels insulted the miserable idol, when it did not want to obey and gave the German troops defeat rather than victory. Thus the magician broke the fetish which was no longer effective. In reality Providence meant for Hitler nothing else than the Darwinian law of the survival of the fittest, justifying the domination of the Arians over all the other races.

In Rudolphi's view, God has created visible orders and a visible world. The God entered the visible flesh. He called into existence a visible church. The creator-God has become flesh. God demands that man become

obedient in his orders to death. Everything else is magic
and fetishism and idolatry. All magic, the manifest and
the cowardly, hidden one, also the piously decorated magic
wants to tempt God.

With Haecker, Rudolphi finds in the third temptation of
Christ the summary of all other temptations for man.
The kingdom, all kingdoms and their glory are offered
for the price of the genuflection before the apostatized
angel. The dark mystery of this world is: the power in
the wrong hands, the power of injustice, the powerlessness
of the right, the powerlessness of the Almighty One. The
Creator of the world is *not* the Lord of the world! The
tempter offers the world and its glory in every moment
of history. It is sweeter than everything else in the
world, in the hour of temptation, to hold the power in
strong hands, made strong by Satan, who says: Power is
given to me and I give it to whom I want. The history
or the histories of this temptation are in the last
analysis the main content of world history. It is not
only a history of magic and fetishism and idolatry but
also a history of the temptation of power. Never is
there taken away from the Christian the sad certainty
that in every moment of history up to the end of this
world, the tempter is allowed to tempt and that the
empires of this world have the tendency toward injustice
and that they do not love the truth. They no longer
even ask the question: What is truth?

According to Rudolphi, when it is so questionable in the
world as nature and particularly as society and history,
who is really the Lord of history, God or Satan, then man
must indeed be afraid. Where man is halfway honest at
all, he will admit that he is afraid. Often, when man
does not confess to this, his *Angst*, his anxiety, right
out, then we must not forget that one usual form of fear
is the loud lie, that it does not exist.

Rudolphi asks: Is the temptation of power the last word
of history? Rudolphi's answer is: No! For Rudolphi,
the last word of history is the *Advent*, in which order
will be restored and in which never again will power and
right be separated, but in which a resolved tranquility
and life will exist in the omnipotence of love. At
present, for the Christian, there remains the misery of
society and history, but also the power of faith as the
only defense against Satan and his temptations of life
by **bread** alone, by God alone and by power alone.

During the war, Rudolphi applied Haecker's theology of
history particularly by preaching almost every morning

during Mass, often after long and frightful nights in the
air shelter, on the saint of the day. Rudolphi published
these sermons after the war in the paper of the diocese
of Limburg and also in a book *Holy Church, Church of the
Saints*.[8] In the last chapter of the book "The Saint N.
Confessor and Worker", Rudolphi extends Haecker's Christian
theory of history to the saint of the future -- the proletarian
saint. Unlike Horkhiemer, Adorno, Benjamin, Habermas, Fromm
who come from bourgeois families, Rudolphi came from a
proletarian background and was at least as close to the
proletariat of Frankfurt's West Side, with and for which
he worked for over thirty years, as any member of the
Frankfurt *Institute for Social Research*, the so-called
"Kaffee Marx".

Rudolphi wants at least to begin to write the life story
of a saint, who is a worker: a worker whose blue togs
smell from oil, who buys for himself a monthly seasonal
ticket for the streetcar, in order early in the morning
to ride with his tender to work, and who at night comes
home and gives his wife a kiss and looks after the homework
of his son Fritz and who takes before himself his sone
Willi, because he has once more broken the windows of one
of the neighbours. Rudolphi wants to talk about a worker,
who is a member of the labour union and the socialist
party and who, after his death, is elevated by the church
to the honour of the alters. Rudolphi asks himself: Is
there such a saint? He must answer: No! By 1949, the
church has no saint who is a worker, a proletarian. There
is still no such representative proletarian saint by 1979.

When Rudolphi becomes aware of this fact, this insight
makes him confounded and perplexed. Why does the modern
church not have a proletarian saint? The church could
say in its defense, that the class of industrial workers
is not yet old enough. It is true, that industrialization
started in England already in 1760 and the first deep
capitalistic crisis took place already in 1825. But the
church could say, that the type of the industrial worker
had just one to two hundred years time, in order to become
a social form in its own right. One or two centuries is
not enough to produce the pre-conditions for a saintly
worker, a proletarian saint. After all, grace presupposes
nature!

Of course, Rudolphi knows only too well that such an
apology fo the church would be a mere evasion of the
problem or simply -- ideology, i.e., untruth. For
Rudolphi, it is, after all, true: "Send out your spirit,
and *everything* will be newly created and you will transform
the *face of the earth*.[9] For Rudolphi, that means that

also the face of the proletariat will be transformed. The church should indeed have proletarian saints!

Rudolphi and many other Catholics had looked a long time for the worker-saint. Already in the early 1920's this concern was expressed in the exicting little book, which the Catholic Herwig called "St. Sebastian from the Wedding" - the image of a proletarian saint. Rudolphi read the book with groups of the Catholic youth movement during the early Nazi period. It was a burning issue in pre-fascist Catholic Germany. It was even a very tormenting concern!

But Rudolphi must admit, that the "St. Sebastian" did not give an answer, which could liberate young Catholics and give them confidence. St. Sebastian's answer did indeed come out of the noise of the machines and out of the worker quarters and the slums of the Berlin of the 1920's. But St. Sebastian was, nevertheless, like the old hermits of the Egyptian desert. Sebastian kept the world distant from himself. The world was only built around Sebastian. It remained for Sebastian only the hostile world. The heavens did indeed glorify the Eternal One, but the earth remained a blasphemous distance away and remote. Rudolphi speaks about the Berlin, in which not only St. Sebastian remained lonely, but in which also Karl Liebknecht and Rosa Luxemburg lived, worked, and were murdered.[10] Rudolphi looks for the worldly proletarian saint, who loves the world as nature, society and history. As long as such a saint was not possible, Reich's Freudian-Marxian liberation message was much more plausible than the Good News of the Christians.[11]

For Rudolphi, the issue of the proletarian saint has not lost anything from its seriousness since the 1920's. [12] Some Christians wanted to solve the problem by giving their Lord and Redeemer a new name: Christ the Worker! The first of May, the feast day for all the workers of the world and their universal solidarity was to become the day of *Christ the Worker*.

But for the hierarchical church, it seemed to be more correct, to celebrate the feast of Christ, the King, at a time when kings became extremely scarce and the last residuals of the Middle Ages were wiped out in advanced capitalistic societies. But the crown on the head of the one, whom the New Testament calls the sone of the carpenter, did not hinder Catholic workers to fold their calloused hands again and again, so that "Your Kingdom come." [13] It would take the pope up to 1979 to assist the

marriage ceremony of a "commoner", while for centuries
he had participated only in weddings of the nobility.
Even for Rudolphi the new name Christ, the worker, sounded
somewhat artificial and propagandist.

According to Rudolphi, saints are called in the language
of the church those transfigured persons, who have lived
the Evangelium of Jesus the Christ to a heroic degree.
They live in the mimesis of Christ. Rudolphi knows
fifteen people of the 19th century, who have been
canonized by the church. All fifteen saints belong to
the clergy or religious orders. Fourteen out of the
fifteen people are members of a monastic order. Eight
out of the fifteen saints are women. The seven male
saints are all priests. Out of the seven men, one was,
be*fore* he was ordained, a baker, Klemens Hofbauer; one
was a farmhand, Konrad of Parzham; one was a farmer,
Johannes Vianney. Rudolphi adds to these three men,
Father Kolping. Rudolphi remembers a song about Kolping:
"He made shoes shiny and fine, when he wandered through
the world. The shoemaker then became a priest". Even
these four occupations fit better into the medieval world,
than the new type of industrial worker of an organized
capitalistic society. The problem seen by Rudolphi
continues today, thirty years later. The first male
saint in the U.S.A., canonized in 1977, is once more a
member of the clergy, a bishop. Should there not have
been among the millions of Catholic proletarians who
lived in the slums of Baltimore, Chicago, Philadelphia,
Detroit, Toronto, etc., in the last one hundred and
fifty years a few anonymous saints and could not one of
them have been canonized by the church as a representative
saint.

Here Rudolphi encounters utter discouragement: "The
shoemaker then became a priest ... listen what a work
he then devised!" Kolping founded the association for
young journeymen. In the same year, Karl Marx proclaimed
the Red International. Could not, so Rudolphi asks, the
shoemaker Kolping have devised the association of young
journeymen instead of the priest? Could not the *baker*
Hofbauer become an apostle? Could not the *fieldhand*
Konrad be a "light of the divinity"? Could not the
villager Vianney become an "envoy of divine love"?
According to Rudolphi, this question has often been
asked in the 20th century, in one form or the other.
But Rudolphi thinks that this question has been asked
in the wrong way.

In Rudolphi's view, the heroism of the "saints" has many
forms. It can be like a blazing fire flame. Rudolphi

thinks of Paul, who was his great model and about whom
he wrote a book. He also remembers Ignatius of Loyola
and Francis of Assisi. Rudolphi cannot imagine Paul as
husband and family father. Rudolphi cannot picture for
himself a Paul playing with his little boy, bouncing
him on his knee to the tune of "Giddy-up horsey!" In
Rudolphi's perspective, a Francis of Assisi would have
given away the sack of potatoes, from which his children
should live during the cold and hungry German post-war
winter of 1946.

For Rudolphi, holiness can mean the burning loneliness
of the soul, which knows only the one single call of
longing: "Restless is my heart, o God, until it rests
in you!" These saints stand outside society. They find
themselves in the isolation of the God-devotion. They
are distant, far away from the work of the world. The
Catholic author Karrer says in a bitter word of St.
Margareta of Alacoque, that from day to day she became
more incapable of joining in the life of the community.
According to Rudolphi, sanctity can mean the building
of the kindgom of God. This is the holiness of the monk-
father Benedict of Nursia. Thus Thomas Aquinas piled up
the temple of the sacred science, of theology. So
Francis Xavier wandered through the wideness of the Far
East.

In Rudolphi's perspective, the stamp of holy heroes is
so manifold, that the seer of Revelation was shocked
by it: "After this, I looked and behold, a great multitude
which no man could remember, from every nation, from all
tribes and peoples and tongues ..."14 Also the church
cannot count this great multitude. But the church can
name individuals. The church makes individuals into her
representatives, so that they may stand as signposts or
as the monuments of God or as the flowers of paradise or
also as the "tree of life with its twelve kinds of fruit,
yielding its fruit each month; and the leaves of the tree
were for the healing of the nations".15 The church names
individuals and calls them holy. These are the representati
saints.

Rudolphi asks, what happens to the great multitude, which
no man can number? They are called holy by the Lord of
the church: "Blessed are the poor in spirit, for theirs
is the kingdom of heaven." "Blessed are those who hunger
and thirst for righteousness, for they shall be satisfied."
"Blessed are those who mourn, for they shall be comforted."1

Christ thinks of the unnamed saints, when he speaks his
deepest words: The kingdom of heaven is like a small

mustard seed, which was sown unpretendingly into the corner of the garden, since the housewife needs it for her small household. But the small herb becomes the dwelling for the birds of heaven.17 The kingdom of heaven is like a leaven. It is insignificant, plain, and wrinkled like a withered potato. But in this lump of leaven, there is the power of fermentation and of secret transformation.18 The kingdom of heaven is the secret seed which becomes mature without the sower being aware of it: "The kingdom of God is as if a man should scatter seed upon the ground and should sleep and rise night and day and the seed should sprout and grow, he knows not how. The earth produces of itself, first the blade, then the ear, then the full grain in the ear. But when the grain is ripe, at once he puts in the sickle, because the harvest has come."19 Here Jesus speaks about the anonymous saints.

Rudolphi cannot name the cannonized industrial worker. But Rudolphi is certain from his work in proletarian parishes in Wiesbaden and Frankfurt: the proletarian saint is there. The saintly proletarian "grows night and day" in the mines, in the factory halls, in the homestead, in the apartment. With the saintly industrial worker grows his partner -- his wife -- in the covenant, which is a mystery in Christ and the church, as Paul knows.20 "The earth produces of itself first the blade, then the ear."

Rudolphi knows, these are no new insights. So it is today in the age of industrialism, and so it was in the age of feudalism and in the age of slave societies. So it was, when people dug catacombs, when Elisabeth experienced the Wartburg, when Robespierre rages with the guillotine, when Tito prohibited the pilgrimages, the only secret weapon of which is the rosary of peasant women. Rudolphi knows the sain N., confessor and worker is approaching in history. Paul stated: "For consider your call, brethren; not many of you were wise according to worldly standards, not many were powerful, not many were of noble birth. But God chose what is foolish in the world to shame the wise. God chose what is weak in the world to shame the strong."21 For Rudolphi, God is on the side of the little people. To the anger of Nietzsche's superman, God finds his way to where the "smell of the poor people" is. According to Paul, "God chose what is low and despised in the world, even things that are not, to bring to nothing things that are ..."22 And truly "For the kingdom of God does not mean food and drink, but righteousness and peace and joy in the Holy Spirit; he who thus serves Christ is acceptable to God."23 Rudolphi rejected the homogeneous and empty time of the evolutionists and approached history with the same apocalyptic expectation as Benjamin, Metz and Peukert.24

In Rudolphi's view, the church's book of heroes tells about these men and women, who are "acceptable to God." The missal of the church calls often to these men and women accepted by God. Paricularly the Evangelium knows of "the poor in spirit."

But according to Rudolphi, after all this is said, it would nevertheless be a great gift, if our of the world of the anonymous proletariat, out of the army of the assembly shops, the shipyards, and the coal pits, out of Berlin's Wedding or Frankfurt's Kamerun or the slums of Detroit or Chicago, or out of the working man's quarters of any large city around the globe, out of socialistic and communistic parties and unions and countries would come a St. Sebastian, a genuine and shining proletarian saint. He would indeed be a wonder of Christ and a sign of Christ.25

After the war, Rudolphi continued to apply Haecker's Christian theory of history to the practice in his parish, in the church in general, in family, society, and state. The theory gave meaning to the practice. The practice brought concreteness and reality to the theory. Rudolphi's sermons and talks, which made him known all over Frankfurt and West Germany, were always of highest theological and political actuality. Rudolphi anticipated in his liturgical practice many of the reforms of Vatican II. Concerning the pastoral practice, Rudolphi thought that each one of his parishoners, particularly each worker, and each wife of a worker, was important enough in his or her own subjecti that his or her biography should be written. As a matter of fact, Rudolphi knew the life stories of most of his parishoners better even than those of the saints he had studies for years as historian and theologian. Rudolphi's parishes bloomed throughout the late 1940's, the 1950's and the early 1960's. Rudolphi anticipated with great warmth and passion the later pastoral orientation of his church.

Rudolphi's practice as a pastor, informed by the Catholic theory of history, as Haecker had articulated it, entailed suffering. Already during the war, Rudolphi did not only suffer from the continual oppression by the Nazi party, but was equally pained, sitting with parishoners and neighbours in his insufficient air-raid shelter, by the dreadful expectation that his two parishes may be destroyed by saturation-bombing. In fact, large parts of the

proletarian sections of his parishes were bombed out.
Shortly after the war, the anti-fascist pastor suffered
deeply, when the American military government evacuated
for good in a few hours hundreds of his parishoners and
occupied their apartments and cut his two parishes apart
by a high barbed wire fence in order to establish a safe
zone for its personnel around its headquarters, the former
I. G. Farben Chemical Corporation Administration Building.
One cold morning when Rudolphi rode along the long barbed
wire fence in order to read Mass in his other parish,
displaced workers pulled him from his bicycle and robbed
him of his only winter coat. Rudolphi did not complain.

The greatest pain came to Rudolphi, when, suddenly one
Sunday morning in the early 1960's, he was removed by
the church authorities from all his offices under the
pretense of his ill health. Rudolphi went into what he
himself considered his exile in the desolate Westerwald
Mountains in Germany. All of the begging of Rudolphi's
parishoners before the ecclesiastical administration to
send their pastor of over three decades back to them,
remained without success. Since the church bureaucracy
never did give the real reasons for Rudolphi's sudden
departure from his parishes, rumours took their place,
which still prevail today and against which his old
parishoners defend lovingly the integrity of their pastor.

His sudden dismissal hurt Rudolphi so much, that during
his short visits with friends in Frankfurt during the
middle '60's, he found it too painful even to look at
his two churches, which he had built with his people
under great stress and with enormous sacrifices during
the Nazi period and which he loved as his real home.
But the ecclesiastical bureaucracy, could as little as
the fascist functionaries before, separate Rudolphi from
his always youthful, passionate, biblical, and prophetic
faith. Out of his painful exile, Rudolphi strengthened
the faith of his parishoners, many of whom had, in the
meantime, spread all over the world and worried about
his fate and the turbulent conditions in church and society,
in the spirit of the theology of history, which he shared
with Haecker. It seemed that Rudolphi's sufferings only
reinforced his apocalyptic faith.

In the late 1960's, Rudolphi returned to Frankfurt a last
time, only to die lonely and neglected in one of the huge
hospitals of the city, where he himself had consoled many
of his ill parishoners. Friends buried Rudolphi in
Frankfurt's main city cemetary, where two decades earlier
he had blessed the thousands of open graves of old men,
women and children slain in their homes during air raids

on the city. Rudolphi died as he had lived in paradoxical
anamnetic solidarity with the Jewish prophets, Jesus,
Paul and the saints of the past and in anticipatory
solidarity with the proletarian saints of the future.

Twelve young men from Rudolphi's parishes followed him
into the priesthood and work today in parishes in and
around Frankfurt. Like Rudolphi they preach the gospel
to the poor and fight the temptations of bread alone --
sex, car and careers -- God alone and power alone in the
advanced capitalistic society of West Germany and try to
prepare the way for the proletarian saint, be it in an
administered or a reconciled society of the future.
Others found the gap between Rudolphi's idea of the
church and the actual bureaucratic church -- which
finally brought about his downfal -- too deep for the
time being, its semi-feudalism as well as its bourgeoise
class-determination too powerful, its conversion to the
spirit of the gospel too unlikely in the near future and
the arrival of the proletarian saint too distant, in
order to be able to follow their pastor into the official
priesthood. They choose less administered forms of
Christian existence as mimesis of the Crucified.

One problem plagued Rudolphi throughout his long hard life
more than anything else: the theodicy problem. Why the
unceasing suffering of the individual subject from
internal and external nature, from family, society, state
and history. Why the continual catastrophies of history?
Rudolphi could resolve this problem as little as Haecker,
Schneider and Guardini or, for that matter, Horkheimer,
Adorno, Benjamin or Habermas.26 Here what Hegel calls the
"religious idealists" and the "religious materialists"
seem to be likewise at a loss.27 Rudolphi could do no
more than to bear with the unresolved theodity problem in
the *Imileti: Christi.*

CHAPTER XVI

THEODICY

Indeed, one fundamental issue binds together Hegel, Marx, Horkheimer, Benjamin and Habermas on one hand and Haecker, Rudolphi, Kung and Peukert on the other hand: the theodicy problem.1 Its core is the justification of God in the face of the terror of the world as nature and particularly as history. The theodicy problem is the common denominator of the critical and functional theory of society and of the negative and the political theology. While the religious materialists develop a negative theodicy from below, the religious idealists propose a positive one, from above. Hegel's philosophy and theology of history combines the last time in Western history of thought a positive and a negative theodicy. To be sure, it is assymetrical in favour of a positive theodicy. Nevertheless since Hegel is not only the great idealist of the Western history of philosophy and theology but also its greatest realist, therefore belongs to him the last word in this book, the nervus rerum of which is after all the theodicy problem as it presents itself in the critical and functional sociology and in negative theology and in the new dialectical theology of intersubjectivity and subjectivity, society and history, the critical political theology.

After Leibnitz's attempt to construct a positive theodicy from above, in still very much metaphysical and as such indeterminate and abstract categories, in order to comprehend the contingencies in the world -- injustice, sickness, death, -- and thereby to reconcile thinking man with the evil which characterizes this world, had been laughed out of court by Voltaire's *Candide*, Hegel replaced it by his own less metaphysical, much more precise and concrete theodicy.2 Up to today it is the most viable alternative to Schopenhauer's metaphysical pessimism which gained such great actuality after World War II inside and outside the Frankfurt *Institute of Social Research.*3 This is so precisely because Hegel's theodicy takes the negative of nature and history and society the awful power of negation as radically serious as Schopenhauer in his philosophy of man, society, state or the Schopenhaurians: Nietzsche in his philosophy of man, society and history. Richard Wagner in his operas and Freud in his psychoanalysis. Hegel did certainly not agree with his great idealistic predecessor Leibnitz, that

ours is the best of all possible worlds. Hegel's and our
own centuries alone -- world wars, depressions, fascism,
death camps, epidemic, systemic diseases, Hiroshima,
Vietnam, leaking atomic reactors -- seem to indicate,
inspite of all scientific and technological progress and
sometimes precisely because of it, that this is rather the
worst of all possible worlds. The critical theory of
society -- following Hegel in many ways -- is fundamentally
the infinite sadness about this worst of all possible worlds
and at the same time the impulse and intent to correct at
least some of its evils. Hegel includes Schopenhauer, but
Schopenhauer does not contain Hegel. Hegel is, so to speak,
the truth of Schopenhauer.

Hegel's whole philosophy is a theodicy, the attempt to
prove that the world is inspite of all its chaos, evilness,
sickness and death nevertheless ultimately governed by
divine reason and providence.4 Hegel tries to establish
this proof in his philosophy of nature as well as in his
philosophy of right, history, art, religion, and in his
history of philosophy and theology. Hegel knows that there
is nowhere a greater need, demand and challenge for a
theodicy as reconciling thought than in world history.
Thus Hegel's philosophy of history is his theodicy par
excellence.

According to Hegel man's reconciliation with the horror of
history can be achieved only through the knowledge of the
affirmative into which the negative disappears as something
subordinate and overcome.5 Man can reconcile himself with
the overwhelming negativity of society and history only
through the consciousness, partially of what is in truth
the ultimate purpose of the world as nature and history,
and partially of the fact that this purpose has been realized
in the world and is now being achieved and will be
accomplished in the future and that the injustice, by which
the world is still characterized today will not have the
last word in history. In Hegel's view for this the mere
faith in Anaxagoras's still abstract principle, that reason
governs the world, or in the Judeo-Christian equally
abstract principle, that divine providence rules the
world, is by far not enough. The word "reason" is as
indeterminate and vague as the word "providence". People
speak of reason and providence without being able to say
what their determination, their concrete content is,
according to which we would be able to decide what in
the particular situations of history is rational and what
is irrational. For Hegel, reason and providence comprehended
in their determination and content, that alone is what
counts in a serious theodicy. Otherwise we have only
words -- flatus vocis. Hegel is very much aware of the

ideological function of empty concepts.

But what precisely is the content or the determination of reason and providence? Hegel determines God's reason and providence merely insofar as it is related to the world as nature and history. Hegel's theodicy is part of his functional or negative theology.6 Furthermore, for Hegel the question concerning the determination of divine reason and providence falls together with the question concerning the ultimate purpose of the world as nature and history. For Hegel following Anselm of Canterbury, it is intrinsic to this concept of the ultimate purpose that it is to be realized.7 Hegel differentiates, nevertheless, between the content of the ultimate purpose, its determination as such, and its actualization.

For Hegel the ultimate purpose of history is the freedom of All, not only the freedom of the One-Eastern despotism, or the freedom of the Few, Western Oligarchism. In Hegel's view freedom is not bourgeoise arbitrariness and selfishness. Freedom is rather the absence of the alienation of man from nature inside and outside of himself, from himself and others and from God. Freedom with others and the wholly Other.8 In Hegel's perspective the human realm of freedom moves over into the Kingdom of God as God's realm of infinite Freedom.9 The human realm of finite freedom must be achieved by human praxis.10 Hegel does indeed, anticipate the Marxian theory - praxis unity.

Hegel agrees with the materialists that the most immediate view of world history can convince us very easily that the actions of men and women do not originate from above, the idea of freedom, but rather from below, from their particular needs, passions, interests, characters and talents.11 In this drama of human practice and history only these needs, passions and interests appear as the real driving forces and as what is most effective. The passions, the purposes of the particular interest, the satisfaction of selfishness are the most powerful subjective factors in praxis and history. Their power consists in that they do not respect in any way any of the limits, which right and personal and social morality want to impose on them. Bourgeoise society is the total mobilization of precisely this selfishness.12

For Hegel the world comprises the physical and the psychic nature.13 Not only the psychic, but also the physical nature continually interferes with history. Systemic

diseases, like cancer, damage the family, by destroying
the mother, or the state by killing outstanding politicians.
In any case, in Hegel's perspective the forces of nature,
destructive as they are, are immediately closer to men
and women, than the artificial and protracted discipline
aiming at order and moderation, right and personal and
social morality. Hegel anticipates Freud's insight,
that men and women are fundamentally, in their natural
will, passions, instincts, interests, hostile to culture
and education.14 According to Freud the Christians of
the "Christian West" have been badly christened.

In Hegel's view, when we consider this drama, this comedy,
this tragedy of human passions and when we look at the
consequences of their violent character, of the folly,
which accompanies not only these violent passions, but
even also, and particularly so, good intentions and
rightful purposes, and when we see how these passions
and this stupidity cause evil, the bad, the ruin of the
most blooming empires and cultures, which the human
spirit has ever produced, then we can only be filled
with great sadness about this transitoriness, this
finitude, this finality.16 In Hegel's view as this
ruin of great empires and cultures is not only the work
of brutal and blind nature, but of men's and women's
natural will, we end up with a moral melancholy, with
an indignation of our good spirit about this drama of
passions, if such a good spirit is in us at all. Hegel
admits to the materialists who stress this melancholical
aspect of action and history, that one can elevate these
consequences of violent passion, and of folly to the
most terrible picture without any rhetorical exaggeration,
by merely putting together correctly the misfortunes,
which the greatest of nations and states as well as
people of highest personal virtue have suffered and are
suffering continually up to today. By painting such a
dark picture of the workd, one can likewise escalate
the feeling of men and women to the deepest, most
helpless and desperate sadness, for which no reconciling
result offers any counterweight. Against such melancholy
we seem to find hold only or out of such sadness we seem to
able to move only by thinking like the old Greeks in
their religion of beauty and fate: That is how it
happened; things are as they are; this is *fate;* we cannot
change it! Then we try to step out of the boredom which
this melancholical, fatalistic reflection produces in
us into our general surface-feeling of life, so
characteristic for our normal life world, as long as it
remains untouched by boundary situations, into the
empirical presence of our particular purposes and
interests, shortly, into the protective incapsulation

of our selfishness. This egoism stands at the quiet bank
of the river of history and from there enjoys the distant
view of the confused heaps of ruins of great cultures. All
this sounds as if Hegel had taken it right out of
Schopenhauer's *The World as Will and Representation.17*

In Hegel's view the general thought, which offers itself
in relation to the restless transformations of individuals
and nations, which exist for a little while and then
disappear, is that of *change* in general.*18* The view of
the ruins of a great culture of the past leads us to
comprehend this category of change from its negative
side. Which traveller, so Hegel asks, has not been
moved among the ruins of Carthage, Palmyra, Persepolis,
Babylon, Rome, Athens, Jerusalem, etc., to considerations
concerning the transitoriness of empires and individual
people, to sadness about a former powerful and rich
life? Such sadness does not stay with personal losses,
as if one looses one's wife or a good friend, or with
the transitoriness of one's own particular purposes.
Here Hegel speaks of the uninterested, universal sadness
concerning the destruction of great and cultivated human life
as well as of the universal solidarity with the victims of
history, with the sufferings of the dead.

But according to Hegel when we look at history as this
slaughterhouse, in which the happiness of nations, the
wisdom of states and the personal virtue of individuals are
sacrificed, then with necessity the question arises in our
mind: for whom, for which ultimate purpose are these enormous
and even monstrous sacrifices of individual and collective
life being made?*19* From the very beginning of his philosophy
of history, from his apriori presupposition on, that divine
reason and providence govern the world, Hegel has determined
the negative events, which the materialists' terrible
picture of action and history offers to the gloomy feeling
and to the reflection concerned with it, right away as the
dimension, in which we must see merely the means for the
substantial determination, the absolute, ultimate purpose
or the true result of world history: freedom as man's
being at home with himself in universal solidarity, finally
as man's being identical with himself in God's infinite
freedom. From the very beginning of his philosophy and
theology of history Hegel has scorned at the possibility
to take exclusively the way of materialistic reflection,
to ascend from the sad picture of particular historical
events to universal reason and providence.

Hegel sees nevertheless clearly the plausibility and

possibility of a materialistic theory of history from below. He decides for an idealistic philosophy of history from above in order to be able to solve the theodicy problem adequately, but an idealistic philosophy to be sure, which includes the valid materialistic concern with the negative aspects of history. Also Hegel makes this idealistic decision, since he is convinced, that it is not really the interest of the reflection of the materialists, no matter how full of feeling, truely to transcend their melancholical position. In reality, so Hegel argues, the materialists do not really want to solve the riddles of divine reason and providence, which rightly are posed by them. It is rather the nature of materialistic theorists of history gloomily to be pleased with themselves in the empty, fruitless sublimities of their own negative result. Hegel does not want to indulge in negative dialectics exclusively.20 Thus, he sublates negative dialectics into positive dialectics.

Hegel differs from Schopenhauer and his followers inside and outside the Frankfurt School when re reduces the theodicy problem to the prevailing dichotomy between the universal principle, ultimate goal, final determination of history, i.e., the realm of freedom in solidarity and the kingdom of God's infinite freedom on one hand, and its realization and actualization through the particular passions, needs, interests and actions of men and women on the other hand; and the solution of the theodicy problem to the reconciliation between universal principle and particular praxis.21 God through the benefolent "cunnin reason and providence turns man's natural will against itself and thus negates the negativity of passions and actions and makes them serve unconsciously or consciously the ultimate goal of human-divine liberation.22 This precisely is the hard work of history.23

Hegel opposes Schopenhauer's metaphysical pessimism by his own theological optimism and only as a theologian of history can Hegel possibly be optimistic in the face of the historical slaughterhouse.24 If Hegel was alive today after the two bourgeoise world wars, which he counselled against, and after Auschwitz and Hiroshima and Vietnam, he would fully agree with Heideggers statement in his last interview with the German journal *The Mirror* published posthumeously: *Only a God can help us.*25 This is possible for Hegel since God himself sacrifices himself and suffers and dies on the Golgatha of world history and precisely thereby negates the negativity of history and turns it into the affirmative -- the human-divine realm of freedom.26 This is the very essence of Hegel's solution to the theodicy problem.

Hegel sees in the different epochs of world history --
the freedom of the One in primitive and archaic Africa
and Asia, the freedom of the Few in intermediate-historical
and modern Greece, Rome and Europe and the freedom of
All in a future post-modern American and Slavic world --
the main moments of the form in which the principle of
concrete universal freedom and solidarity realizes itself
through particular and singular human praxis.27 According
to Hegel human evolution is nothing else than the
development of the notion of freedom: from singular
over particular to universal freedom. In Hegel's view
the objective freedom of states, including societies
and families, the laws of real freedom, demand at the
end of modernity the subordination of the accidental
personality - subjective will, passions, interests - since
in civil society it has in general become merely formal.
If the objective spirit, the state, including society,
marriage and family, is rational in itself, then the
insight of the subjective spirit of the individual must
internally correspond to the objective reason. The
unity of subject and object must be established. Then
also the essential element of the subjective freedom of
the individual is not only preserved, but even enhanced.
Subjective freedom is real only through the mediation of
objective freedom and vice versa.

In his philosophy and theology of history as theodicy
Hegel considers the progression of the notion of freedom
exclusively and resists the very attractive challenge
to portray more closely the happiness of individuals, of
marriages and families, the periods in which the great
nations bloomed in their brightest colours, the beauty
and greatness of subjects, the interest of their fate
in suffering and joy. In Hegel's view, philosophy of
history has to deal only with the splendour of the *idea
of freedom*, as it reflects itself in the course of history
and in the actions of men and women through which it is
realized. Philosophy in contrast to historeography works
itself out of the disgust with the particular movements of the
immediate passions of the people in the empirical reality
upward to the consideration of the very idea of universal
freedom and its actualization. It is the general
interest of the philosopher and the theologian of history
to know the process of the self-developing idea of
freedom, which exists only in peoples' consciousness of
freedom and in their praxis.

For Hegel it is the true theodicy, the true justification
of God in history, that world history is precisely this
evolutionary process and the real becoming of man's **free
spirit**, under the always changing drama of particular

historical events. According to Hegel, during the
bourgeoise enlightenment it became a famous word, that
half a philosophy leads people away from God -- and it
is this half philosophy which puts, like Kant, knowledge
into a mere approximation to the truth -- but that the
true philosophy guides people to God.[29] For Hegel the
same is true in relation to the state, including society
and family. As little as reason, so Hegel argues, is
content with mere approximation, which in biblical terms
is neither cold nor warm and therefore must be spit out
so little is reason satisfied with the cold desperation,
which admits, that in history things go badly or at best
in a mediocre way, but that in it one cannot get anything
better and that therefore one must make peace with
reality.[29] According to Hegel, historical-philosophical-
theological knowledge can produce a much warmer peace.
Such warm peace Hegel's philosophy of history as theodicy
wants to give. In Hegel's view only the rational insight
can reconcile man's spirit with the world as history and
nature, that what has happened in the past and what is
happening every day in the empirical present and what
will happen in the future, is not only without God, but
is essentially his own work.[30]

At the end of Hegel's philosophy of history as theodicy
one central question arises: Is it possible to reconcile
Hegel's mainly positive, religious-idealistic theodicy
from above, which in principle contains all religious-
idealistic theodicy attempts before and after him
including those of scholastics and neo-scholastics, of
Haecker, Rudolphi, Guardini, Schneider, Kung, Metz and
Peukert, with the negative, religious-materialistic
theodicy attempts from below as presented by Marx,
Horkheimer, Adorno, Benjamin and Habermas. Our answer
is affirmative. Such reconciliation is possible in the
sign of the messiah!

CHAPTER XVII

MESSIAH

Hegel states in his *Encyclopædia* concerning the contemporary split between religious idealists and religious materialists:

> "... the pure religious idealist and the pure religious materialist are only the two shells of the mussel, which contains the pearl of Christianity."[1]

Hegel's statement is programmatic for the present historical situation of Christianity in advanced capitalistic and socialistic society, particularly for the relationship between critical theorists interested in religion and negative theologians or political theologians of the subject concerned with historical materialism: Redemption not only in the spirit, but also in the flesh; salvation not only in the flesh, but also in the spirit; redemption *and* emancipation.[2]

Historical materialists, like Horkheimer, Benjamin or Habermas can show critical theologians like Haecker or Rudolphi, Guardini or Schneider, Küng, Peukert or Metz, that there is not only an idealistic way from above to the truth of religion in general and Christianity in particular, be it Platonic-Augustinian or Aristotelian-Thomistic, but also a materialistic approach from below, be it Marxian or Freudian.[3] It seems to us, the time has come to try once more, as Hegel before, to resolve the contradiction of long standing in the West between pure idealism and pure materialism, redemption and happiness, divine and worldly wisdom, knowledge and interest, truth and meaning, theory and praxis, thought and need, idea and production, spirit and flesh, man and nature, the religious and the secular, the individual and the collective, the subject and the object.[4] This is possible, since in all great idealisms, philosophical or religious, there are present strong materialistic elements, and in all great materialisms, philosophical or scientific, there are contained powerful subjective- or objective-idealistic moments. In any case, idealism without materialism is as such as abstract and untrue as materialism without idealism.

The critical theologians Haecker, Rudolphi, Küng, Metz
or Peukert understand very well the dialectical
contradictions in organized capitalistic society between
rich and poor classes, luxury and misery, producer and
consumer, owner and worker and the immense human suffering
they entail.5 On the other hand, for the historical
materialists Horkheimer, Adorno, Benjamin, Marcuse,
Fromm or Habermas, there is nothing foreign in the saint's
hunger and thirst for perfect justice.6

Shortly before his sacrificial suicide in 1941, Benjamin
wrote his short "Theses of the Philosophy of History"
and "Theological-Political Fragment".7 Both writings
constitute part of the foundation of the critical theory
as well as of the political theology. They are so to
speak the common ground on which political theology and
critical theory differ and also agree. Certainly Metz
and Peukert are, not only critical of Parsons' and
Luhmann's functional evolutionism, but also of Horkheimer's,
Benjamin's and Habermas's dialectical materialistm.8 But
their political theology of the subject is nevertheless
fundamentally a specifically Christian explication of
Benjamin's theses of the philosophy of history and of the
theological political fragment.9

According to Benjamin's theses of the philosophy of
history, historical materialism can be a match for anybody
if it takes theology into its service.10 This is so inspite
of the fact, that theology is, as Benjamin states with an
abyss-like smile, today, as everybody knows, small and
ugly and cannot let itself be seen in public. In Adorno's
judgement Benjamin was the man who could have discovered
and set free the theological glowing fire of the critical
theory.11 To some extent he did this in his last writings
on the philosophy of history and in the political
theological fragment.

For Benjamin, in the idea of happiness swings unalienably
along the concept of redemption. The past brings with
it a temporal index through which it is directed toward
redemption. To our generation as to any other, who lived
before us, has been given a weak messianic power, to
which the past generations and individuals have a claim.
This claim cannot be fulfilled cheaply. The historical
materialist Benjamin knows this. His friends in the
Frankfurt School know this. The political theologians
are aware of this.

In Benjamin's historical-materialistic perspective only
the redeemed humanity will inherit its past completely.
For the unredeemed mankind the past remains partially

blocked off, repressed. That means: Only the redeemed
humanity will be able to cite its past in each of its
moments. Each lived moment of the past turns into a
citation of l'ordre du jour -- which day is the youngest
one.

In his theses on the philosophy of history Benjamin
quotes a materialistic statement by the young idealist
Hegel of 1807, the Hegel of the *Phenomenology of the
Spirit*: First search for food and cloth, then the
kingdom of God will fall to you by itself. Benjamin's
close friend, Bert Brecht, engaged continually in such
materialistic reversals of statements from the bible,
which he read daily.

In Benjamin's view the messiah does not only come as
redeemer, but also as the conqueror of the Anti-Christ.
Only to that historian it is given to kindle the spark of
hope in the past, among the dead, who is permeated by the
knowledge: Also the dead will not be safe from the
enemy, the Anti-Christ, when he wins. This enemy, so
Benjamin knows living through the age of fascism, has
not ceased to be victorious.

Benjamin knows of a picture by Paul Klee, the name of
which is *Angelus Novus*. It impressed Benjamin more than
any other picture. It constitutes a sign of a breakthrough
in his life work and particularly in his philosophy of
history. To Benjamin the picture represents an angel who
looks as if he was in the process of moving away from
something, at which, at the same time, he stares. His
eyes are wide open and so is his mouth and his wings are
stretched out and extended far. Benjamin thinks that
the angel of history must look like that. The angel has
his face turned toward the past. Where a chain of
particular events appears before us in the process of
history, the angel sees one huge, universal catastrophy,
which heaps continuously ruins over ruins throwing them
before his feet. The angel would like to stay and to
come to rest and to awaken the dead and to put together
again what has been destroyed. But a storm blows from
paradise, which gets caught up in the angel's wings.
The storm is so strong and powerful, that the angel is
no longer able to close his wings. Without the angel
being able to resist, the storm drives him into the
future, to which he turns his back, while the heap of
ruins before him grows into heaven. According to
Benjamin, what we call progress, is this storm.

Benjamin opposes the vulgar marxist idolatry of the social
democrat Josef Dietzge: that work is the name of the

saviour of modern time or that in the improvement of
work consists the wealth which can now achieve, what so
far no redeemer could do. He does not accept the social
democratic attempt to attribute to the working class the
role of the redeemer of the *future* generations. Thereby
the social democracy cuts through the sinew of the working
class's best energy. The working class unlearned in the
school of social democracy its hate as well as its will
to sacrifice. This is so, since both nourish themselves
from the image of the enslaved ancestors, and the
sufferings of the dead, not from the ideal of the
liberated grandchildren.

According to Benjamin, the historical materialist
approaches an object where it comes toward him as a
monad. In the object's monadic structure, the historical
materialist recognizes the sign of a messianic standstill
in the historical process, i.e., of a revolutionary
chance in the struggle for the oppressed past. He
perceives this messianic standstill or revolutionary
chance in order to blast a definite epoch out of the
homogeneous course of history. The historical materialist
breaks a particular life out of the epoch, or a specific
work out of the work of a total life. The result of the
historical materialist's procedure consists in that, in
the particular work is preserved and sublated the whole
life work, in the life work the epoch, and in the
epoch the total course of history. The nourishing fruit
of that what is historically comprehended has *time* for
its precious seed in its interior, but deprived of taste.

For Benjamin, the *now-time*, which as model of the messianic
time sums up in a gigantic abbreviation the history of the
whole human species falls together very sharply and
precisely with the configuration, which constitutes the
history of mankind in the universe. The historical
materialist comprehends the constellation, into which
his own epoch has entered with a very particular earlier
epoch. He lays thereby the foundation for a conception
of the present as now-time, in which splinters of the
messianic time are interspersed.

Benjamin, a Jew himself, knows that the Jews were
forbidden to explore the future. Contrary to this
exploration the *Torah* and their prayers taught the Jews
to remember. This remembrance disenchanted the future
for the Jews. Those who have fallen to the enchantment
of the future, who search for information from the
soothsayers and fortune-tellers. But for the Jews the
future did therefore not become a homogeneous and empty
time. This is so, since for the Jews, in the future

172

every second was the small door through which the messiah could enter.

According to Benjamin's theological-political fragment, only the messiah himself completes all historical happening.[12] He does this by, first of all redeeming, completing and creating the relationship between the historical event and the messianic dimension. Therefore, nothing historical can intend to relate itself to the messianic realm. Thus for Benjamin, the Kingdom of God is not the *telos* of the historical dynamic. The kingdom of God cannot be posited as the goal of the historical process. In the historical-materialist perspective the Kingdom of God is not goal, but *end*. Therefore, the order of the profane cannot be constructed in accordance with the thought of the Kingdom of God. In Benjamin's view the historical materialist Ernst Bloch has rightly denied the political significance of theocracy with all intensity in his early work *Spirit of Utopia*.[13] For Benjamin as for Bloch the theocracy has no political, but alone a religious meaning.

In Benjamin's perspective, the order of the profane must direct itself toward the idea of happiness. The relationship of this profane order of happiness to the messianic dimension is one of the central doctrines of the philosophy of history as Benjamin understands it. Through this relationship a mystical concept of history is conditioned, the problem of which can be represented by the following image. When one direction of an arrow signifies the goal, in which is at work the dynamic of the profane realm, another arrow the direction of the messianic intensity, then of course the search for happiness tends away from that messianic impulse. But as one power can through its way promote another one on its way in the opposite direction, so can also the profane order reinforce the coming of the messianic realm. Thus the profane is indeed not a category of the Kingdom of God itself. But it is a most adequate category for the very silent *approach* of the messianic realm. This is so, since in happiness all finite life tends toward its destruction. But finite life is destined to find its destruction only in happiness.

In Benjamin's view, it is true that, of course, the immediate messianic intensity of the human heart, of the interior of the single man or woman, goes through unhappiness in the sense of suffering. But to the spiritual *restitutio in integrum*, which introduces into immortality, corresponds a worldly restitutio in integrum, which leads into the eternity of desctruction. For

Benjamin the rhythm of this eternally, in its spatial and temporal totality passing secular realm, the rhythm of the messianic nature, is happiness. This is so, since nature is messianic out of its eternal and total transitoriness. According to Benjamin it is the task of world politics understood in the broad Aristotelian or Hegelian sense, to strive after this eternal and total transitoriness also for those stages of man, which are nature. The name of the method of such world politics must be "nihilsm" as the acceptance of the transitoriness of the world as nature.

Six years after his friend Benjamin's death, Theodor Adorno writes at the very end of his *Minima Moralia*, that philosophy particularly philosophy of history, as it can alone still be done responsibly in the face of the present desperation, would be the attempt to see all things in such a way, as they present themselves from the point of view of the redemption or the messianic realm.*14* For Adorno knowledge has no other light than that which shines from the messianic redemption on the world. Everything else exhausts itself in mimetic reconstruction and remains a piece of technique. Adorno continues the "messianic" line of thought of his friend Benjamin.

According to Adorno perspectives would have to be established in a new philosophy of history, in which the world would in a similar way reveal its alienation, its splits and cracks, as it will once lay as needy and distorted in the messianic light. That alone is of importance for historical-materialist thought at this time, to gain such perspectives without arbitrariness and violence, completely out of the feeling-contact with the objects.

One one hand this is the most simple thing to do for Adorno, since the present condition calls, in a way not to be refused, for such knowledge, such philosophy, such messianic philosophy of history. This is so, since the complete negativity of our time, once completely faced, as already recommended by Hegel, shoots together into the   of its opposite.*15* But on the other hand, to gain such perspectives is also the most impossible thing to do, since it presupposes a standpoint, which is removed from the ban of existence, be it only to the smallest extent. But it is only too obvious that any possible knowledge must be obtained by persistence, also be characterized by the same distortion and neediness, from which it wants to escape.

According to Adorno, the more passionately the thought

of historical materialism closes itself heremetically
up against its being conditioned by present society for
the sake of the unconditional, the more unconsciously
and therefore the more fatefully it falls to the side
of the world as it is. It becomes positivistic, Historical-
materialistic thought, must even still comprehend its own
impossibility for the sake of its possibility. For
Adorno in relation to the demand, which is thereby
directed to the historical materialism, the question
concerning the reality or unreality of the redemption
and the messianic realm and the messiah is itself almost
indifferent.

There is no doubt, the materialist and idealist views of
history and religion, Judaism, Christianity or any other
religion do differ. The critical theologian cannot be
indifferent, like the historical materialist, concerning
the reality or unreality of the messiah. Certainly
Metz and Peukert understand Benjamin's and Adorno's
philosophy of history and religion differently from
Habermas. Redemption and emancpation, messianic
dimension and marxian realm of freedom are not the same.
But critical theology and dialectical theory of society
stand nevertheless in a dialectical relationship with
each other. They are not only different or even
contradictory. They can also not be without each other.
They need each other. They reproduce each other and
become fully true only as mediated through each other.

The critical philosophers and sociologists of the
Frankfurt School - Horkheimer, Adorno, Benjamin, Marcuse,
Fromm, Habermas - can remind critical theologians, like
Haecker, Rudolphi, Küng, Peukert and Metz of the
fundamentally eschatological character of the church to
which they belong, no matter how bureaucratic it may
appear. They can show the theologians, that the church
was not always feudal or bourgeoise, but that once in
its early stages in the Roman world it was proletarian
and as such indeed produced proletarian saints who
remembered and anticipated the messiah, and even paid
for this with their lives.16 The critical theorist can
help the theologian to articulare and answer questions
like: Why is a feudal or bourgeoise church not very
likely willing to name proletarian saints, no matter
how many of such saints hoping for the messiah may
actually be present in the working classes of advanced
capitalistic or socialistic societies? Why can proletarian
heroes be easier found in the liberation movements in
Africa, South America, South East Asia, than in the
established mainline churches of Europe and North
America. Why are religious cults catering to the

proletariat in organized capitalistic society driven into internal and external emmigration and even into mass suicide?17 Historical materialists can strengthen the hope of the political theologians, that a proletarian church may very well come about in the future, which will not be authoritarian, dogmatic, bureaucratic and traditionalistic and will be able to produce and to name representative worker saints.18 They can point out, that this proletarian church is even already present now in Christian brothers and sisters tortured and murdered today together with Marxists in Brazil, Argentina, Chile and elsewhere.19

On the other hand, theologians of history like Haecker and Rudolphi, Peukert and Metz can help historical materialists to re-discover in their own critical theory the glowing fire of an unideological, non-positivistic, authentic, radical theology. They may point out to the critical theorists, that it is very unlikely, that man's freedom history originated from the mammals, from nature, from matter alone. They can support the critical theorists' longing for complete justice and his hope for redemption and the messianic future and thereby help them to conquer the overwhelming positivistic temptation. The Christian theorists of history can help the historical materialists to correct the dialectics of enlightenment, particularly in its fascist consequences. Together they can help people to free themselves from their fears and to make themselves masters of their fate. Practical theologians can remind the critical theorists of the real proletarians of flesh and blood in the trivialties of their daily lifeworld of labour and tools and needs and cares, who are easily forgotten over high level academic discourse concerned with culture, e.g., Mahler's symphonies. They can encourage critical sociologists to communicate intelligibly not only with their colleagues, but also with workers and to translate their theory more adequate into their ordinary perception and understanding and logic and grammar and particularly into concrete praxis and give practical answers to their daily problems no matter how banal they may be.

Theologians who are waiting for the proletarian church and the worker-saint and critical theorists who carry in themselves the longing and the help for redemption and perfect justice and universal solidarity and happiness and the age of the messiah, can certainly enter into fruitful dialogue with each other and indeed have done so in the past.20 But more than that, critical theorists and political theologians can cooperate with each other practically in the antagonistic advanced modern society. Critical theorists have no difficulty to recognize the

polemical and revolutionary imperatives of the so-called
Sermon on the Mount.21 Critical theologians can accept
the categorical imperative intrinsic to the dialectical
theory of society: Act as if the interest in the solidarity
with humanity and the emancipation of humanity were your
own existential interest.22 Adorno states rightly the
feeling which binds together critical Christians and
dialectical sociologists: That in all seriousness no human
being should be hungry any longer; that in all seriousness
no wars should be fought any longer; and that in all
seriousness no man, woman or child should any longer be
sent to concentration camps.23

Political theologians and historical materialists can fight
together for the innocent victims and against the victorious
and triumphant murders. Together they can remember the
dead and their sufferings and the injustices from which
they died and together then can see the past and the present
in the redemptive messianic light and let themselves be
driven by the messianic impulse. Together critical theorists
and political theologians can try practically at least
to mitigate alternative Future I -- the totally cybernetically
controlled, bureaucratic and militaristic signal-society,
to oppose as powerfully as possible the trend toward
alternative Future II -- ABC wars; and to promote as
wholeheartedly and passionately as possible alternative
Future III -- the reconciled, rational, free humanistic
world federation. Such political praxis can reinforce the
quiet coming of the time of the messiah, the Kingdom of
God: where those who mourn shall be comforted; where
the meek shall inherit the early; where the hungry and
thirsty for righteousness shall be satisfied; where the
merciful shall obtain mercy; where the peacemakers shall
be called the sons of God and where the pure of heart
shall see God.24

FOOTNOTES

Introduction

1. J. Habermas, *Strukturwandel der Öffentlichkeit*,
Neuwied: Hermann Luchterhand Verlag 1976, 17-18,
21-23, 24-25, 52-53, 58-59, 60-61, 65-66, 111,
113-115, 116, 142-143, 144-150, 154-155, 158-163,
159, 174-175, 263-265.
   - J. Habermas, *Toward a Rational Society*, Boston:
Beacon Press, 1970, 41
   - J. Habermas, *Technik und Wissenschaft*, Frankfurt
a.M.: Suhrkamp Verlag, 1975, 39-43, 54, 65-70,
71-72, 74-77, 108, 109-110, 137-138, 148-150,
153-155.
   - J. Habermas, *Zur Logik der Sozialwissenschaften*,
Frankfurt a.M.: Suhrkamp Verlag 1973, 275-276,
284-285.
   - J. Habermas, etc. *Zwei Reden*, Frankfurt a.M.:
Sukrhamp Verlag 1974, 34-75.
   - G.W.F. Hegel, *Vorlesungen über die Philosophie der
Religion*, Bd.I, Stuttgart-Bad Cannstatt: Friedrich
Frommann Verlag 1965, SW 15).
   - G.W.F. Hegel, *Vorlesungen über die Philosophie
der Religion*, Bd. II, Stuttgart-Bad Cannstatt:
Friedrich Frommann Verlag 1965 (SW 16).
   - M. Horkheimer, *Critical Theory*, New York: Herder
and Herder 1972, 129-131.
   - M. Horkheimer, "Zu Theodor Haecker: Der Christ
und die Geschichte" in M. Horkheimer (ed.)
Zeitschrift für Sozialforschung, München: Kösel
Verlag 1970, V, 372-382. (ZFS)
   - M. Horkheimer, "Europa und das Christentum," in
M. Horkheimer, *Notizen 1950bis 1969 und Dämmerung*,
Frankfurt am.M. S. Fischer Verlag, 316-319.
   - M. Horkheimer, "Was ist Religion," in Horkheimer,
Notizen, op. cit., 92-93.
   - M. Horkheimer, "Jesus" in Horkheimer, *Notizen*,
op. cit., 96-97.
   - R. Niebuhr, (ed.), *Marx and Engels on Religion*,
New York: Schocken Books 1967, 41-58.
   - K. Marx, *Das Kapital*, Berlin 1961, BdI, 389, n. 89.
   - K. Marx, *Capital*, New York: The Modern Library
1906, 91-95.

2. H. Peukert, *Wissenschaftstheorie-Handlungstheorie-*

Fundamentale Theologie, Düsseldorf: Patmos Verlag
1976, 283-323.
- H. Peukert, "Einleitung des Herausgebers," in H.
Peukert (ed.) Diskussion zur "Politischen Theologie",
Mainz: Matthias-Grunewald Verlag 1969, VII-XIV.
- H. Peukert, "Zur formalen Systemtheorie und zur
hermeneutischen Problematik einer "politischen
Theologie," in Peukert, Diskussion, op. cit., 82-95.

3. G.W.F. Hegel, Vorlesungen über die Philosophie
   der Geschichte, Stuttgart: Fr. Frommann Verlag 1961,
   42, 48-50, 112 (SW 11).

4. Peukert, Wissenschaftstheorie, op. cit., 15-17,
   Part II.
   - W. Pannenberg, Theology and the Philosophy of
   Science, Philadelphia: The Westminster Press 1976,
   3-22, part one, 301-326.

5. H. Küng, Existiert Gott?, München: Piper Verlag
   1978, 119-143.
   - J.B. Metz, Glaube in Geschichte und Gesellschaft,
   Mainz: Matthias Grünewald Verlag 1978, 3-12.
   - Peukert, "Zur formalen Systemtheorie," op. cit.,
   82-95.
   - Peukert, Wissenschaftstheorie, 15-17, 283-323,
   parts II, III.
   - Pannenberg, Theology, op. cit., 3-22, part two.
   - Pannenberg, Grundfragen Systematischer Theologie,
   Güthersloh: Gutersloher Verlagshaus, 1967.
   - W. Pannenberg, Christentum und Mythos, Güthersloh:
   ·Güterloher Verlagshaus, Gerd Mohn, 1972.
   - H. Küng, Christ Sein, München: R. Piper Verlag
   1974, 48-80.

Chapter I - Claims of a Critical Theory

1. Küng, Existiert Gott?, op. cit., FI, 2.
   - Peukert, Wissenschaftstheorie, op. cit., 227-229.
   - Peukert, "Zur formalen Systemtheorie", op. cit.,
   82-95.

2. Peukert, Wissenschaftstheorie, op. cit., 227-229.
   - L. Kolakowski, The Alienation of Reason, Garden
   City, New York: Doubleday and Co. Inc. 1968,
   chaps. 1-8.

3. Peukert, Wissenschaftstheorie, op. cit., 227-229.
   - R. Döbert, Systemtheorie und die Entwicklung
   religiöser Deutungssysteme, Frankfurt: Suhrkamp
   Verlag 1973, 40, 152.

- Habermas, *Zwei Reden*, op. cit., 34-48.

4. Peukert, *Wissenschaftstheorie*, op. cit., 227-228.
- J. Habermas, *Legitimation Crisis*, Boston: Beacon Press 1975, 11-12.
- SW 15, 24-36.

5. Peukert, *Wissenschaftstheories*, op. cit.
- J. Habermas, *Philosophisch-politische Profile*, Frankfurt a.M.: Suhrkamp Verlag 1973, 28-29.
- Habermas, *Zwei Reden*, op. cit., 44-48.

6. Peukert, *Wissenschaftstheorie*, op. cit., 228-229.
- K. Löwith, *Die Hegelsche Linke*, Stuttgart-Bad Cannstatt: Friedrich Frommann Verlag 1962.
- Habermas, *Zwei Reden*, op. cit., 44-59.
- Habermas, *Legitimation Crisis*, op. cit., chaps. 6,7.
- Habermas, *Strukturwandel*, op. cit., chaps. I, IV.

7. Peukert, *Wissenschaftstheori*, op. cit., 228.
- J. Habermas, *Theory and Practice*, Boston: Beacon Press 1973, 189-191.
- G.W.F. Hegel, *Wissenschaft der Logik*, Stuttgart-Bad Cannstatt: Friedrich Frommann Verlag.
- SW 16, 354-356.

8. Peukert, *Wissenschaftstheorie*, op. cit., 228-229, 1964, Chap. I, (SW 5).
-G.W.F. Hegel, *Phänomenologie des Geistes*, Stuttgart-Bad Cannstatt: Friedrich Frommann Verlag 1964, 569-601, 602-620 (SW2).
- J. Habermas, *Zur Rekonstruktion des Historischen Materialismus*, Frankfurt a.M.: Suhrkamp Verlag 1976, 92-97-126.
- SW 15, 24-36.
- SW 16, 353.

9. Peukert, *Wissenschaftstheorie*, op. cit., 228-229.
- Habermas, *Profile*, op. cit., 28-29.
- R.J. Siebert, "Horkheimer's Sociology of Religion," in *Telos* 30 (Winter 1976) 127-144.
- R.J. Siebert, "The New Marxist Conception of Christianity: Hope Versus Positivism I" in the *Anglican Theological Review*, October 1977, 237-259.

10. E. Bloch, *Experimentum Mundi*, Frankfurt a.M.: Suhrkamp Verlag 1975, 206-212.
- E. Bloch, *Das Prinzip Hoffnung*, Frankfurt a.M.: Suhrkamp Verlag 1959, chaps. 53, 54, 55.

11. Peukert, *Wissenschaftstheorie*, op. cit., 228-229.

- Habermas, *Profile*, 28-29.
- J. Habermas, *Kultur und Kritik*, Frankfurt a.M.: Suhrkamp Verlag, 1973, 332-344.

12. Habermas, *Zwei Reden*, op. cit., 65-75.
    - J. Habermas, *Technik und Wissenschaft als "Ideologie"*, Frankfurt a.M.: Suhrkamp Verlag, 1976, 65-73, 73-79, 108, 137-138, 148-168.

13. Peukert, *Wissenschaftstheorie*, op. cit., 228-229.
    - J. Habermas, *Legitimation Crisis*, Boston: Beacon Press 1975, 105.
    - R.J. Siebert, "Communication without Domination", in *Concilium*, January 1978.

14. Peukert, *Wissenschaftstheorie*, op. cit., 229.
    - Metz, *Glaube*, op. cit., 7, 66, 90, 107, 117, 137, 172, 174, 208.
    - Küng, *Existiert Gott?*, op. cit., Chaps. II, III; F I.
    - Habermas, *Zur Rekonstruktion*, op. cit., 271-
    - Habermas, *Zwei Reden*, op. cit., 65-75.

Chapter II - *Religion and State*

1. SW 2, 517.
   - R.J. Siebert, *Hegel's Philosophy of History: Theological, Humanistic and Scientific Elements*, Washington, D.C.: University Press of America, 1979, chaps. I, II and III
   - R.J. Siebert, "Die Zukunft der Ehe und der Familie: Schwinden sie dahin oder strukturieren sie sich um?" *Concilium*, 141, 1979, 22-25.
   - R.J. Siebert, *Hegel's Concept of Marriage and Family: The Origin of Subjective Freedom*, Washington, D.C.: University Press of America, 1979, chaps. 1-25.
   - R.J. Siebert, "From Aquinas to Hegel: The Principle of Subjectivity" in *The Michigan Academician*, 1975, 409-436.
   - R.J. Siebert, "Hegel and the Rebellion and Counter-Rebellion of Youth" in *Perspectives*, Vol. 3, No. 2, 1971, 53-77.
   - R.J. Siebert, "Hegel and Theology", in *The Ecumenist* Vol. 12, No. 11, November-December, 1973, 1-6.
   - R.J. Siebert, "Hegel's Political Theology: Liberation", in *The Ecumenist*, XIII, No. 3, (March-April 1974) 33-41.

2. SW 15, 104-114, 114-220, 220-268, 19-22.
   - SW 16, 223-247.
   - SW 16, 327-353.
   - SW 2, 602-620.

3. SW 15, 256-267.
   - G.W.F. Hegel, *Grundlinien der Philosophie des
   Rechts*, Stuttgart-Bad Cannstatt: Friedrich Frommann
   Verlag 1964, 446-465. (SW 7)
   - G.W.F. Hegel, *Vorlesungen über die Philosophie der
   Geschichte*, Stuttgart: Fr. Frommann Verlag 1961,
   37-120, 260-264, 409-430. (SW 11)

4. SW 15, 256-267.
   - SW 7, 328-337.
   - SW 11, 70-82.

5. SW 15, 257.
   - W. Benjamin, *Illuminationen*, Frankfurt a.M.:
   Suhrkamp Verlag 1961, 280.
   - E. Bloch, *Geist der Utopie*, Frankfurt: Suhrkamp
   Verlag 1964, chaps. I, II, III, IV

6. Ibid.
   - SW 16, 207-209.
   - SW 2, 517-526.

7. SW 15, 257.
   - SW 11, 44-47.

8. SW 15, 258-260.

9. Ibid.
   - SW 5, 35-65.

10. SW 15, 258-260.
    - SW 2, 81-138.

11. SW 15, 258-260.
    - SW 7, 337-432.

12. SW 15, 258-267.

13. Ibid., 260-267.
    - G.W.F. Hegel, *Enzyklopädie*, Hamburg: Verlag von
    Felix Meiner 1959, 434-436.

14. SW 15, 258-260.

15. Ibid., 259-260.
    - SW 11, 568.

16. SW 15, 259-260.
    - SW 7, 328-446, 1-13.
    - G.W.F. Hegel, *Enzyklopädie der philosophischen Wissenschaften im Grundriss*, Stuttgart: Fr. Frommann Verlag 1956, 349-490.
    - G.W.F. Hegel, *Vermischte Schriften aus der Berliner Zeit*, Stuttgart: Fr. Fromman Verlag 1958, 473-518.

17. SW 15, 259-260.
    - J. Habermas, *Toward a Rational Society*, Boston: Beacon Press 1969, chaps. 1, 4, 5, 6.
    - Habermas, *Theory*, op. cit., chaps. 3, 5.
    - M. Horkheimer, *Notizen 1950-1969 und Dämmerung*, Frankfurt a.M.: S. Fischer Verlag 1974, 225-354.
    - K. Marx, *Die Frühschriften*, Stuttgart: Alfred Kroner Verlag 1953, chaps. III, IV, V, VI, VII, VIII, IX.
    - R.J. Siebert, "Communication sans Domination", *Concilium*, 131, 1978, 117-131.

18. SW 15, 67-68.
    - G.W.F. Hegel, *Vorlesungen über die Geschichte der Philosophie*, Stuttgart-Bad Cannstatt: Friedrich Frommann Verlag 1965, 551-611, 611-646, 646-683.
    - G.W.F. Hegel, *Jenaer Kritische Schriften*, Hamburg: Felix Meiner Verlag 1968, 5-92.
    - F. Schleiermacher, "Religion as a Faculty", in J.D. Bettis (ed.), *Phenomenology of Religion*, New York: Harper and Row, Publishers 1969, 139-168.

19. SW 15, 67-68.
    - Schleiermacher, *Religion*, op. cit., 139-168.
    - Siebert, *Hegel's Political Theology*, op. cit.
    - Metz, *Glaube*, op. cit.,
    - R.J. Siebert, "Political Theology" in *The Ecumenist*, Vol. 9, No. 5, July-August 1971, 65-71.

20. SW 15, 114, 104-114.

21. Ibid. 114, 44-64.
    - SW 11, 39-43.

22. SW 15, 227-228.

23. Ibid. 228.
    - R.B. Blackney, *Meister Eckhart*, New York: Harper and Brothers Publishers 1941, 206.

24. SW 15, 228.

25. Ibid. 271-278, 75-100.
    - SW 16, 207-209.

26. SW 15, 278.

27. Ibid.
    - Hegel, *Enzyklopädie*, op. cit., 432.
    - SW 16, 191-207.

28. SW 15, 100.
    - SW 16, 191-207, 207-218, 218-223.
    - SW 2, 569-601.

29. SW 16, 191-209.

30. Metz, *Glaube*, op. cit., 144, 149-158, 162, 193.

31. R.J. Siebert, "The New Marxist Conception of Christianity
    I", in *Anglican Theological Review*, July 1977, 237-259.
    - R.J. Siebert, "The New Religious Dimension in Western
    Marxism I", in *Horizons*, Vol. 3, No. 2, Fall 1976.
    - J.R. Siebert, "Jacob and Jesus: Recent Marxist Readings
    of the Bible", in The Bible and Liberation - Political
    and Social Hermeneutics, prepared as a radical Religious
    Reader by the Community for Religious Research and
    Education, Berkeley, California: a, 1976, 145-156.

Chapter III - Basis and Superstructure

1. E. Bloch, *On Karl Marx*, New York: Herder and Herder,
   1971, chaps. 4, 5, 8.
   - E. Bloch, *Man On His Own*, New York: Herder and
   Herder 1970, chap. I.
   - E. Fromm, *Marx's Concept of Man*, New York:
   Frederick Ungar Publishing Co. 1967, 1-83.
   - Niebuhr, *Marx*, op. cit., 41-43.
   - Marx, *Die Frühschriften*, op.cit., 339-341.
   - E. Bloch, *A Philosophy of the Future*, New York:
   Herder and Herder 1970, chap. 10.
   - SW 7, 316-317.
   - SW 15, 258-260.

2. Niebuhr, *Marx*, op. cit., 41.

3. Ibid. 41-42.

4. Ibid. 42.

5. Ibid.

6. Ibid.

7. Marx, *Das Kapital*, op. cit., 389, n. 89.

8. Ibid.
    - E. Bloch, *Man on His Own*, op. cit., chaps. I, II, III.
    - Bloch, *Experimentum Mundi*, op. cit., chap. 43.
    - E. Bloch, *On Karl Marx*, New York: Herder and Herder 1971, chaps. 4, 5, 8.
    - M. Horkheimer, *Die Sehnsucht nach dem ganz Anderen*, Hamburg: Furche Verlag 1970, 54-89.
    - E. Fromm, *The Dogma of Christ*, New York: Holt, Rinehart and Winston, 1963, 3-91.
    - E. Fromm, *You Shall be as Gods*, Greenwich, Conn.: Fawcett Publications 1960.
    - M. Horkheimer and Theodor W. Adorno, *Dialectic of Enlightenment*, New York: Seabury Press 1972, 3-80.
    - W. Schmidt, *Die Religion der Religions Kritik*, München: Claudius Verlag 1972, 28-49, 71-120.
    - J. Habermas, Dieter Henrich, *Zwei Reden*, Frankfurt a.M.: Suhrkamp Verlag 1974, 25-75.

9. Marx, *Das Kapital*, op. cit., 389, n. 89.
    - SW 15, 68

10. Marx, *Capital*, op. cit., 91.
    - Niebuhr, *Marx*, op. cit.

11. Marx, *Capital*, op. cit., 91-92.
    - SW 15, 279-324.

12. Marx, *Capital*, op. cit., 91-92.

13. Ibid. 92.
    - K. Marx, *Das Kapital*, Berlin: Dietz Verlag 1961, Bd. III, 873-874.

14. Marx, *Capital*, op. cit., 92-93,
    - G.W.F. Hegel, *Jenaer Schriften*, Berlin: Akademie Verlag 1972, 431-463.

15. Marx, *Capital*, op. cit., 93/2.

16. Schmidt, *Die Religion*, op. cit., chaps. III, IV, VIII, IX.

Chapter IV - Infinity and Finality

1. Rudolf J. Siebert, *Horkheimer's Critical Sociology of Religion: The Relative and the Transcendent*, Washington, D.C.: University of America Press 1979, ix, chaps. I, II, III, IV, V.

- M. Horkheimer and Th. W. Adorno, *Dialectic of Enlightenment*, New York: The Seabury Press 1972, 43-80, 168-208.
- Horkheimer, "Zu Theodor Haecker", op. cit., 372-382.
- M. Horkheimer, *Zur Kritik der instrumentellen Vernunft*, Frankfurt a.M.: S. Fischer Verlag 1967, 216-228, 229-238, 239-247.
- M. Horkheimer, *Critical Theory*, op. cit., chaps. II, IV, V, VI.
- M. Horkheimer, *Critique of Instrumental Reason*, New York: The Seabury Press 1974, chaps. 2, 3, 4.

2. Horkheimer, *Critical Theory*, op. cit., 129.

3. Ibid. 131.

4. Ibid.

5. Ibid.
- Kolakowski, *The Alienation*, op. cit., chaps. 1-8.
- M. Horkheimer, *Dawn and Decline, Notes 1926-1931 and 1950-1969*, New York: The Seabury Press 1978, 119-120, 125, 143, 144-145, 151-152, 173, 180-181.
- Horkheimer, *Notizen*, op. cit., 101-104, 116-117.
- Habermas, *Technik*, op. cit., 155-168.
- R.J. Siebert, "Max Horkheimer, Theology and Positivism I", in *The Ecumenist*, January-February, 1976, 19-24.
- R.J. Siebert, "Max Horkheimer, Theology and Positivism II", in *The Ecumenist*, March-April, 1976, 42-45.
- R.J. Siebert, "Horkheimer's Sociology of Religion", *Telos*, (Summer 1976), 127-144.

6. W. Post, *Kritische Theorie und Metaphysischer Pessimismum*, Munchen: Kösel Verlag 1971, 9-16, 17-43.
- M. Horkheimer, *Aus der Pubertät*, Munchen: Kosel Verlag 1974, 55-87, 91-145.

7. Horkheimer, *Aus der Pubertät*, op. cit., 7, 18, 19, 20, 21, 22, 25, 27, 29, 30, 44, 46, 47, 48.
- Horkheimer, *Zur Kritik*, op. cit., 248-268.

8. Horkheimer, *Critique*, op. cit., chap. 4.
- Horkheimer, *Aus der Pubertät*, op. cit., 7-25.
- A. Schopenhauer, *The World as Will and Representation*, New York: Dover Publications, Inc. 1969, Vol. I, First and Second Book.
- A. Schopenhauer, *The Fourfold Root of the Principle*

of Sufficient Reason, La Salle, Ill.: Open Court 1974, Chaps. I and II.
- A. Schopenhauer, Counsels and Maxims, New York: MacMillan and Co. (no year) 1-2, chap. I.

9. Horkheimer, "Zu Theodor Haecker," op. cit., 372-382.
- Th. Haecker, Der Christ und die Geschichte, Leipzig: Hegner 1935.
- K. Muth, "Satire und Polemik" in Hochland 20 (1922) 95-100.
- W. Schmarwiler, Theodor Haecker's Christliches Menschenbild, Frankfurt 1962.

10. W. Becker, "Der Überschritt von Kiergaard zu Newman in der Lebensentscheidung," in I.F. 1948, 251-270.
- Th. Haecker, Tag und Nachtbücher, Frankfurt a.M.: Suhrkamp Verlag 1975, 9-23.

11. Horkheimer, Zu Theodor Haecker, op. cit., 279-382.

12. Ibid.
- M. Reding, "Utopie, Phantasie, Prophetie-Das Prinzip der Hoffnung im Marxismus," in Frankfurter Hefte, 16. Jhrg. H.1 (Januar 1961, 11-13). (FH)

13. Horkheimer, Zu Theodor Haecker, op. cit., 380-382.

14. Ibid.

15. Ibid. 381

16. Ibid. 381-382.
- R.J. Siebert, "The Christian Revolution: Liberation and Transcendence," in The Ecumenist, (September-October 1976) 85-91.

17. Horkheimer, Zu Theodor Haecker, op. cit., 381-382.

18. Ibid.
- H. Mayer, "Nachdenken uber Adorno," in FH 25, 4 (April 1970), 268-280, esp. 280.
- J. Habermas, Zur Rekonstruktion des Historischen Materialismus, Frankfurt a.M.: Suhrkamp Verlag, chap. 4.

19. Horkheimer, "Zu Theodor Haecker," op. cit., 381-382.

20. Ibid.

21. Ibid.
- M. Horkheimer, Die Sehnsucht nach dem ganz Anderen,

Hamburg: Furche Verlag 1971, 83-89.

22. Horkheimer, Zu Theodor Haecker, op. cit., 381-382.

23. Ibid.
   - P. Tillich, *Der Mutzum Sein*, Stuttgart:Steingrüben Verlag, 1954.

Chapter V - Realistic Humanism

1. W. Benjamin, *Angelus Novus*, Frankfurt a.M.: Suhrkamp Verlag 1972, 467-474; 185-189; 517-519.
   - Th. Haecker, *Vergil, Vater des Abendlandes*, Leipzig: Verlag Jacob Hegner 1931, 457-461, 404-407, 384-395, 396-403.
   - W. Benjamin, *Briefe*, Frankfurt a.M.: Suhrkamp Verlag 1966, II 725-726; 512-513, 736-737.
   - W. Benjmain, *Charles Baudelaire: A Lyric Poet in the Era of High Capitalism*, London: New Left Books 1973, 157-176.
   - W. Benjamin, *Illuminationen*, Frankfurt a.M.: Suhrkamp Verlag 1961, 319, 280-281, 409-436.
   - W. Benjamin, *Ursprung des deutschen Trauerspiels*, Frankfurt a.M.: Suhrkamp Verlag 1963, 257-262, 174-211, 149-173.
   - W. Benjamin, *Gesammelte Schriften*, Frankfurt a.M.: Suhrkamp Verlag 1974, I, 2, 693-704, III, 275-278, IV, 1, 409-416.
   - W. Benjamin, *Berliner Chronik*, Frankfurt a.M.: Suhrkamp Verlag 1970, 115-122, 123-134.

2. Benjamin, *Illuninationen*, op. cit., 439-443.
   - R.G.L. Waite, *The Psychopithic God Adolf Hitler*, New York, N.Y.: New American Library 1977, chaps. I, II.
   - E. Fromm, *The Anatomy of Human Destructiveness*, New York: Rinehart and Winston 1973, chap. 13.

3. Benjamin, *Angelus Novus*, op. cit., 467-471.

4. Ibid.
   - SW 16, 156-188.

5. Benjamin, *Angelus Novus*, op. cit., 467-471.
   - Benjamin, *Briefe* ,op. cit., 725-726.
   - Horkheimer, Zu Theodor Haecker, op. cit., 372-382.

6. Benjamin, *Angelus Novus*, op. cit., 471.
   - G.W.F. Hegel, *Vorlesungen über die Geschichte der Philosophie*, Stuttgart-Bad Cannstatt: Friedrich Frommann Verlag 1965, III, 173-174, 180-190. (SW 17, 18, 19).

- R.J. Siebert, "From Aquinas to Hegel: The Principle of Subjectivity" in *The Michigan Academician*, VIII, No. 4 (Spring 1975) 409-436.

7. Benjamin, *Angelus Novus*, op. cit., 471-474.

8. Ibid.
- W. Dirks, and others, "Zu Reinhold Schneider's autobiographischen Schriften" in *FH* 33, 11 (November 1978, 52-52).

9. Benjamin, *Angelus Novus*, op. cit., 471-474.
- H. Marcuse, *Reason and Revolution*, Boston: Beacon Press 1969, 412-413, 418-419.
- C. Schmitt, *Begriff des Politischen*, Munchen 1932, 50.
- C. Schmitt, *Staat, Bewegung, Volk*, Hamburg 1933, 12.

10. Benjamin, *Angelus Novus*, op. cit., 472-473.
- SW 16, 257-277.
- M. Horkheimer, *Die Sehnsucht nach dem ganz Anderen*, Hamburg: Furche Verlag 1971, 64-67.
- Schopenhauer, *The World*, op. cit., I. 329, 407; II, 580, 604-605, 620-621, 638.
- H. Mayer, "Nachdenken uber Adorno" in *FH* 25, 4 (April 1970) 268-280.
- H. Scheible, "Max Horkheimer's fruhe und spate Aufzeichnungen" in *FH* 33, 6 (June 1978) 50-54.

11. Benjamin, *Angelus Novus*, op. cit., 472-474.

12. Benjamin, *Illuminationen*, op. cit., 443.

13. Benjamin, *Illuminationen*, op. cit., 280-281.

14. Benjamin, *Gesammelte Schriften*, op. cit., I, 2, 693-704.
- W.F. Schoeller (ed.) *Die Neue Linke*, Munchen: Kindler Verlag 1969, 168-173, esp. 171.
- Benjamin, *Briefe*, op. cit., 671-683, esp. 676.

15. Schoeller, *Die Neue Linke*, op. cit., 170-173.
- Benjamin, *Briefe*, op. cit., 663, 351, 355, 663, 671-673, 676, 664; 520-522, 602-603, 641-643, 656-658.

16. H. Küng, *Existiert Gott?* München: R. Piper and Co. Verlag 1978, 18, 363-367, 376-379, 539, 540-542, 553, 559, 613, 616-167, 619, 673, 724, 756, 760, 804, 805, 828, 853, 857, 372, 377, 539-540, 559, 805, 822, 828, 831; 533, 559, 615, 617-618,

818, 827, 838; 331, 356-361, 609-610, 801, 803, 816, 837; 137, 511, 601, 636-638, 779, 822, 823, 831, 836, 839, 840.
- Metz, *Glaube*, op. cit., 44, 91, 99, 107, 152, 154, 171, 182-184; 34, 43, 52, 206; 34, 43, 62, 67, 94, 107-108, 113-114, 171-172, 183, 191, 206; 67, 96, 107, 171; 114; 7, 66, 90, 107, 117, 137, 172, 174, 208.
- Peukert, *Wissenschaftstheorie*, op. cit., 227-229; 278-282.
- R.J. Siebert, "Religion in the Perspective of Critical Sociology" in *Concilium*, I, No. 10 (January 1974) 56-59.
- R.J. Siebert, "The Christian Revolution: Liberation and Transcendence" in *The Ecumenist*, (September-October 1976), 85-91.
- R.J. Siebert, "Max Horkheimer: Theology and Positivism I" in *The Ecumenist*, XIV, No. 3, (March-April 1976)
- R.J. Siebert, "Max Horkheimer: Theology and Positivism II" in *The Ecumenist*, XIV, No. 5, (July-August 1976)
- R.J. Siebert, "Horkheimer's Sociology of Religion" in *Telos*, (Summer 1976)
- R.J. Siebert, "Fromm's Theory of Religion", in *Telos*, (Summer 1977).
- R.J. Siebert, "Hans Küng: Toward a Negative Theology", in *The Ecumenist*, (July-August 1979)
- R.J. Siebert, "Peukert's New Critical Theology I" in *The Ecumenist*, (May-June 1978) 52-58.
- R.J. Siebert, "Peukert's New Critical Theology II" in *The Ecumenist*, (July-August 1978) 78-80.

Chapter VI - Beyond Ideology Critique

1. Habermas, *Theory*, op. cit., 189-191.
    - R.J. Siebert, Christian Revolution, op. cit. 85-91.
    - R.J. Siebert, "Communication Sans Domination" in *Concilium*, 131, 1978, 117-131.
    - R.J. Siebert, "Habermas's Critical Theory of Religion" in *Telos*, 1979.
    - Siebert, *Horkheimer's Critical Sociology*, op. cit., Chaps. VII, VIII.

2. Ibid.
    - Siebert, *Hegel's Philosophy of History*, op. cit., Chap. I.
    - Löwith, *Die Hegelsche Linke*, op. cit., 1-20.

3. Habermas, *Theory*, op. cit., 190.
    - SW 15, 24-34.

- SW 16, 353-356.

4. Habermas, *Theory*, op. cit., 190.
- P. Tillich, *The Socialist Decision*, New York: Harper and Row, 1977, part one and two.

5. SW 7, 5-8.
- R.J. Siebert, *Hegel's Philosophy of History*, op. cit., chap. I.

6. Habermas, *Theory*, op. cit., 190.
- SW 17, 306-316.

7. Habermas, *Theory*, op. cit., 190-191
- SW 16, 353-356.

8. Habermas, *Theory*, op. cit., 190.
- SW 16, 355.

9. Habermas, *Theory*, op. cit., 190.

10. SW 16, 354-356, 223-247, 247-308, 308-356.
- SW 2, 18-20, 569-601.

11. Habermas, *Theory*, op. cit., 190-191.

12. Ibid.
- SW 16, 356.

13. Habermas, *Theory*, op. cit., 191.
- SW 16, 356

14. Habermas, *Theory*, op. cit., 190-191.
- SW 16, 354, 247-308, 308-354.
- SW 2, 18-20, 569-601.
- SW 18, 429-473.

15. SW 16, 354.
- R.J. Siebert, "Hegel's Philosophy of History: Its Historical Consequences," in the *Encyclopaedia Moderna*, (June 1977)
- Siebert, *Hegel's Philosophy of History*, op. cit., chaps. I1, III.

16. SW 16, 247-308, 308-356, esp. 354-355.

17. Ibid., 355-356.
- SW 11, 129, 149.
- G.W.F. Hegel, *Ästhetik*, Frankfurt a.M.: Europäische Verlagsanstalt GmbH 1951, Bd. II, 423.
- Siebert, *Horkheimer's Critical Sociology of Religion*

op. cit., chap. IX.

18. Habermas, *Theory*, op. cit., 235-236.
   - SW 19, 646-683
   - SW 16, 298-300, 354-355
   - SW 11, 88-120.

19. Habermas, *Theory*, op. cit., 236.
   - SW 11, 42, 48-50.

20. Habermas, *Theory*, op. cit., 236-237.

21. Ibid.
   - K. Marx, *The 18th Brumaire of Louis Bonaparte*,
   New York: International Publishers 1972, 15-26,
   26-41.

22. Habermas, *Theory*, op. cit., 239
   - Habermas, *Philosophisch-politische Profile*, op.
   cit., 147-167.
   - Marx, *Die Frühschriften*, op. cit., 339-341, esp.
   340.

23. Habermas, *Theory*, op. cit., 239.
   - Marx, *Die Frühschriften*, op. cit., 340.
   - SW 7, 310-323, esp. 320, 261-286.

24. Habermas, *Theory*, op. cit., 239.
   - SW 7, 310-323.

25. Habermas, *Theory*, op. cit., 239-240.
   - Bloch, *Man*, op. cit., chaps. III, IV, V, VI,
   VIII.
   - SW 7, 35-37.

26. Habermas, *Theory*, op. cit., 239-240.
   - Siebert, *Horkheimer's Critical Sociology*, op.
   cit., chaps. VIII, IX.

27. Habermas, *Theory*, op. cit., 239-240.
   - M. Jay, *The Dialectical Imagination*, Boston:
   Little, Brown and Co., 1973, xii.
   - SW 16, 46-95, 191-356.
   - SW 15, 342-254, 355-400, 400-417.

28. Habermas, *Zur Rekonstruktion*, op. cit., chap. 4.
   - SW 17, 22, 38-48, 48-57, 58-80.
   - Habermas, *Legitimation Crisis*, op. cit., part III,
   chap. 2.
   - Jürgen Habermas/Niklas Luhmann, *Theorie der Gesellscheft
   oder Sozialtechnologie - Was leistet die Systemforschung*,

Frankfurt a.M.: Suhrkamp Verlag 1975, 221-238.
- SW 16, 207-209.
- Siebert, *Horkheimer's Critical Sociology of Religion*, op. cit., chaps. I, II.

29. Habermas, *Zur Rekonstruktion*, op. cit., chaps. 3 and 4; part IV.
- Habermas, *Legitimation Crisis*, op. cit., part III.
- Habermas, *Theorie der Gesellschaft*, op. cit., 101-141, 142-146, 171-202.

Chapter VII - The Identity Crisis

1. Habermas, *Zwei Reden*, op. cit., 34-41.
- J. Habermas, "On Social Identity" in *Telos*, (Spring 1974) 91-103.
- Habermas, *Zur Rekonstruktion*, op. cit., 63-91, 92-126; part IV.
- Habermas, *Technik*, op. cit., 65-73.
- Habermas, *Legitimation Crisis*, op. cit., 17-31.

· 2. Habermas, *Zwei Reden*, op. cit., 35-36.
- SW 15, **278**; 279-324, 434-437, 437-472.

3. Habermas, *Zwei Reden*, op. cit., 36-37.
- SW 15, **324-342**, 342-354, 355-400, 400-417, 417-434, 434-437, 437-472.

4. Habermas, *Zwei Reden*, op. cit., 36-37
- SW 16, **95-156**, 156-188.
- SW 15, **324-472**.
- SW 16, **95-156**, 247-308.

5. Habermas, *Zwei Reden*, op. cit., 36-37.
- SW 16, **95-156**.
- Habermas, *Zur Rekonstruktion*, op. cit., chap. 4.

6. Habermas, *Zwei Reden*, op. cit., 36-37.
- Habermas, *Zur Rekonstruktion*, op. cit., chap. 4.
- SW 15, **434-437**.
- SW 16, **95-156**.

7. J. Habermas, *Technik und Wissenschaft als Ideologie*, Frankfurt a.M.: Suhrkamp Verlag 1976, 9-47.
- Habermas, *Zwei Reden*, op. cit., 36-37.
- Habermas, *Theory*, op. cit., Chap. 4.
- G.W.F. Hegel, *Jenaer System Entwurf I*, Hamburg 1975, 282-326.
- G.W.F. Hegel, *Jenaer Schriften*, Berlin: Akademic Verlag 1972, 431-520

8. Habermas, *Theory*, op. cit., chap. 4
   - Habermas, *Zwei Reden*, op. cit., 36-37
   - Habermas, *Technik*, op. cit., 9-47

9. Habermas, *Zwei Reden*, op. cit., 36-37
   - Habermas, *Zur Rekonstruktion*, op. cit., 92-126
   - SW 15, 342-472
   - SW 16, 46-188

10. Habermas, *Zwei Reden*, op. cit., 36-37
    - SW 18, 42-122
    - R.J. Siebert, *Hegel's Concept of Marriage and Family: The Origin of Subjective Freedom*, Washington, D.C.: University Press of America, chaps. 1-3.

11. Habermas, *Zwei Reden*, op. cit., 36-37.
    - SW 15, 417-421
    - Siebert, *Hegel's Concept*, op. cit., chapter 1-3

12. Habermas, *Zwei Reden*, op. cit., 36-37.
    - Habermas, *Zur Rekonstruktion*, op. cit., chap. 4

13. Habermas, *Zwei Reden*, op. cit., 36-37.
    - SW 7, 182-183, 265-267
    - SW 11, 44-47, 409-430
    - Hegel, *Enzyklopädie*, op. cit., 387-388.
    - Siebert, *Hegel's Concept*, op. cit., chaps. 1, 2, 3, 7, 18, 31.
    - H. Küng, *Menschwerdung Gottes*, Freiburg: Herder 1970, chaps. I, II, III, V, VI, VII.
    - M. Theunissen, *Hegel's Lehre vom absoluten Geist als theologisch-politischer Traktat*, Berlin: Walter de Bruyter and Co. 1970, 60-100

14. SW 11, 44-47
    - Siebert, *Hegel's Philosophy of History*, op. cit., chap. II
    - Siebert, *Hegel's Concept*, op. cit., chaps. 1-3, 18, 31

15. SW 7, 265-267.
    - Hegel, *Enzyklopädie*, op. cit., 388.
    - Siebert, *Hegel's Philosophy of History*, op. cit., chap. I

16. SW 11, 45-46.
    - SW 16, 247-308, 308-353
    - Hegel, *Enzyklopädie*, op. cit., 387-388.

17. Habermas, *Zwei Reden*, op. cit., 37-38.
    - Habermas, *Zur Kritik*, op. cit., chap. 4

18. Habermas, *Zwei Reden*, op. cit., 37-38.
    - SW 7, 266.
    - Hegel, *Enzyklopädie*, op. cit., 388.
19. Habermas, *Zwei Reden*, op. cit., 38.
    - Habermas, *Legimitmation Crisis*, op. cit., 117-130.
    - Horkheimer, *Zur Kritik*, op. cit., 239-247.
    - Siebert, *Hegel's Concept*, op. cit., chap. 1.
    - Hegel, *Enzyklopädie*, op. cit., 388.
    - SW 16, 300/1, 247-308, 308-356.
    - Horkheimer, *Dawn*, op. cit., 168-170.
20. Habermas, *Zwei Reden*, op. cit., 38.
    - SW 16, 308-356.
21. Habermas, *Zwei Reden*, op. cit., 38.
    - Habermas, *Zur Rekonstruktion*, op. cit., chap. 4.
22. Habermas, *Zwei Reden*, op. cit., 38-39.
    - Habermas, *Technik*, op. cit., 65-73.
    - Habermas, *Theorie der Gesellschaft*, op. cit., 239-269.
23. Habermas, *Zwei Reden*, op. cit., 39-40.
    - Habermas, *Zur Rekonstruktion*, op. cit., chap. 4
24. Habermas, *Zwei Reden*, op. cit., 40
    - Habermas, *Zur Rekonstruktion*, op. cit., chap. 4
    - SW 15, 22-26.
    - SW 16, 353-356
24. Habermas, *Zwei Reden*, op. cit., 40
    - Habermas, "Legitimation Crisis", op. cit., 121.
    - T. Rendtorff, *Theorie des Christentums*, Gutersloh, 1972, 96-98.
    - J.B. Metz, *Theology of the World*, New York: The Seabury Press 1973, Part III.
    - E. Düssel, *Filosofía de la Liberación*, Mexico, 1977, 11-24.
    - G. Gutierrez, *A Theology of Liberation*, New York, 1973, part I.
    - Tillich, *The Socialist Decision*, op. cit., ixxxvixxxi-xxxvii.
    - Peukert, *Diskussion*, op. cit., 231-246, 247-266, 267-301, 302-317
    - E. Kogon (ed.), "Revolution und Theologie-Das Neue in unserem Zeitalter/Ein Symposion," in *FH*, 22, 9, (September 1967) 619-630.
    - W. Kasper, "Politische Utopie und Christliche Hoffnung," in *FH*, 24, 8, (August 1969) 563-572.
    - E. Höflich, "Karl Marx fur die Kirche," in *FH* 24,

11, (November 1969) 777-735.
- E. Hoflich, "Heilsverkundigung als politische
Gewissensbildung," in *FH* 24, 12 (December 1969)
843-854
- W. Pannenberg, *Gottesgedanken und menschliche
Freiheit*, Gottingen: Vandenhoeck und Ruprecht 1972,
chaps. II, IV, V.
- R.J. Siebert, "Political Theology," in *The Ecumenist*,
July-August 1971, 55-71.
- R.J. Siebert, "Hegel's Political Theology:
Liberation", in *The Ecumenist*, March-April 1974,
33-40.
- R.J. Siebert, "Christian Revolution: Liberation
and Transcendence," in *The Ecumenist*, (September
October 1976), 85-91.
- Metz, *Glaube*, o'. cit., part II and III.

26. Schmidt, *Die Religion*, op. cit., chaps, III, IV, VIII,
IX.
- Siebert, "Horkheimer's Sociology", op. cit., 127-
144.
- Siebert, "Religion in the Perspective of Critical
Sociology, op. cit., 59-59
- Siebert, *Horkheimer's Critical Sociology of Religion*,
op. cit., chaps. IV, V, VI.

27. Habermas, *Legitimation Crisis*, op. cit., 121.
- Habermas, *Zwei Reden*, op. cit., 40.
- Habermas, *Zur Rekonstruktion*, op. cit., chap. 4.

28. Habermas, *Legitimation Crisis*, op. cit., 121.
- Peukert, *Wissenschaftstheorie*, op. cit., 315-323.
- Peukert, *Diskussion*, op. cit., chap. V.
- Metz, *Glaube*, op. cit., 47-48, 57-59, 64-65, 68-69,
72-74, 101-103, 109-110, 117-118, 126-127, 209-210.

29. Peukert, *Wissenschaftstheorie*, op. cit., 13, 227-229.
- Siebert, *Peukert's New Critical Theology*, op. cit.,
52-58, 78-80.

30. Peukert, *Wissenschaftstheorie*, op. cit., 13, 278-280.
- W. Benjamin, *Gesammelte Schriften 1, 2*, Frankfurt
a.M.: Suhrkamp Verlag 1974, 693-704.
- Benjamin, *Illuminationen*, op. cit., 280-281.
- Benjamin, *Gesammelte Schriften*, op. cit., I, 693-
704.

31. Habermas, *Zwei Reden*, op. cit., 41.
- Habermas, *Zur Rekonstruktion*, op. cit., chap. 4.

32. Habermas, *Zwei Reden*, op. cit., 41.

- Marx, *Capital*, op. cit., 91-92.
- Marx, *Das Kapital*, op. cit., 873-874.

33. Habermas, *Zwei Reden*, op. cit., 41-42.
    - Habermas, "On Social Identity", op. cit., 94.
    - SW 15, 24-36, 256-267.
    - SW 16, 354-356.

34. Habermas, "On Social Identity", op. cit., 94.
    - G.W.F. Hegel, *Wissenschaft der Logik*, Stuttgart-
    Bad Cannstatt: Friedrich Frommann Verlag, 1965,
    132-139 (SW 4).

35. Habermas, "On Social Identity", op. cit., 94.
    - Th. W. Adorno, E. Kogon, "Offenbarung oder autonome
    Vernunft," in *FH*, 13, 7, Juli 1958, 486-488.

36. Habermas, "On Social Identity", op. cit., 94.
    - Habermas, *Zur Rekonstruktion*, op. cit., chap. 4.

37. - A. Schmidt, *Zur Idee der Kritischen Theorie*,
    Munchen: Carl Hanser Verlag 1974, 141-142.
    - Post, *Kritische Theorie*, op. cit., 97-153.
    - Siebert, *Horkheimer's Critical Sociology of
    Religion*, op. cit., chap. IX.

38. Schmidt, *Zur Idee*, op. cit., 141-142.
    - M. Horkheimer and Th. W. Adorno, *Dialectic of
    Enlightenment*, New York: The Seabury Press 1972,
    chaps. I, IV, V.
    - Siebert, *Horkheimer's Critical Sociology of
    Religion*, op. cit., chap. IX.

39. Schmidt, *Zur Idee*, op. cit., 141-142.
    - Horkheimer, *Dialectic*, op. cit., V.
    - Horkheimer, *Notizen*, op. cit., 101-104, 116-117.

40. R.J. Siebert, "Communication", op. cit., 117-131.

41. Schmidt, *Zur Idee*, op. cit., 141-142.
    - Siebert, *Horkheimer's Critical Sociology*, op. cit.,
    chaps. I, II, III, VIII.

42. Schmidt, *Zur Idee*, op. cit., 141-142.
    - Horkheimer, *Die Sehnsucht*, op. cit., 83-89.
    - Jay, *Dialectical Imagination*, op. cit. XI-XII.
    - H. Marcuse, *One Dimensional Man*, Boston: Beacon
    Press 1966, chaps. 1-7.
    - E. Fromm, *The Revolution of Hope*, New York: Harper
    and Row, Publishers, 1968, chap III.

43. Schmidt, *Zur Idee*, op. cit., 141-142.
   - Horkheimer, *Die Sehnsucht*, op. cit., 54-89.

44. Horkheimer, *Die Sehnsucht*, op. cit., 88-89.
   - H.C.F. Mansilla, "Swei Begegnungen in der Schweitz," in *FH*, 28, 4, 239-240.
   - Siebert, "Horkheimer's Sociology", op. cit., 127-144.
   - Siebert *Horkheimer's Critical Sociology*, op. cit., chap. IV.

45. Schmidt, *Zur Idee*, op. cit., 141-142.
   - Horkheimer, *Die Sehnsucht*, op. cit., 61.

46. Schmidt, *Zur Idee*, op. cit., 141-142.
   - Horkheimer, *Die Sehnsucht*, op. cit., 61-62.

47. Schmidt, *Zur Idee*, op. cit., 141-142.
   - Horkheimer, *Die Sehnsucht*, op. cit., 54-62.

48. Horkheimer, *Die Sehnsucht*, op. cit., 54-71.
   - Siebert, *Horkheimer's Critical Sociology*, op. cit., IV, V, VI.

49. Schmidt, *Zur Idee*, op. cit., 142.
   - Seibert, *Horkheimer's Critical Sociology*, op. cit., chaps. IV-VII.

50. Schmidt, *Zur Idee*, op. cit., 142.
   - Siebert, "Horkheimer's Sociology," op. cit., 127-144.
   - Siebert, *Horkheimer's Critical Sociology*, op. cit., chaps. IV, IX.

51. Habermas, "On Social Identity", op. cit., 95-103.
   - Horkheimer, *Kritik*, op. cit., 248-268.
   - Horkheimer, *Die Sehnsucht*, op. cit., 64-89.

52. Horkheimer, *Die Sehnsucht*, 54-62.
   - Habermas, *Zur Rekonstruktion*, op. cit., chap. 4

53. Th. W. Adorno, E. Kogon, "Offenbarung oder autonome Vernunft", in *FH*, 13, 6, June 1958, 392-402.
   - Horkheimer, *Die Sehnsucht*, op. cit., 57-59.

54. Habermas, *Zwei Reden*, op. cit., 41-42.

55. Ibid.

56. SW 15, 24-34.
   - SW 16, 247-277

- SW 19, 368-411

57. Habermas, "On Social Identity", op. cit., 95.
    - Habermas, *Zur Rekonstruktion*, op. cit., 42-45.

58. Habermas, *Zwei Reden*, op. cit., 42-45.
    - SW 15, 34-36, 256-267.

59. Habermas, "Social Identity," op. cit., 95.
    - Habermas, *Zur Rekonstruktion*, op. cit., chap. 4.

60. G. Lukacs, *Der Junge Hegel*, Neuwied: Hermann
    Luchterhand Verlag 1948, chaps. I, II, III.

61. Hegel, *Ästhetik*, op. cit., II, 461.

62. SW 7, 266-267.
    - Hegel, *Enzyklopädie*, op. cit., 387-388.
    - Siebert, *Hegel's Philosophy*, op. cit., Chaps. II,
    III.

63. SW 7, 182-183.
    - Siebert, *Hegel's Philosophy*, op. cit., chap. III.
    - Seibert, *Hegel's Concept*, op. cit., chap I.
    - Siebert, *Horkheimer's Critical Sociology*, op. cit.,
    chap. VII

64. SW 7, 2650267.

65. Ibid. 266-267.

66. Ibid.
    - Hegel, *Ästhetik*, op. cit., II, 423.
    - SW 11, 129.
    - SW 16, 354-356.

67. Hegel, *Ästhetik*, op. cit., II, 423.

68. Habermas, *Zwei Reden*,
    - Habermas, *Zur Rekonstruktion*,

69. Habermas, *Zwei Reden*, op. cit., 45-46.
    - Hegel, *Enzyklopädie*, op. cit., 440-441.
    - SW 6, 301-310.
    - SW 2, 569-620.
    - SW 16, 308-354.

70. Habermas, "Social Identity", op. cit., 96.
    - Habermas, *Zur Rekonstruktion*, op. cit., chap. 4.

71. Habermas, *Zwei Reden*, op. cit., 47-48.

- Siebert, *Hegel's Philosophy*, op. cit., chaps. II, III.
72. Habermas, *Zwei Reden*, op. cit., 47-48.
    - Hegel, *Enzyklopädie*, op. cit., 316.
73. SW 16, 300-308.
    - SW 2, 572, 577-601.
74. Kung, *Menschwerdung*, op. cit., 69-70.
    - Siebert, *Hegel's Philosophy*, op. cit., chap. II.
75. Habermas, *Zwei Reden*, op. cit., 49-50.
    - SW 15, 256-267
    - SW 7, 328-337.
76. Habermas, *Zwei Reden*, op. cit., 49-50.
    - Habermas, "Social Identity", op. cit., 96-99.
    - Habermas, *Zur Rekonstruktion*, op. cit., chap. 4.
77. Hegel, *Enzyklopädie*, op. cit., 433.
    - SW 16, 218-223.
    - SW 11, 69-82.
    - Seibert, *Hegel's Philosophy*, op. cit., Chap. IV.
78. Küng, *Menschwerdung*, op. cit., 522-557.
    - Siebert, *Hegel's Philosophy*, op. cit., chap.II.
79. Hegel, *Enzyklopädie*, op. cit., 433.
80. Habermas, *Zwei Reden*, op. cit., 65-68.
    - Habermas, *Zur Rekonstruktion*, op. cit., chap. 4.
81. Habermas, *Zwei Reden*, op. cit., 66-68.
    - SW 15, 259-260.
    - Habermas, "Social Identity", op. cit., 99.
82. Habermas, "Social Identity", op. cit., 99-100.
    - Hegel, *Enzyklopädie*, op. cit., 433.
83. Hegel, *Enzyklopädie*, op. cit., 433.
    - SW 16, 218-223.
84. Habermas, *Zwei Reden*, op. cit., 68-69.
    - Habermas, *Zur Rekonstruktion*, op. cit., chap. 4.
85. Habermas, *Zwei Reden*, op. cit., 68-69.
    - SW 15, 256-267.
86. Habermas, "Social Identity", op. cit., 100.
    - Habermas, *Zur Rekonstruktion*, op. cit., chap. 4.

87. Habermas, Social Identity, op. cit., 100.
     - SW 15, 342-472, 44-75, 75-100.
     - SW 16, 46-188, 223-356.

88. Habermas, Social Identity, op. cit., 100.
     - SW 15, 24-36.
     - H. Küng, Being a Christian, Garden City, New York:
     Doubleday and Co. Inc., 1976, parts A, D.

Chapter VIII - Communications Community

1.   Habermas, Zwei Reden, op. cit., 71-75.
     - Habermas, Social Identity, op. cit., 102.
     - Habermas, Zur Rekonstruktion, op. cit., chap. 4.

2.   Habermas, Social Identity, op. cit., 103.
     - Habermas, Zwei Reden, op. cit., 74-75.
     Habermas, Zur Rekonstruktion, op. cit., chap. 4.

3.   Habermas, Zwei Reden, op. cit., 75.
     - Habermas, Legitimation Crisis, op. cit., 105.
     - Habermas, Zur Rekonstruktion, op. cit., chap. 4.

4.   Habermas, Legitimation Crisis, op. cit., 105.

5.   Ibid.
     - J. Habermas, Theorie der Gesellschaft oder
     Socialtechnologie, Frankfurt a.M.:   Suhrkamp Verlag
     1975, 279-290.
     - J. Habermas, Kultur und Kritik, Frankfurt a.M.:
     Suhrkamp Verlag 1973, chaps. I, II, IV.

6.   Habermas, Legitimation Crisis, op. cit., 110-111.

7.   Ibid., 130-131.
     - Habermas, Theorie der Gesellschaft, op. cit.,
     326-328.
     - Habermas/Luhmann, Theorie der Gesellschaft, op.
     cit., 291-405.

8.   Habermas, Legitimation Crisis, op. cit., 110-111.

9.   Ibid.
     - K.O. Apel, "Das Apriori der Kommunikationsgemeinschaft
     and die Ethik" in Transformation der Philosophie,
     2: 358:360, 420-421.

10. Habermas, Legitimation Crisis, op. cit., 105-110-111.
     - Horkheimer, Zur Kritik, op. cit., 248-268.

11. Bloch, Man, op. cit., chaps. II, VIII.

- J. Habermas, ed., *Antworten auf Herbert Marcuse*, Frankfurt a.M.: Suhrkamp Verlag 1969, 9-16.
- Habermas, *Philosophisch-politische Profile*, op. cit., chaps. 6, 7.
- E. Fromm, *The Revolution of Hope*, New York: Harper and Row Publishers 1968, chap. VI.

12. Post, *Kritische Therie*, op. cit., 136-153.
    - Schmidt, *Zur Idee*, op. cit., 137-142.
    - Siebert, "Horkheimer's Sociology", op. cit., 127-412.
    - Mansilla, "Zwei Begegnungen," op. cit., 239-240.

13. Schmidt, *Die Religion*, op. cit., chaps. VII, IX.

14. Niebuhr, *Marx*, op. cit., 41-42.
    - Horkheimer, *Critical Theory*, op. cit., 129-131.
    - Horkheimer, "Zu Theodor Haecker" op. cit., 378-382.

15. H. Ley, etc., *Kritische Vernunft und Revolution*, Koln: Pahl-Regenstein, 1971, 9-12, 234-263.

16. Habermas, *Legitimation Crisis*, op. cit., 77-78.

17. SW 19, 169.
    - SW 15, 227-228.

18. Habermas, *Legitimation Crisis*, op. cit., 77

19. Habermas, *Legitimation Crisis*, op. cit., 78.

20. Ibid.
    Adorno, "Offenbarung," op. cit., 397-398.
    - W. Benjamin, *Schriften I*,

21. Habermas, *Legitimation Crisis*, op. cit., 78-79.

22. Ibid., 118-119.
    - Th. F. O'Dea, *The Sociology of Religion*, Englewood Cliffs, N.J.: Prentice Hall, Inc. 1966, chap. I
    - Habermas/Luhmann, *Theorie der Gesellschaft*, op. cit., 171-202.

23. Habermas, *Legitimation Crisis*, op. cit., 119.

24. Ibid.
    - Niebuhr, *Marx*, op. cit., 41-42.

25. Habermas, *Legitimation Crisis*, op. cit., 119-120.

26. Ibid.
    - Horkheimer, *Dialectic*, op. cit., 3-42, 43-80.

27. Habermas, *Legitimation Crisis*, op. cit., 119.
    - O'Dea, *Sociology*, op. cit., 11-13.
    - SW 15, 24-34.

28. Habermas, *Legitimation Crisis*, op. cit., 119-120.

29. Horkheimer, *Die Sehnsucht*, op. cit., 81-89.
    - Siebert, *Horkheimer's Critical Sociology*, op. cit.,
    IX.

30. H. Marcuse, *One Dimensional Man*, Boston: Beacon
    Press 1966, chaps. 1-4.
    - Fromm, *The Revolution*, op. cit., chap. III

31. Horkheimer, *Die Sehnsucht*, op. cit., 81-89.
    - Siebert, *Horkheimer's Critical Sociology*, op. cit. IX.

32. Habermas, *Legitimation Crisis*, op. cit., 117-130.
    - Horkheimer, *Dawn*, op. cit., 132, 133, 125-126, 141,
    160, 168, 229, 227.

33. Ibid. 119-120.

34. Ibid.

35. R.J. Siebert, "Horkheimer's Sociology", op. cit.,
    129-130.
    - B.F. Skinner, *Beyond Dignity and Freedom*, New York:
    Knopf 1971.

36. Küng, *Existiert Gott*, op. cit., C, D, E.
    - Metz, *Glaube*, op. cit., part I.
    - Siebert, *Peukert's New Critical Theology*, op. cit.,
    52-58.

37. Habermas, *Legitimation Crisis*, op. cit., 120-121.

38. Ibid., 121.

39. Ibid.
    - Metz, *Theology*, op. cit., 107-155.
    - Gutierrez, *A Theology*, op. cit., part 4.
    - I. Fetscher, etc. (ed.), *Marxisten und die Sache
    Jesu*, Munchen: Kaise-Grunewald 1974, 7-16, chap. I.
    - Peukert, *Wissenschaftstheorie*, op. cit., 303-323.
    - Metz, *Glaube*, op. cit., part II, III.

40. Habermas, *Legitimation Crisis*, op. cit., 121.
    - Habermas, *Zwei Reden*, op. cit., 40-41.

- H.E. Bahr, (ed.), *Religionsgespräche Zur gesellschaftlichen Rolle der Religion*, Darmstadt: Hermann Luchterhand Verlag 1975, 9-30.

41. Bahr, *Religionsgespräche* op. cit., 3-30.
    - Adorno, "Offenbarung," op. cit., 484-498.
    - Horkheimer, *Die Sehnsucht*, op. cit., 68-69.
    - Schmidt, *Die Religion*, op. cit. CH. III,IV,VII,VIII,IX.

42. Habermas, *Legitimation Crisis*, op. cit., 121-122.

43. Ibid.
    - J. Habermas, *Knowledge and Human Interests*, Boston: Beacon Press, 1971, part II.

44. Habermas, *Legitimation Crisis*, op. cit., 121-122, 105.
    - Siebert, "Hegel's Political Theology", op. cit., 33-40.
    - Siebert, "Political Theology," op. cit., 65-71.
    - Siebert, "Christian Revolution", op. cit., 85-91.
    - Kasper, "Politische Utopie," op. cit., 563-572.
    - Siebert, *Horkheimer's Critical Sociology*, op. cit., chap. 9.
    - Siebert, *Hegel's Concept*, op. cit., chaps. 5, 7, 8, 21, 25.
    - Siebert, *Hegel's Philosophy of History*, op. cit., chaps. I, II.

45. Habermas, *Legitimation Crisis*, op. cit., 122.

46. Ibid.
    - Horkheimer, *Die Sehnsucht*, op. cit., 81-89.
    - Fromm, *The Revolution*, op. cit., 27-32.
    - Marcuse, *One-Dimensional Man*, op. cit., chaps. 1-7.

47. Horkheimer, *Die Sehnsucht*, op. cit., 88-89, 54-56.

48. Bahr, *Religionsgesprache*, op. cit., 9-10.

49. Ibid., 13.
    - Hoflich, "Karl Marx", op. cit., 777-785.
    - Metz, *Glaube*, op. cit., part II, esp. pgs. 8, 9.

50. Bahr, *Religionsgesprache*, op. cit., 14-16.
    - SW 7, 266.
    - Seibert, *Hegel's Philosophy*, op. cit., III.
    - Siebert, *Hegel's Concept*, op. cit., chaps. 1, 18.
    - Siebert, *Horkheimer's Critical Sociology*, op. cit., chap. VII.

51. Bahr, *Religionsgesprache*, op. cit., 15-16.

- Habermas, *Legitimation Crisis*, op. cit. part III, 4.

52. Bahr, *Religionsgespräche*, op. cit., 15-16.
    - Kasper, "Politische Utopie," op. cit., 563-572.
    - Metz, *Glaube*, op. cit., 112.

53. Bahr,*Religionsgespräche*, op. cit., 15-16.
    - Horkheimer, *Die Sehnsucht*, op. cit. 83-89.

54. Horkheimer, *Die Sehnsucht*, op. cit., 81-89.

55. Ibid., 54-56.
    - Bahr, *Religionsgespräche*, op. cit., 15-16.
    - Siebert, *Horkheimer's Critical Sociology*, op. cit., chap. IX.
    - Metz, *Glaube*, op. cit., 209-211.

56. Bahr, *Religionsgespräche*, op. cit., 15-16.

57. Ibid., 16.

58. Ibid. 21-22.

59. Ibid., 27.

60. Ibid., 29-30.

61. Ibid.
    - Habermas, *Zwei Reden*, op. cit., 50-51.

62. Bahr, *Religionsgesprache*, op. cit., 29-30.

63. Ibid.

64. Ibid., 30.
    - W.V. Casey, (ed.), *The Berrigans*, New York: The
    Hearst Corporation 1971, 7-11, 13-30.

65. Habermas, *Zur Rekonstruktion*, op. cit., 333.

66. Ibid., 333-345.
    - Habermas, *Legitimation Crisis*, op. cit., part III.

67. Habermas, *Zur Rekonstruktion*, op. cit., 330.
    - J. Habermas, "Wahrheitstheorien," in *Festschrift
    fur W. Schultz*, Pfullingen, 1973, 11.
    - K.O. Apel, "Das Apriori der Kommunkkationsgemeinschaft
    und die Ethik," in K.O. Apel, *Transformation der
    Philosophie*, Frankfurt a.M.:   1973mBd. II.
    - L. Kohlberg, *Die kognitive Entwicklung des Kindes*,
    Frankfurt a.M.:   1974.

- R. Döbert, *Systemtheorie und die Entwicklung*
religiöser Deutungssysteme, Frankfurt a.M.: 1973.

68. Habermas, *Zur Rekonstruktion*, op. cit., 330-335.

69. Ibid., 333-335.

70. Ibid., 334-335.

71. Ibid.
- Habermas, *Legitimation Crisis*, op. cit., 105.

72. Habermas, *Zur Rekonstruktion*, op. cit., 334-336.

73. Ibid., 335-336.

74. Ibid., 336.

75. Ibid.
- Siebert, "Communication", op. cit.

Chapter IX - Ultimate Reality

1. T. Parsons, Introduction, in M. Weber, *The Sociology*
of Religion, Boston: Beacon Press 1964, xix-lxvii
- T. Parsons, *Structure and Process in Modern Societies*,
Chicago: The Free Press of Glencoe 1960, chap. 10.
- T. Parsons, etc. (ed.), *Theories of Society*, New
York: The Free Press of Glencoe, Inc. 1961, Vol. I,
645-684; Vol. II, 1077-1164, 1385-1402.
- T. Parsons, *The Structure of Social Action*, New
York: The Free Press 1966, chaps. V, VI, XI, XIV, XV.
- T. Parsons, etc., (ed.), *Toward a General Theory*
of Action, New York: Harper and Row 1962, 3-39,
47-275.
- T. Parsons, *Essays in Sociological Theory*, London:
The Free Press of Glencoe 1964, chap. X.
- T. Parsons, *The Social System*, London: The Free
Press of Glencoe 1964, 163-167, 367-384.
- S. Budd, *Sociologists and Religion*, London:
Collier-MacMillan Publishers 1973, 34, 46-48, 57,
79-80, 121-124, 135, 154.
- N.S. Timasheff, *Sociological Theory*, New York:
Random House 1967, 238-248.
- T. Parsons, The Present Status of Structural-
Functional Theory in Sociology, in L.A. Coser, *The*
Idea of Social Structure, New York: Harcourt Brace
Jovanoviich 1975, 67-83.
- N. Luhmann, *Funktion der Religion*, Frankfurt a.M.:
Suhrkamp Verlag 1977, chap. I.

- N. Luhmann, Religion als System, Thesen, in N.W. Dahm, etc., *Religion - System und Sozialisation*, Darmstadt: Hermann Luchterhand Verlag 1972, 11-14.
- N. Luhmann, "Religiöse Dogmatik und gesellschaftliche Evolution", in Dahm, *Religion*, op. cit., 15-132.
- T. Parsons, *Societies, Evolutionary and Comparative Perspectives*, Englewood Cliffs, New Jersey: Prentice Hall Inc. 1966, 8, 9, 29, 33, 38-40, 45, 48, 49, 71-72, 59-61, 104, 105-106, 78, 79-80, 81, 84, 85, 86, 98, 63-64, 68, 88, 92-93.
- T. Parsons, *The System of Modern Societies*, Englewood Cliffs, New Jersey: Prentice Hall Inc. 1971, 5, 10, 15, 18, 99-100, 51, 54-56, 58, 88, 128, 29, 46, 47, 119, 22, 21, 49-57, 67, 72, 86, 88-91, 93, 98-99, 54-56, 48-49, 28, 2, 9, 98-99.
- R.W. Friedrichs, Social Research and Theory: End of the Detente? in *Review of Religious Research*, Vol. 15, No. 3 (Spring 1974) 113-126.
- B. Johnson, Sociological Theory and Religious Truth in *Sociological Analysis*, 1977, 38, 4: 368-388.

2. L. Kolakowski, *The Alienation of Reason. A History of Positivist Thought*, Garden City, New York: Doubleday and Co. Inc., 1968, chaps. I and VIII.

3. Parsons, *The System*, op. cit., 1-2.
    - Parsons, *The Structure of Social Action*, New York: The Free Press 1968, Vol. I and II, chaps. II, III, IV, V, VI, VIII, XI, XIII, XIV, XV.

4. G.W.F. Hegel, *Ästhetik*, Frankfurt a.M.: Europaische Verlaganstalt GmbH 1951, Vol. I, 95, Vol.II, 423.
    - SW 11, 129-130, 149, 447.

5. Parsons, *Societies*, op. cit., 114-115; chap. VI.

6. Habermas/Luhmann, *Theorie der Gesellschaft*, op. cit., 142-290.
    - J. Habermas, *Zur Logik der Sozialwissenschaften*, Frankfurt a.M.: Suhrkamp Verlag 1973, 164-184.
    - Habermas, *Zur Rekonstruktion*, op. cit., chaps. 1, 2, 6, 8, 9, 10.

7. G.W.F. Hegel, *Enzyklopädie der Philosophischen Wissenschaften*, Hamburg: Verlag von Felix Meiner 1959, 431-439, esp. 432.

8. Parsons, *Societies*, op. cit., 1-29.
    - Parsons, *The System*, op. cit., 1-28.
    - SW 7, part III.
    - SW 11, part IV.

- SW 15, 19-36, 75-100.
- G.W.F. Hegel, *The Phenomenology of Mind*, New York: Harper and Row, Publishers, 1967, 685-785.

9. SW 11, 88-120.
- Habermas, *Zur Rekonstruktion*, op. cit., chaps. 5, 7, 8.

10. G.W.F. Hegel, *Science of Logic*, New York: Humanities Press 1976, 28, 417-443.
- Th. W. Adorno, *Negative Dialectics*, New York: The Seabury Press 1973, Part two.
- Hegel, *Phenomenology*, op. cit., 75.

11. D. Martindale, "Limits of and Alternatives to Functionalism in Sociology", in D. Martindale (ed.), *Functionalism in the Social Sciences*, Philadelphia, February 1965, 144-162.
- D. Martindale, The Roles of Humanism and Scientism in the Evolution of Sociology, in G.K. Zollschen, etc. (ed.), *Explorations in Social Change*, Boston: Houghton Mifflin Co. 1964, 468-470, 487.

12. Parsons, *Societies*, op. cit., 7, 8, 9, 10, 28-29.
- Parsons, *The System*, op. cit., 5, 10, 11.

13. P. Tillich, *Biblical Religion and the Search for Ultimate Reality*, Chicago: The University of Chicago Press 1955, 12-13, chap. VIII.
- Luhmann, *Funktion*, op. cit., 17-18, 69, 85.

14. SW 11, 42-43, 48-50, 112-115, 569.

15. Martindale, *The Roles*, op. cit., 461-473, 478, 487.

16. Hegel, *Enzyklopädie*, op. cit., 317-388, 389-439, 440-463.

17. SW 15, 114-118.

18. Horkheimer, *Zur Kritik*, op. cit., 7-9, part I.

Chapter X - Meaning

1. Habermas/Luhmann, *Theorie*, op. cit., 13-18.
- Luhmann, *Funktion*, op. cit., 17-20, 69-71, 78-79, 84-87, 89-90, 110-111, 121-123, 138-139, 157-158.

2. Habermas, *Zur Logik*, op. cit., 164-184.

3. Horkheimer, *Notizen*, op. cit., 92-93, 96-97.

- Niebuhr, Marx, op. cit., 41-42.
- SW 15, 256-267.

4. SW 11, 47-69, 39-40.

Chapter XI - Evolution of Religion

1. Parsons, Societies, op. cit., 21-24, 26-27, 33, 38,
    39, 40, 44, 45, 47, 48, 49, 50; 59, 60, 61, 63, 64,
    68, 71, 72; 77, 78, 79, 80, 84, 85, 88, 92, 93, 94,
    97, 98, 104, 105, 106.
    - Parsons, The System, op. cit., 2, 9, 10, 14, 15,
    18, 21, 22, 28, 29, 30, 31, 32, 33, 34, 35, 38, 39,
    40, 41, 43, 45, 46, 47, 48, 49, 50, 51, 52, 53, 54,
    55, 56, 57, 58, 59, 67, 69, 70, 71, 72, 73, 74, 79,
    80, 84, 86, 87, 88, 89, 90, 91, 92, 93, 98, 99, 100,
    118, 119, 124, 128, 139, 140, 141, 142.
    - T. Parsons, in International Encyclopedia of the
    Social Sciences, New York 1968, Vol. 2, 425-447.
    - T. Parsons, Christianity and Modern Industrial
    Society in E.A. Tiryakian, Sociological Theory,
    Values and Socio-Cultural Change, London: The Free
    Press of Glencoe 1963, 33-70.
    - T. Parsons, Sociological Theory and Modern Society,
    New York: The Free Press, 1967, chap. 12.
    - Parsons, The Social System, op. cit., 525-535.

2. R.J. Siebert, "Fromm's Theory of Religion" in Telos,
    (Summer 1977)
    - R.J. Siebert, "Jacob and Jesus: Recent Marxist
    Readings of The Bible" in The Bible and Liberation -
    Political and Social Hermeneutics, prepared as a
    Radical Religious Reader by the Community for
    Religious Research and Education, Berkley, California,
    1976, 145-156.

3. Horkheimer/Adorno, Dialectic, op. cit., 120-167.
    - Marcuse, One Dimensional Man, op. cit., chaps. 5-7.
    - M. Horkheimer, Critical Theory, New York: The
    Seabury Press, 1972, chap. IX.

4. H. Peukert, Diskussion zur Politischen Theologie,
    Mainz: Matthias Grunewald Verlag 1969, 82-95, 247-
    266, 267-301.
    - J.B. Metz, Theology of the World, New York: The
    Seabury Press 1969, part three.
    - Metz, Glaube, op. cit., part I.

5. Habermas, Zur Rekonstruktion, op. cit., 4, 12.
    - G. Radnitzky, Contemporary Schools of Metascience,

New York: Humanities Press, 1970, Vol. II, esp. 164, 170.

6. SW 16, 354-356.
   - SW 7, 261-262, 311-323.
7. Hegel, *Ästhetik*, op. cit., Vol. II, 423.
   - SW 15, 24-36.
   - SW 16, 355-356.
   - Horkheimer, *Die Sehnsucht*, op. cit., 54-56, 83-89.
   - Metz, *Glaube*, op. cit., part III.
   - Metz, *Theology*, op. cit., chap. VI.
   - Siebert, *Horkheimer's Critical Sociology*, op. cit., IX.
   - Siebert, *Hegel's Concept*, op. cit., chaps. 5, 6, 7, 8, 25, 30, 31.

Chapter XII - Intersubjectivity

1. Luhmann, *Funktion*, op. cit., chap. 4.

2. W. Dirks, "Der Traum vom guten Staat", in *FH*, 33, 6 (June 1978), 42-48.

3. Habermas, *Zur Rekonstruktion*, op. cit., 112-114.
   - Dobert, *Systemtheorie*, op. cit., part II, esp. 87-157.

4. Habermas, *Zur Rekonstruktion*, op. cit., 114-115.
   - Horkheimer/Adorno, *Dialectic*, op. cit., chap. I.
   - M. Horkheimer, *Critique of Instrumental Reason*, New York: Seabury Press 1974, chap. I.
   - M. Horkheimer, *Zur Kritik der instrumentellen Vernunft*, Frankfurt a.M.: S. Fischer Verlag 1967 part I.

5. Habermas, *Zur Rekonstruktion*, op. cit., 114-115.
   - K. Marx, *Das Kapital*, Berlin: Dietz Verlag 1961, 5-9, 10-18, 19-20, 21-23, 24-28, 29-35.

6. Luhmann, *Funktion*, op. cit., 222-224, chap. 4.
   - Parsons, *The System of Modern Societies*, op. cit., chap. 8.
   - Habermas, *Zur Rekonstruktion*, op. cit., chap. 4.

7. Habermas, *Zur Rekonstruktion*, op. cit., chaps. 4, 6, 12.
   - Habermas/Luhmann, *Theorie der Gesellschaft*, op. cit., 285-290.
   - Habermas, *Zur Logik*, op. cit., chaps. 9, 10.
   - Habermas, *Legitimation Crisis*, op. cit., part III, chaps. 4, 5, 6.

- J. Habermas, *Toward a Rational Society*, Boston: Beacon Press 1970, chaps. i, 6.
- J. Habermas, *Knowledge and Human Interests*, Boston: Beacon Press 1968, part III.

8. Küng, *Existiert Gott?* op. cit., part G.
   - Metz, *Glaube*, op. cit., part III.
   - Peukert, *Wissenschaftstheorie*, op. cit., part III, C, D.

Chapter XIII - Negative Theology

1. W. Jens, (ed.), *Um Nichts als die Wahrheit. Deutsche Bischofskonferenz contra Hans Kung*, Munchen: Zurich Verlag R. Piper, 1978.
   - H. Küng, *The Church*, Garden City, New York: Image Books 1967, parts A, B.
   - H. Küng, *Christ Sein*, München: R. Piper and Co. 1974, part A, II, parts C, D.
   - Küng, *Existiert Gott?* op. cit., parts F, G.
   - H. Küng, *Menschwerdung Gottes*, Freiburg: Herder 1970, chap. VIII, 611-670.

2. Küng, *Christ Sein*, op. cit., parts B, C, D.

3. Küng, *Existiert Gott?* op. cit., part G.II, III.

4. Ibid., 729-767, esp. 740-754.

5. Ibid., 748, 750.

6. Küng, *Menschwerdung*, op. cit., chaps. V-VIII, 611-670.

7. Küng, *Existiert Gott?* op. cit., part B.

8. M. Horkheimer und Th. W. Adorno, *Dialektik der Aufklärung*, Frankfurt a.M.: S. Fischer Verlag 1969, 187-188.
   - Horkheimer, *Zur Kritik*, op. cit., 311-312.
   - SW 11, 34-47.

9. SW 15, 19-36.
   - SW 16, 223-354.

10. W. Dirks und E. Stammler, (eds.), *Warum bleibe ich in der Kirche?* Munchen: Manz Verlag 1971, 42-48.
    - W. Dirks, "Hans Küng: Der Fall und ein Buch" in *FH*, 33, 7, (Juli 1978) 63-66.
    - E. Kogon, "Rudolf Augstein's, Herausforderung" in *FH*, 28, 4, (April 1973) 249-257.
    - W. Dirks, "Was meine ich, wenn ich sage: Ich glaube

an den Sohn Gottes?" in *FH*, 28, 4, (April 1973) 257-260.

11. Küng, *Existiert Gott?* op. cit., 729-254.
    - Küng, *Menschwerdung*, op. cit., chaps. II, III, V, VII, VIII, 611-670.
    - Küng, *Christ Sein*, op. cit., part C, D.

12. Küng, *Existiert Gott?* op. cit., 119-154.

13. E. Bloch, *Das Prinzip Hoffnung*, Frankfurt a.M.: Suhrkamp Verlag 1959, chaps. 53, 54, 55.
    - E. Bloch, *Experimentum Mundi*, Frankfurt a.M.: Suhrkamp Verlag 1975, chap. 43.
    - SW 15, 24-36.

14. SW 15, 34-36.
    - SW 6, 355-356.

15. SW 15, 34-36.
    - SW 16, 223-308.
    - Küng, *Menschwerdung*, cp. cit., 558.
    - Küng, *Christ Sein*, op. cit., 367, 348, 316, 285.

16. SW 15, 34-36.
    - Küng, *Existiert Gott?* op. cit., parts G, E.
    - Küng, *Christ Sein*, op. cit., Part D.

17. Küng, *Existiert Gott?* op. cit., 730-731, 733-734, 736-739, 740-760.

18. SW 11, 42-43, 48-50, 569.
    - K. Marx, "German Ideology" in E. Fromm's, *Marx's Concept of Man*, New York: Frederick Ungar, Publishing Co. 1967, 215.
    - Horkheimer, Zur Theodor Haecker, op. cit., 372-382.
    - W. Benjamin, *Gesammelte Schriften*, Frankfurt a.M.: Suhrkamp Verlag 1961, 280-281.
    - W. Benjamin, *Illuminationen*, Frankfurt a.M.: Suhrkamp Verlag 1961, 280-281.

19. Horkheimer, *Die Sehnsucht*, op. cit., 56-57, 59-60.
    - H. Scheible, "Max Horkheimer's frühe und späte Aufzeichnungen" in *FH*, 33, 6 (Juni 1978) 50-54.
    - Voltaire, *Candide*, New York: The New American Library 1961, 15-101.

20. Horkhiemer, *Zur Kritik*, op. cit., 248-268, esp. 259-261.
    - Schopenhauer, *The World*, op. cit., I, 87, 221, 283, 296, 306, 313-314, 358-359, 406-407; II, 463-464, 576-577, 590-591.

- SW 11, 42, 48-50, 112-113, 569
- SW 15, 100

21. W. Dirks and others, "Zu Reinhold Schneider's autobiographischen Schriften" in FH, 33, 11, (November 1978) 52-53.

22. H.R. Schlette, Romano Guardini - Werk und Wirkung, Bonn: Bouvier Verlag Herbert Grundmann 1973, 26.

23. W. Reich, The Cancer Biopathy, New York: Farrar, Strauss and Giraux, 1971, chaps, V, VI, VIII, IX, X.

24. Metz, Theology, op. cit., chaps. V, VI.
    - Metz, Glaube, op. cit., part III.

Chapter XIV - Universal Solidarity

1. Peukert, Wissenschaftstheorie, op. cit., 16.
   - Metz, Theology, op. cit., part I, II.
   - Metz, Glaube, op. cit., 204-211.
   - Siebert, "Peukert's New Critical Theology, op. cit., 52-58, 78-80.

2. Peukert, Wissenschaftstheorie, op. cit., part I.

3. Ibid., part II.
   - Kung, Existiert Gott? op. cit., 553-560, 119-154.
   - Metz, Glaube, op. cit., 3-12; 112, 67.

4. Peukert, Wissenschaftstheorie, op. cit., 16, 283-323.

5. Ibid., 303.
   - Habermas, Zur Rekonstruktion, op. cit., 101.
   - Metz, Glaube, op. cit., 13-28.

6. Peukert, Wissenschaftstheorie, op. cit., 303.

7. Ibid., 307.
   - SW 15, 19-21, 104-114.
   - SW 16, 208-247.

8. Peukert, Wissenschaftstheorie, op. cit., 283-307.

9. Ibid., 307-308.
   - SW 11, 43-47.
   - SW 2, 153-158.

10. Peukert, Wissenschaftstheorie, op. cit., 307-309.
    - Radnitzky, Contemporary Schools, op. cit., II, 164, 170.

11. Peukert, *Wissenschaftstheorie*, op. cit., 307-310.

12. Ibid., 310.
    - Hegel, *Jenaer Systementwurfe I*, op. cit., 282-326.
    - G.W.F. Hegel, *Jenaer Schriften*, Berlin: Akademie
      Verlag 1972, 458-463.
    - Habermas, *Theorie*, op. cit., chap. 4.

13. Peukert, *Wissenschaftstheorie*, op. cit., 310-311,
    289-302.
    - Schmidt, *Die Religion*, op. cit., chaps. I, II, III,
      IV, V, VIII, IX.
    - Siebert, *Horkheimer's Critical Sociology*, op. cit.,
      III, IV, V, VIII.
    - Siebert, Fromm's Critical Theory, op. cit.,

14. Peukert, *Wissenschaftstheorie*, op. cit., 311-312.
    - SW 15, 68.

15. Peukert, *Wissenschaftstheorie*, op. cit., 310-312.
    - SW 11, 37-47.
    - SW 5, 327-353.
    - SW 4, 45-46.
    - R.J. Siebert, "Hegel and Theology" in *The Ecumenist*
      XII, No. 1 (November-December 1973) 1-6.
    - R.J. Siebert, "Hegel's Political Theology: Liberation"
      in *The Ecumenist*, XII, No. 3 (March-April 1974) 33-41.

16. Peukert, *Wissenschaftstheorie*, op. cit., 311-312.
    - Habermas, *Zwei Reden*, op. cit., 44-75.

17. Peukert, *Wissenschaftstheorie*, op. cit., 311-313,
    part I, II.
    - Pennenberg, *Theology*, op. cit., part I, II.

18. Peukert, *Wissenschaftstheorie*, op. cit., 312-313,
    294-302.
    - J.B. Metz, *Freiheit in Gesellschaft*, Freiburg:
      Herder 1971, 7-20.
    - Metz, *Glaube*, op. cit., 37-39, 72-73, 77-86, 98-99,
      139-140, 162-163, 165-166, 172-175, 179-180.

19. Peukert, *Wissenschaftstheorie*, op. cit., 312-313,
    294-302.
    - Metz, *Glaube*, op. cit., 181-203.
    - Siebert, Jacob and Jesus, op. cit., 145-146.

20. Peukert, *Wissenschaftstheorie*, op. cit., 289-303.
    - Siebert, Jacob and Jesus, op. cit., 289-303.

21. Peukert, *Wissenschaftstheorie*, op. cit., 313-314.

- Kung, *Christ Sein*, op. cit., 308-331, 332-400.

22. Peukert, *Wissenschaftstheorie*, op. cit., 314-315.
    - Metz, *Glaube*, op. cit., 8, 72-74, 99-100, 158, 175, 182, 190.

23. Peukert, *Wissenschaftstheorie*, op. cit., 315.
    - Metz, *Unsere Hoffnung*, in *Synode*, 6, 1975, I, 3.

24. Peukert, *Wissenschaftstheorie*, op. cit., 323, 278-282.
    - Habermas, *Kultur*, op. cit., 302-344, esp. 332-339, 339-344, 399.

25. Peukert, *Wissenschaftstheorie*, op. cit., 323.
    - Horkheimer, *Die Sehnsucht*, op. cit., 81-89.
    - Benjamin, *Gesammelte Schriften*, op. cit., I, 2, 693-704.
    - Benjamin, *Illuminationen*, op. cit., 280-281.

26. Peukert, *Wissenschaftstheorie*, op. cit., 323.
    - Kung, *Christ Sein*, op. cit., 81-108.
    - SW 15, 75-100.

Chapter XV - Proletarian Saints

1. G.W. Rudolphi, "Die Versuchung Christi" in *FH*, 3, 5, (Mai 1948) 475-476.
   - G.W.F. Rudolphi, *Heilige Kirche, Kirche der Heilige*, Frankfurt a.M.: Verlag Josef Knecht 1949, 433-436.

2. Horkheimer, Zur Theodor Haecker, op. cit., 372-382.
   - Haecker, *Vergil*, op. cit.,
   - Th. Haecker, *Die Versuchungen Christi*, Berlin: Morus Verlag 1946,
   - Haecker, *Der Christ*, op. cit.,
   - Kung, *Christ Sein*, op. cit., part D.
   - Metz, *Glaube*, op. cit., 204-211.
   - Peukert, *Wissenschaftstheorie*, op. cit., part III, D.
   - Horkheimer, *Die Sehnsucht*, op. cit., 55-56.
   - Siebert, *Horkheimer's Critical Sociology*, op. cit., chaps. III, IV, VI, VII, VIII, IX.
   - Th. W. Adorno/E. Kogon, "Offenbarung oder autonome Vernunft" in *FH*, 13, 7, (Juli 1958) 484-498, esp. 498.
   - Habermas, *Zur Rekonstruktion*, op. cit., 115-121.

3. Benjamin, *Gesammelte Schriften*, op. cit., I/2, 693-704.

4. Rudolphi, *Die Versuchung*, op. cit., 475-476.
   - Haecker, *Die Versuchungen*, op. cit.,
   - Matthew 4, 1-11.

5. G.W.F. Hegel, *The Phenomenology of Mind*, New York: Harper and Row 1967,
   - Kung, *Menschwerdung*, op. cit., 497.
   - K. Rosenkranz, G.W.F. *Hegel's Leben*, Darmstadt 1963, 407.

6. A. Schmidt, "Zeitschrift fur Sozialforschung. Geschichte und gegenwärtige Bedeutung" in M. Horkheimer (ed.), *Zeitschrift für Sozialforschung*, Munchen: Kosel Verlag 1970, I, 8-17.

7. Matthew 6, 25.
   - SW 11, 39-43, 569.

8. Rudolphi, *Heilige Kirche*, op. cit., 433-436.

9. Psalm 104, 30.

10. L.H. LaRouche "Luxemburg and the Crisis in Political Science," in R. Luxemburg, *The Industrial Development of Poland*, New York: Capaigner Publications Inc., 1977, 13-58.

11. W. Reich, *The Mass Psychology of Fascism*, New York: Farrar, Strauss and Giroux 1970, chaps. VI, VII.
    - W. Reich, *Sexual Revolution*, New York: Farrar, Strauss and Giroux, 1971
    - W. Reich, *Sex-Pol Essays 1929-1934*, New York: Random House 1972.
    - W. Reich, *The Invasion of Compulsory Sex Morality*, New York: Farrar, Straus and Giroux, 1971.

12. Rudolphi, *Heilige Kirche*, op. cit., 434-436.

13. Matthew 6, 10.

14. Revelation 7, 9.

15. Revelation 22, 2.

16. Matthew 5, 3-4, 6.

17. Matthew 13, 31.

18. Matthew 13, 33.

19. Mark 4, 26-29.

20. Ephesians 5, 32.

21. I Corinthians 1, 26-27.

22. I. Corinthians 1, 28.

23. Rudolphi, *Heilige Kirche*, op. cit., 434-436.
    - Benjamin, *Gesammelte Schriften*, op. cit., I/2, 693-436.
    - Benjamin, *Illuminationen*, op. cit., 280-281.
    - Metz, *Glaube*, op. cit., 10-11, 52, 60, 71-72, 115,
    149-158, 162, 206.

24. Matthew 5, 3.

25. Acts 4, 30.
    - Romans 15, 19.
    - II Corinthians 12, 12.

26. Horkheimer, *Die Sehnsucht*, op. cit., 37-38.

27. G.W.F. Hegel, *Enzyklopädie der philosophischen
    Wissenschaften im Grundriss*, Stuttgart: Fr. Frommann
    Verlag 1956, 344 (SW)

Chapter XVI - Theodicy

1. SW 11, 39-43, 47-51, 568-569.
   - SW 15, 100
   - Marx, *German Ideology*, op. cit., 213-216.
   - Horkheimer, *Die Sehnsucht*, op. cit., 37-53, 54-89.
   - Metz, *Glaube*, op. cit., 109, 112.

2. SW 11, 42.
   - Voltaire, *Candide*, op. cit., 15-101.
   - Horkheimer, *Dawn*, op. cit., 119-120.

3. Horkheimer, *Zur Kritik*, op. cit., 248-268.
   - Horkheimer, *Dawn*, op. cit., 149-150, 188, 218-219.
   - Horkheimer, *Die Sehnsucht*, op. cit., 64-65.
   - Schopenhauer, *The World*, op. cit., I, 323-324;
   II, 170, 356, 620-621.

4. SW 11, 39-43, 47-51, 568-569.
   - SW 15, 100.
   - SW 7, 27-28, 32-34, 35-36.
   - G.W.F. Hegel, *System der Philosophie*, Stuttgart-Bad
   Cannstatt: Friedrich Frommann Verlag 1965, 1-22,
   29-65, 66-69.
   - SW 17, 19-22, 23-26, 27-34, 35-80.

5. SW 11, 42-47.

6. Ibid.
   - Horkheimer, *Zur Kritik*, op. cit., 311-312.

7. SW 11, 43-47.
   - SW 16, 312-218.
   - SW 19, 162-169.

8. SW 11, 43-47.
   - R.J. Siebert, "Change, Value and Adult Education"
   in *Chrysallis*, I, No. I, (Summer 1975), 14-25.

9. SW 11, 43-47.
   - SW 16, 354.

10. SW 11, 43-47.
    - Siebert, Hegel's Political Theology, op. cit., 33-41.
    - R. Ahlers, "The Overcoming of Critical Theory in
    the Hegelian Unity of Theory and Praxis" in *Clio*,
    Vol. 8, No. 1, (Fall 1978) 71-96.

11. SW 11, 47-50.

12. Ibid.
    - SW 7, 261-262, 262-270, 270-276, 311-323.

13. SW 11, 43, 48-50.

14. Ibid.
    - H. Marcuse, *Eros and Civilization*, New York:
    Vintage Books 1962, chaps. II, III.

15. Marcuse, *Eros*, op. cit., 64.
    - S. Freud, *Moses and Monotheism*, New York: Alfred
    A. Knopf, 1949, 145.

16. SW 11, 48-51.

17. Ibid.
    - Schopenhauer, *The World*, op. cit., I, 192, 319;
    II, 217, 359, 381, 383, 389, 395, 568.
    - Horkheimer, *Zur Kritik*, op. cit., 248-268.

18. SW 11, 112-113.

19. SW 11, 49-51.

20. G.W.F. Hegel, *Wissenschaft der Logik*, Hamburg: Verlag
    von Felix Meiner, 1960, I, 6, 11, 20-21, 35-36, 87,
    90; II, 58-60, 491.
    - Hegel, *Enzyklopädie*, op. cit., 44, 73, 102-103,
    184, 316.
    - Th. W. Adorno, *Negative Dialectics*, New York:
    The Seabury Press 1973, part two; part three, II.

21. SW 11, 37-47, 568-569.
    - Horkheimer, *Zur Kritik*, op. cit., 259-268.
    - Horkheimer, *Die Sehnsucht*, op. cit., 15-16, 64-66.

22. SW 11, 63-69.
    - Hegel, *Enzyklopadie*, op. cit., 180.

23. Hegel, *Phenomenology*, op. cit., 64.

24. SW 11, 37-50, 568-569.

25. Ibid.
    - Hegel, *Ästhetik*, op. cit., II, 423.
    - R. Augstein/G. Wolff, "Nur noch ein Gott kann uns
    vetten. Spiegel Gesprach mit Martin Meidegger am 23.
    September 1966" in *Der Spiegel*, No. 23/1976, 193-219.

26. Hegel, *Jenaer Schriften*, op. cit., 395-396.
    - Hegel, *The Phenomenology*, op. cit., 750-785, esp.
    752-753, 781-782.
    - SW 16, 296-308.
    - R.J. Siebert, "Hegel and the Rebellion and Counter-
    Rebellion of Youth", in *Perspectives*, XXX, No. 2
    (Fall 1971), 53-77.

27. SW 11, 43-47, 69-120, 568-569, 129, 447.
    - Hegel, *Ästhetik*, op. cit., II, 423.

28. SW 11, 568-569.
    - SW 7, 35-36.

29. SW 7, 36.
    - Revelation 3, 15-17.

30. SW 11, 569.

Chapter XVII - Messiah

1. Hegel, *Enzyklopädie*, op. cit., 344. (SW)

2. Marcuse, *Eros*, op. cit., 63-65.
   - E. Fromm, *Die Entwicklung des Christusdogmas*,
   Wein: Internationaler Psychoanalytischer Verlag
   1931.
   - Horkheimer, *Notizen*, op. cit., 96-97, 91-92.
   - Metz, *Theology*, op. cit., chaps. V, VI.
   - Metz, *Glaube*, op. cit., 204, 211.
   - Küng, *Christ Sein*, op. cit., 545-594.

3. Küng, *Existiert Gott?* op. cit., 539-542, 533-539.

- Metz, *Glaube*, op. cit., 34, 43, 52, 206; 34, 43, 62, 67, 94, 107-108, 113-114, 171-172, 183, 191; 44, 91, 99, 107, 152, 154, 171, 182-183; 7, 66, 90, 107, 117, 157, 172, 174, 208.

4. SW 15, 24-36.
- Kung, *Menschwerdung*, op. cit., 558.
- Kung, *Christ Sein*, op. cit., 285.

5. SW 7, 311-323.
- Metz, *Glaube*, op. cit., 5, 15, 18, 25, 26-27, 30-43, 65, 67, 83, 90, 136, 205.

6. Horkheimer, Zu Theodor Haecker, op. cit.,
- H. Marcuse, "Marxism and the New Humanity: An Unfinished Revolution" in J.C. Raines and Th. Dean, *Marxism and Radical Religion*, Philadelphia: Temple University Press 1970, 9-10.

7. Benjamin, *Gesammelte Schriften*, op. cit., I/1, 693-704.
- Benjamin, *Illuminationen*, op. cit., 280-281.

8. Metz, *Glaube*, op. cit., 3-12.
- Kung, *Existiert Gott?* op. cit., C, D.

9. Metz, *Glaube*, op. cit., part III.
- Peukert, *Wissenschaftstheorie*, op. cit., 278-282.
- Benjamin, *Gesammelte Schriften*, op. cit., I/1, 693-704.
- Benjamin, *Illuminationen*, op. cit., 280-281.

10. Benjamin, *Gesammelte Schriften*, op. cit., I/1, 693-704.

11. H. Brenner, "Theodor W. Adorno als Sachwalter des Benjaminschen Werkes" in W.F. Schoeller, *Die Neue Linke nach Adorno*, Munchen: Kindler Verlag 1969, 168-173.
- W. Benjamin, *Briefe*, Frankfurt a.M.: Suhrkamp Verlag 1966, Bd. II, 676.

12. Benjamin, *Illuminationen*, op. cit., 280-281.

13. E. Bloch, *Der Geist der Utopie*, op. cit., chaps. I, II, III
- E. Bloch, *Man On His Own*, New York: Herder and Herder 1970, chaps. VI, VII.
- E. Bloch, *A Philosophy of the Future*, New York: Herder and Herder 1970, chaps. 12, 13.

14. Th. W. Adorno, *Minima Moralia*, Frankfurt a.M.: Suhrkamp Verlag 1971, 333-334.

14. Ibid.
    - Siebert, *Hegel's Philosophy*, op. cit., 22-23.

16. Fromm, *Die Entwicklung*, op. cit., chaps. III, IX.
    ⁓ Marcuse, *Eros*, op. cit., 63-65.

17. "Hurry, My Children, Hurry" in *Time*, Vol. 113, No. 13,
    (March 26, 1979) 27-28.

18. E. Fromm, *To Have On To Be*, New York: Harper and
    Row Publishers 1976, 201-202.

19. Marcuse, Marxism, op. cit., 9-10.

20. Adorno/Kogon, Offenbarung, op. cit., 484-496.

21. Matthew 5, 1-12.

22. Radnitzky, *Contemporary Schools*, op. cit., II, 164,
    176.

23. Adorno/Kogon, Offenbarung, op.cit., 496.

24. Matthew 5, 1-12.
    - Benjamin, *Gesammelte Schriften*, op. cit., I/1, 693-704.
    - Benjamin, *Illuminationen*, op. cit., 280-281.
    - Bloch, *A Philosophy*, op. cit., chaps. 10-15.
    - Bloch, *Man*, op. cit., chaps. III, IV, V, VI.
    - R.J. Siebert, "Communication Without Domination,"
    in G. Baum and A. Greeley, *Communication in the
    Church*, New York: The Seabury Press 1978, 81-94.
    - R.J. Siebert, "The Christian Revolution: Liberation
    and Transcendence" in *The Ecumenist*, (September-October
    1976) 85-91.
    - Metz, *Glaube*, op. cit., part III.

ABOUT THE AUTHOR

Rudolf J. Siebert was born in Frankfurt a.M. Germany in
1927. He studies History, Theology, Philosophy and
Philology at the Universities of Mainz and Münster,
Germany and at the Catholic University of America,
Washington, D.C., U.S.A. He graduated from the Theological
Faculty of Mainz in 1965. He first taught in Germany
and then in the U.S.A. and Canada. He has concentrated
in his teaching and writing on the critical theory of
society and the political theology. Since 1965 Siebert
is a professor in the religion department of Western
Michigan University, Kalamazoo, Michigan, teaching
courses in the philosophy, sociology and psychology of
religion. Siebert initiated and is directing the
international course on the Future of Religion in the
Inter-University Centre of Post-graduate Studies in
Dubrovnik, Yugoslavia. He is the founder of the Centre
for Humanistic Future Studies at Western Michigan
University. Rudolf and Margaret (+ October 20, 1978)
Siebert are the parents of seven children.

9316